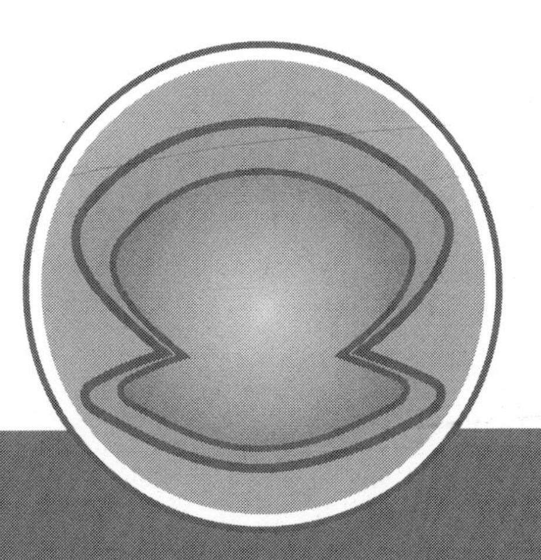

REMAIN CLAM!

Did you notice the title of this book? Did you notice what was wrong with it? Or did you think the title was Remain Calm? Don't be embarrassed if you did. MANY people, grown-ups and kids alike, make the same mistake. Why? Well, the brain wants the title to make sense. Remain Calm makes sense; Remain Clam doesn't. Also, most of us only glance at or skim things like titles, instructions, or epigraphs [which is what this paragraph is]. If we do read more closely, we might read too quickly or too anxiously and flip letters automatically. This is what some dyslexic people do, and when we're stressed, we all become a little bit dyslexic: letters switch, negatives and positives flip, and up becomes down. So? Why does this matter? It matters because test makers on every level are all too aware of this tendency, which is especially common in young minds. They know if you feel rushed, stressed or distracted that you'll be prone to miss details, get things backwards or answer the question you imagine rather than the one on the page. That means it is VERY important that you find a way to quiet your mind, focus on ALL the words and, by all means, no matter what:

Remain Clam!

'IBID/

adverb

adverb: ibid.; symbol: ib.

Bad enough I named my books "Remain Clam," but did I also have to name my company ibidPREP?

What on earth does "ibid" mean?

The term "ibid" is short for the Latin "ibidem" which means "in the same place." It is used in bibliographies and footnotes to mean "look back to the previous citation."

At ibidPREP, we use it to mean "look back to what you already know, have already learned, or should have learned." Our tutors show students the way back into their own minds in order to access knowledge that, more often than not, they already have. Under the pressure of test taking conditions, we almost always know more than we think we know, and, more importantly, we forget that we're allowed to look back into our own minds and think!

An ibidPREP Book

2231 Broadway, 3B

New York, NY 10024

ibidprep.com

3rd Edition

ISBN 978-1-7339173-3-9

REMAIN CLAM!

4th Grade Edition

INTRODUCTION:

TEST TAKING AND THE STUDENT MIND

I grew up a classic underachiever, partly because I thought so highly of myself that nothing I could contemplate doing was good enough for me to do. Therefore, I often did nothing. I certainly didn't prepare for my standardized tests; I was far too arrogant for that. I know now that a couple of practice tests and some review would probably have helped me gain a lot of points. I don't want my students ever feeling as if they didn't reach for every last point. We may not always reach our goals, but it will never be for lack of trying. The goals we reach for are never soft. Many tutoring courses artificially manipulate their diagnostics to ensure the appearance of gains among their students. I prefer the challenge of challenging my students.

As fun as it might be, complaining about tests is a waste of your time, and having a negative attitude going into your tests usually leads to a negative result coming out. The best way to use your energy is by studying and learning how to get better at taking the test in front of you, in this case whatever Middle School Entry Test you're facing. Remember that all tests are inherently unfair. Most are skewed toward better prepared, calmer and more confident students. If tests were not unfair or skewed, everyone would excel equally.

Test Taking & the Student Mind

Underachievers—a.k.a. the Slackers

Students often come to me with their minds stressed and self-images wobbling. They are filled with notions of what kind of students they are and what their potential is or isn't; they all dread becoming numbers that don't represent them. Obviously, you are not a number, but neither are you your potential. You are what you are right now.

My job is to convince my underachievers [as I had to convince myself] to try and, in so doing, begin to end their boring cycles. Even though one of the credos[1] of the underachiever is "If I ever did try, I'd ace this test," that isn't always true. No one succeeds every time; once you learn to try, it just means that you must **always** try. Though there are no guarantees of success, I can guarantee you one thing: if you **don't** try, then it is certain you **won't** succeed.

Overachievers—The Anxious Test Takers

In addition to underachievers, I also work with a lot of students caught in the grip of test anxiety. These students are usually good students and hard workers, but they often, well, stink at tests like these. Why? Because there are certain things for which we cannot prepare, namely questions and topics that require improvisational flair. The overachiever likes to be prepared for everything, and when she's not [no one ever is], she can be a bit emotionally brittle and begin to chastise herself for not knowing something [or thinking she doesn't know it because it's not familiar to her] or get mad at her mom, her school, her tutor...All this emotionality only detracts from focus and impairs performance on tests. This is where the overachiever can learn a little from the underachiever—aka "slackers." Underachievers are used to and often completely comfortable not knowing everything. They are often able to shrug off unfamiliar looking topics and wing it when needed. That's a good thing.

All of You

Almost all students—slackers, overachievers and every student in between—come to me with preconceived notions of their own abilities: "I suck at math," "I'm terrible at grammar," "I'm slow," etc. Most of these preconceptions have been formed through years of parent/teacher conferences or odd family dynamics: "My sister is the smart one," "I'm the reader," "I'm not so mathish." *Ugh.* Often these diagnoses have only the slightest basis in reality and, if we believe them, lead us into self-fulfilling-prophecy territory. Students are told that they are bad at math, so they stop applying themselves, and then they really *do* become bad at math. Or students have a little difficulty getting the hang of reading, so they stop reading! Instead of conforming to artificial definitions, keep your mind open to its possibilities. If you do, who knows where you can go?

Even into adolescence, most kids' minds are amorphous[2] mushes that have yet to be formed to any reasonable degree. Telling kids that they have math minds or verbal minds is about as productive or accurate as looking at a sack of flour and saying it is only ever going to be bread and then looking at another sack of flour and saying it will only ever be cookies.

THE MIND IS A MUSCLE —USE IT

Even for those students who seem to breeze through tests, it's not because they never think; it's because they're used to thinking and working through problems. The finest problem-solving methods and approaches will not help unless you implement them. The mind is indeed a muscle that can be strengthened and improved through use. If my flabby belly can be tightened with fewer bagels and more sit-ups, your mind can wrap itself around fractions.

But I'm Not Good at Test Taking...

Being good at test taking is not an innate[3] trait like having brown eyes or webbed toes. Some students may have done poorly on one or two tests when they were little and have since gotten stuck with the "poor test taker" label. Some may have started out with some test-taking anxiety only to see it snowball as they've gotten older and the tests have come to have more consequences. Whatever the case, none of this means you are doomed to a life of underperforming on tests. As you read and implement the lessons in this book, you will begin to fight fear and your preconceived[4] notions with knowledge and experience. The first step in learning how to use your brilliant young mind properly is to find a way to **Remain Clam!**

---

[2] without a clearly defined shape or form

[3] in-born, natural

IT REALLY IS LIKE EXERCISE!

If you focus only on the muscle groups you are strong in, then those muscles will get very strong , and the rest of you will turn to flab.

How to Use This Book

This book is designed to walk you through all the types of questions you will face on the Middle School Test and review the material that will be covered on it. Use this book either in conjunction with a class or a tutor or on your own [you may also even bring your parents in on the process!] There are plenty of practice questions for each facet of the tests and answers to the questions are at the back.

As you review your practice, evaluate your strengths and weaknesses. Give yourself a pat on the back for every question you get right, and try to honestly figure out what you did on the problems you missed. Don't just note the correct answer and forget it. You won't learn that way.

Also try to avoid just doing question after question or test after test. If you don't review your tests and learn from your mistakes, you'll just keep making the same ones over and over. **Practice. Review. Repeat. Improve!**

NO TURTLING

You see it every day. We've turned into a nation of turtles, and somehow we're proud of it. Someone on a talk show mentions math, and someone else waves her flippers around like a turtle flailing on its back: "Oh, I can't do any of that math stuff. I'm just awful at it. Hahahahaha!" And for some reason that's okay. That kind of helplessness in the face of something vaguely challenging is really doing great things for us individually and as a nation. Not. I'm not saying that math isn't hard, or that you're a nincompoop if you have problems with it. What I am saying is, stop flipping onto your back at every obstacle. TRY!was outside in the sun, but I didn't play golf, so I didn't wear a hat and got a sunburn because of it." He replied, "But you didn't play golf yesterday." I laughed and said, "You know, when I talked just now all you heard was 'Blah, blah, blah, golf!'" **He laughed and grudgingly agreed.**

HOW TO USE THIS BOOK

& TEST FORMAT

It's about process. As much about HOW you do something as WHAT you do. In order to distinguish among students, these tests prey on students' tendency to make careless errors, not pay attention, and RUSH! Therefore, students who learn HOW TO: pay attention, execute properly, and NOT rush—WIN!!!

Read this book, and I do mean READ, in order to prep and guide yourself in the basic knowledge required on the 4th grade ELA and Math exams and the rigors of HOW TO TAKE TESTS. Then practice, practice, practice, but practice WELL. It doesn't help to do a lot of work if you keep making the same mistakes over and over again. Pay attention to what you're doing and honestly try to evaluate your weaknesses [and strengths!].

Remain Clam! contains exercises for every topic and type of question on these exams. Once you have worked through every topic and type of question, please feel free to contact ibidPREP to schedule a practice test to take with us or on your own.[1]

If we send you a test to take on your own, that means getting out of your bed or off the couch. You need to find a quiet spot in which you won't be interrupted [this may involve leaving your house entirely and seeking out the sanctuary of the nearest library, school, church or ashram[2]]. It also means uncovering the last little dirty secret almost every student clings to—in order to properly test, prep, study, read, learn, look or listen to ANYTHING, you must first turn off the computer, phone and TV. If you cannot learn to create a temporary media-free zone in your life [we call it "going acoustic" in my house], YOU WILL NEVER DO YOUR BEST ON THESE TESTS.

As you finish and correct your exercises and tests, focus on the questions you get wrong [remember to give yourself a pat on the back for the ones you get right]. Don't just look at the correct answer to your incorrect questions, say "Oh yeah," and move on. Really analyze your mistakes and try to figure out why you made them in terms of the things discussed in this book. Did you rush? Did you skim? Did you panic because it looked difficult? Was it a subject/topic you need to go back and review? Tackle every wrong question one by one and really try to grasp your errors on each so that you don't continue to make those same errors for the rest of your test-taking life!

Also, please don't fall into the trap of thinking that doing a lot of tests and questions is necessarily a good thing. If you are not learning from your mistakes, then you are simply going to repeat them and not improve your performance. It is far better to do one or two tests under super-realistic conditions, analyze your results REALLY closely, and then perhaps do one more test than to do a bunch of tests, one right after the next like a crazy person!

[1] info@ibidprep.com

[2] religious retreat [Hindu]

Here's what to expect from your 4th Grade New York State Tests

ELA Test Format

This test isn't one of those test experiences that is over in one go. No, you have to go in on two separate days to do this thing!

Here's the deal:

Day 1—Book One:

Book One is made up of four reading passages and a total of 24 multiple-choice questions—about six questions per passage.

Day 2—Book Two:

Book Two consists of three reading passages, six short-response questions and one extended-response essay to write. For info on how short- and extended-responses are graded, please see pg. 151.

	Book One	Book Two
Number of Passages	4	3
Multiple-Choice Questions	24	0
Short-Response Questions	0	6
Extended-Response Questions	0	1
Total Questions	24	10

Math Test Format

The math test takes place over two days and two books, too.

Day 1—Book One:

Book One contains 30 multiple-choice questions.

Day 2—Book Two:

Book Two contains 15 questions: eight multiple-choice questions, six short-response questions and one extended-response question. For information on how short- and extended-response questions are graded, see pg. 253.

	Multiple Choice	Short Response	Extended Response	Total
Book One	30	0	0	30
Book Two	8	6	1	15

ibidPREP Book Key

One of the main goals of this book is to try to get students to stop skimming through texts and tests and encourage them by any means necessary to READ ALL THE WORDS in order to better comprehend reading passages, ensure that they're answering the questions asked and get them to avoid partially correct answer choices. I firmly believe that students can and should develop the mental strength to plow through dense text no matter what.

However, to make reading this book a little more enjoyable, I have broken up our dense text by presenting it in various graphic forms. There is something of a method to our breakouts, and that format is explained below.

Brains generally feature amusing though often incredibly wise anecdotes I've gleaned from my experiences with students and in everyday life.

These spiky splashes include pithy aphorisms and reminders that I hope will stick in your mind.

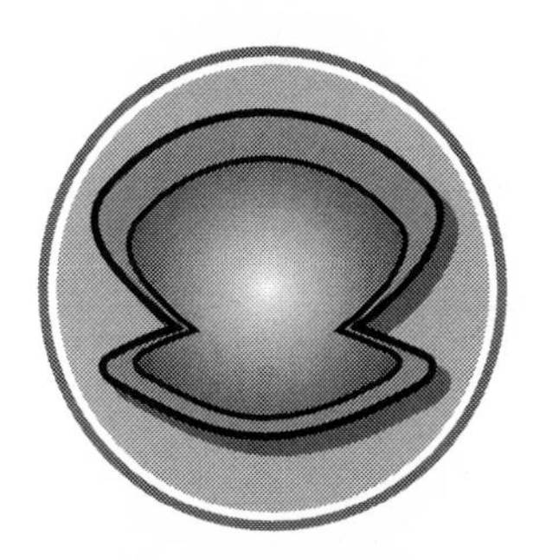

Clamshells contain sets of information that you MUST KNOW in order to excel on your exam. MUST KNOW information usually covers basic knowledge that students should have come across long ago. If you haven't truly learned this info, you should do so asap. It will make your life much easier.

Gray boxes and margins indicate practice sets and exercises.

HOW TO AVOID

PART I
CARTOON CATS & OTHER CREATURES!

1 THE CAT & THE RAKE

There is an old expression:

Fool me once, shame on you; fool me twice, shame on me.

For many of my students the rule seems to be: *Fool me a thousand times, and I'll keep coming back for more.*

Some students make the same mistakes over and over and over again, which is why the makers of these tests are so fond of building the same pitfalls into every section. Think of those poor cartoon cats chasing the mouse through the yard. They've been around that backyard so many times that you'd think by now they would know there is going to be a rake lying in the grass just waiting for them to step on and thwack them in the head. Yet episode after episode, those cartoon cats step on the same darn rake. Don't be that cartoon cat.

2 WATER FLOWING DOWN A HILL

When contending with tests, think of yourself as water flowing down a hill [I swear this is as Zen as I'm gonna get]. When water hits a tree, it doesn't stop, head back up the hill or freak out; it merely finds a way around, under or over the tree. You should too. If your approach to a problem fails, try something else. If that doesn't work, find another hill.

I often ask my students what water flowing down a hill does when it hits a tree. Most answer the basic "Goes around," "Goes under," etc. When I asked one student, a broad-shouldered soccer player, what the water did when it encountered a tree, she told me: "It knocks the tree down." She did just fine on her tests.

EXAMICIDE

3 ADRENALINE IS GOOD FOR only THREE THINGS, NONE OF WHICH IS TEST-TAKING...

Adrenaline is a magical substance. In moments of danger, it can give us strength and energy unimaginable in ordinary circumstances. For teenagers who have so many other hormones raging in their system, adrenaline surges are fairly common occurrences. Only problem is adrenaline evolved to aid prehistoric man in peril, not 21st century students taking tests.

Adrenaline worked great in frightening situations when most of our frightening situations involved lions, tigers and bears or other dudes with spears. Now, however, most of our frightening situations involve accidentally posting those pics from spring break, forgetting to erase our texts or taking standardized tests. If a caveman left his cave in the morning and right outside the cave he saw a mountain lion, his brain would shut down and adrenaline would take over. Adrenaline would give his brain one of three simple commands for his body to execute: fight, flee or freeze. That means the dude could use the adrenaline to get mad strong, pick up a rock and bash the lion [Me Kill Test Before It Kill Me], use the adrenaline to power his legs and get the heck out of there [Me Rush Through Test Before It Kill Me] or stand very, very still in the hope that the lion would not notice him [Me Freeze and Completely Choke on Test, So Test Not Kill Me]. A little adrenaline bump will certainly perk you up and keep you going during test times, but a total surge is not good for most test situations because all your energy and strength is in your body and your mind is completely focused on fighting, fleeing or freezing, NOT solving complex problems.

This is where Remain Clam! comes into play.

See next Examicide on Page 158!

CHAPTER ONE

READING COMPREHENSION

It is very important for all tests [and learning and school and life] that you have a reading life. That means that you spend some part of most every day reading something outside of school. It really does not matter what you read: books, newspapers, fiction, nonfiction, graphic novels, blogs, textbooks. Whatever you like. What does matter is that you're always paying attention to what you read and making sure that you don't let words or ideas just slide by. If there's something in your reading you don't quite follow, stop and try to figure it out, or ask your parents, teachers, friends, caregivers—anyone—what the passage or words might mean. Remember: fools think they are wise people, but wise people know they are fools! [And if you don't understand what ***that*** means, don't be afraid to ask!]

There is one more thing that matters in how you go about your reading life: no more being read to! I'm REALLY sorry about that because it really is a nice thing, but it's very important that you start reading to and for yourself. Why? Because it is very important that you learn to become an **active** reader who is not afraid to work through hard or boring material.

When your mom or dad or grandma or big sister or whoever reads to you, it's a little like watching TV. All this interesting stuff just sort of washes over you, and you don't have to do much [it's also a little like being a baby bird whose mom does everything including chewing your food for you]. As you start to become bigger kids and more independent students, it's time to start chewing your own food and working through your own books!

Boring Reading

Many, many students tell us that they like to read but only stuff they ***like*** to read. That makes a lot of sense. Unfortunately, that usually just means the fun stuff like Percy Jackson or Harry Potter or Eloise. Good stuff, but not the kind of thing you're going to find on tests. Sometimes on tests you find interesting stories, but more often you find passages about things you don't like. Some kids love reading about sea turtles, some students would rather chew their arms off than read about sea turtles. The point is, you don't get to choose. You get what you get and you don't get upset! The important thing is to always try to stay involved and engaged in your reading. It makes taking these tests that much easier, and you never know where you might just find something new or interesting!

How to Read

Most of your teachers in school try to help you with your tests. However, while teachers are very good at teaching students about history and math and spelling, they're not always so good at teaching kids about tests. That's okay, they're not supposed to be. We are. If teachers have ever told you anything about not reading passages or reading questions first or any other games like that, we'd like to ask you to forget all those tricks for now. Let us help you learn to read better instead.

The Three T's

The best readers are constantly asking questions of themselves and, more important, the material in front of them. "Why is this mind-numbingly boring?" "Why is that author going on for so long about this tiny thing?" "Why is he asking us this question?" "Why am I having problems getting through this part?"

Good readers do not accept confusion as a natural state while reading. If something doesn't make sense, they stop and try to figure it out. These are the points at which ALL readers need to slow down and break down what is being said. Don't worry, though; spending extra time on thorny sections is often made up for by being able to spend less time on other parts. There are indeed many parts of a reading that you may go through at a good pace because they are saying predictable things or repeating themselves.

As you are reading, the questions you always need to have at the back of your mind are the **three T's:**

- What is the **THEME** of this piece [**what** is its TOPIC]? First things first: figure out what the whole thing is about. Is it about sea turtles? Cool 4th graders hanging out prepping for a test? Or is it about pirates and how they fix their hair? Make sure you're clear on WHAT the piece is about, then figure out:

- What is the **THESIS** of the piece [**why** is the author writing this? **What** is the point the piece is trying to make about its TOPIC?] The WHY is the author's opinion or the point she is trying to make about her THEME. In other words, WHY the author has gone to all the trouble of writing the piece in the first place. Perhaps: sea turtles are amazing creatures that should be protected. Or: 4th graders prepping for a test are cool but need to practice their reading processes—how they read—if they want to do well on their tests!

- What is the **TONE** of the piece [**how** does the author convey her THESIS—objectively, ironically, skeptically, critically, analytically, angrily, humorously...]? This question is much easier to answer once you can tell what kind of writing it is. If it's fiction, the tone could be all kinds of things depending on the character telling the story. It could be silly or funny or even confused. If the piece is a nonfiction piece, like something from a textbook or newspaper, then most of the time the tone is going to be neutral, fairly serious and objective. If the piece is an opinion piece, the tone could be neutral, but it might also be a little angry [never too angry] or excited or even amused and humorous. Think of tone like the tones in a pencil drawing from darkest dark to the almost bare white of a page. The darkest tones are the serious, angry, harsh tones. The grey middle tones are the neutrals, and the lightest, almost white tones are the humorous, easygoing tones

Break it down!

It is impossible to eat a steak in one bite. In order to eat it and enjoy it, you need to cut it into smaller pieces and the tougher the steak, the smaller the bites. It's the same for reading. It is impossible to comprehend a passage in one go. You have to break it down to pieces and the more complex the section the smaller the piece. Sometimes we need to go through a section paragraph by paragraph, sentence by sentence or even word by word. It is vital for all your reading that you feel comfortable doing this and not worry about time. If you do break down your reading and chew slowly through the complex parts, you will undoubtedly end up unlocking the whole passage!

Reading Comprehension: Finding The Three T's Passage

Please read the following passage and identify the Three T's: Theme, Thesis and Tone. Write about the Three T's on the questions that follow.

Polar Life

The challenges facing life at the poles are far different from those at the equator. At the poles, the climate undergoes vast changes every year in temperature and in levels of sunlight. Winters are astonishingly cold and darkness lasts for weeks on end. In summer, the temperatures warm dramatically and the sun simply circles the sky without setting for several whole weeks.

Creatures have evolved many clever strategies for dealing with their shifting climate. Polar mammals have developed thick fur that changes colors with the seasons in order to camouflage them against snow and grass. Most birds simply leave, flying thousands of miles every fall to spend their winters in warmer climes. In Antarctica, the famous exception is the penguin, who stubbornly braves the cold in loving devotion to its egg. They are quite admirable parents. Plants, on the other hand, are tiny, huddled together, and have extremely brief growing seasons. Taken collectively, life at the poles shows the beautiful and impressive tenacity of life in the face of the hardest of conditions.

Reading Breakdown Sheet

What is this passage about [**THEME]**?

___

What is the main point of the passage [**THESIS**]?

___

___

___

What is the **TONE** of the piece and what type of writing is this, most probably?

___

How to Answer

With reading comprehension questions, it is not always possible or wise to do what kids usually do: read the question and then pick through the answers for something reasonable. First of all, it's not always clear what the question is. Second, the answer choices for the questions are often so unclear and poorly worded that by the time you get to answer choice (D), you might be hard-pressed to know what to think or to even clearly remember the question. Here's a better way to proceed:

1. Read the question and restate it in your own words.
2. Ask the question in your own words, so you're sure what it is they're asking
3. If possible, answer the question for yourself ***BEFORE*** you look at the answer choices. If you don't have an answer to the question without looking at the text, look at the text, THEN come up with an answer.
4. Once you've determined your answer, ***THEN*** look at the answer choices and select the one whose meaning is closest to yours. Be careful: the answer choice may word your answer differently from what you expect.

Interpretation

Although we are delighted by our students' interpretations (opinions, ideas, etc.) of the world, we are not interested in those interpretations if they are made without any foundations—if they are not based on anything. Interpreting information and texts does not mean immediately sticking your own opinion on everything that's put in front of you. It does not mean seeing everything you read through your eyes only. At ibidPREP, interpretation means taking in what is placed before you [book, film, discussion, experience] and letting all the words and information go into your brain, so you may establish what the reading is trying to say from its author's viewpoint [not your own]. Once you are able to explain what someone else's viewpoint is, then your interpretation will have a lot more strength!

If You're Going to Get It Wrong, Get It Wrong Quickly

Studies [mine] show that the longer a student takes to answer a reading comprehension question, the greater the odds are that that student is going to get it wrong. Therefore, if you're going to get a reading comprehension question wrong–if you have no feel for the question, if you were able to get rid of only one bad answer, if the remaining answers are all blurring together, don't agonize; don't sit there thinking "A no B no D...darn it, C." In these situations, GUESS ONE and MOVE ON [aka GTHOOT–get the heck out of there!] Some questions are just lost causes, and it's not worth suffering over them when there are others to tackle [unless you have extra time at the end of the test after you've checked all your other answers]. When you guess like this, you might get it wrong, but you will save time, energy and confidence.

Stop the Multiple Choice Madness [and Other Bad Habits We Pick Up in School]

Conventional wisdom has it that multiple choice questions are great if you're not entirely sure about what you are doing. They give you something to get you moving in the right direction. Right? Wrong. Not on these tests. If you have no idea or only a partial idea of what you're doing on a question, the answer choices are going to be there to distract, annoy, confuse you further OR sucker you into the wrong answer right away. The multiple choice answers help give you a confidence boost only when you already know what you are doing in a question.

When your teacher gives a multiple choice test, she is probably using those multiple choices to help you. The answers act as prompts that are meant to steer students toward the correct answers and reward those who, even though they may not remember the exact answer to a question, have a general sense of the topic and what are reasonably correct answers. This is NOT AT ALL what goes on in most standardized tests!

Almost every kid, when left to his or her own devices, will tackle most multiple choice problems pretty much the same way: look at the problem, get a rough idea of what's being asked, and then pick through the answers for something that looks good. I would like to break you of that habit, not because it doesn't work on the problems on which it works, but because it really doesn't work on the problems on which it doesn't work. If you don't know the answer to a question and start picking through the answers, you are very likely to pick an answer that is partially correct and therefore completely incorrect. Most standardized tests are loaded with incorrect answer choices placed there to tempt and weed out the lazy.

How to combat these false answers? Come up with your own answer first! Don't just jump to the answer choices. For reading especially: figure out your own answer to the question FIRST, before you start shopping around from among the multiple choice selections. Then pick the answer choice that is closest to your own answer. You'll save time, energy and points!

STOP FLIPPING

So many students never finish their reading sections because they sit there wrestling among bad and worse answers. Even worse, they flip back and forth and back and forth from the reading to the questions to the reading to the questions. Once you start over-flipping, you're dead. Your brain during the test and, truth be told, most times, is like a colander (spaghetti strainer, sieve). You would not use a colander to carry soup from the kitchen to the table. If you did, you would probably try to run to the table before everything leaked out. You certainly wouldn't go back and forth and back and forth to the kitchen trying to top off the soup each time. Eventually, everything would drain out, and you'd end up in a puddle of soup, confused, out of time, lacking in confidence, soupless and wrong.

In the Reading Comprehension It Is More Often a Question of Finding the Least Wrong Answer Than Finding the Right Answer

The reading comprehension passages on standardized tests are taken from previously published materials: novels and articles mostly from national publications or fairly well known books. However boring and pointless the readings might seem to the young reader, they are, at least, somewhat well written. The pieces have been written by an author who has made a career out of writing. Each particular piece was chosen for publication by an editor whose job it is to find good and interesting writing that will attract readers. The piece, once selected for publication, is reviewed by editors and proofreaders who read the piece for errors, statements that aren't true, and plain bad writing. While all this is true for the reading passages on these tests, the same cannot be said about the QUESTIONS for these tests.

Reading comprehension questions are written by the same kind of people who bring you the math questions. Namely, teachers, out of work educators and wild-eyed zombies looking to make a few extra bucks writing test questions. While there is nothing wrong with that, and while their questions are closely examined, it is also true that there is not much chance that the questions to reading passages are going to be as clear or as well written as the passages they are about. So, it is often the case that NONE of the answers truly hits the mark, and I'm not talking about the answers that are put in to confuse and distract you, I'm talking about the answers that are actually meant to be correct. This is why it is very important NOT to get hung up looking for the ***perfect*** answer; it might not be there. It is far more important to get good at choosing the least wrong answer!!

One of the best ways to find the least wrong answer is to find the **wrong wrong** answers and eliminate them. These include answers that:

- include absolutes[9] that can't be proven. An absolute USUALLY cannot be proven because, as with most things in life, there is ALMOST always an exception. [Look for answers that include words that make things NOT so absolute. Words like USUALLY and ALWAYS as used above!]
- include direct repetition of quoted text.
- are just plain dopey.
- are 80–90% correct but contain one or two words that make them 100% WRONG. If you like to just read the beginnings of answers and then grab and go, these answers will get you every time.

Eliminating bad answers can usually help you shake out at least one or two answers. The ones that are left are generally not as tough to choose from as you might think. After you've done enough practice, you can begin to smell the right answers. That's right; there is a certain odor to these kinds of answers. It smells not too vague but not too specific. It limits what it's saying to cover its back and is generally about 90% right.

The other thing about wrong answers is that they often seem correct at first glance. That is, 90% of the answer seems correct, but perhaps one or two wrong or misplaced words make the entire answer wrong. Readers who skim the answers, just like readers who skim the passages, are sunk. Make sure you read through the entire answer to be certain that everything it is saying is correct:

Most clouds are made of cool water vapor and cottony puffs.

While it is true that clouds are made of cool water vapor, they are definitely not made of cotton. The passage would certainly not have said that they were!

Reading For Details

We read for many reasons, not just to be entertained or because our teachers tell us to. We also read to get information and learn things. Texts that try to teach us something are usually full of facts, and it is important that we learn to take them in.

When you read for details, do not try to hold each number or fact in your mind as you read. Just remember where it is in the text, so that you may find it when you need it.

Read the following text about Zeami Motokiyo and keep track of where the details are!

[9] Absolutes are those things we say that make it sound as if something is all one way or the other: "You ALWAYS say that!" "It is NEVER good to guess." "ALL students hate tests."

READ ALL The WORDS

[Including the italics at the beginnings of passages]

One student of mine had reading issues and processing issues and issue issues and needed extra time and so on and so on. I worked with her a while before I started noticing a number of things, mostly that she was an incredibly passive reader. The words on the page scrolled past her eyes, but she never took it upon herself to process what those words were saying. Eventually, I thought I figured it out and asked her, "Do you watch much TV?" It turned out she watched about four hours of TV a night! TV is great, ridiculously good, but a lot of it is like baby bird food: all pre-chewed for you, completely passive, which is why it's so good for vegging at the end of the day. It does not, however, promote an active mind.

Eventually, I was able to cajole this student into actually letting the words on the page into her brain. Then one day it all seemed to click, her reading score shot up, AND she didn't really need the extra time [skimming really ends up taking MUCH longer than reading well]. Stunned, I asked her what had clicked for her. She blithely (showing a cool and casual indifference) replied, "Oh. I just started reading all the words."

Oh.

Zeami Motokiyo and Noh Theater

You might have heard about fathers expecting their children to "join the family business." Maybe you are such a son or daughter yourself! The family businesses you usually hear about are law firms, doctor's offices, stores, and things like that. But have you heard about fathers recruiting their children for theater groups?

This is what happened to Zeami Motokiyo in Japan in the 1400s. When he was growing up, Zeami's father Kan'ami had a theater company. Zeami wanted to change it from a group that did circus-like shows into one that did more serious plays. This new form was called "Noh," a word which means "skill" or "talent." While Kan'ami perfected the style of his Noh theater group, he also taught Zeami how to act. The company quickly became well known for its unique style and impressive young performer.

But what exactly is Noh theater? It is a classical form of performance, like opera or ballet, and it combines drama, music, and dance to tell ancient Japanese myths and stories. These stories usually take two forms: either they are about humans in everyday situations, or they are about gods, spirits, and ghosts in supernatural situations. Noh performers wear masks to indicate what type of person they are—old, young, woman, man—and they have their own language of complicated dance steps and hand gestures to show what they are feeling.

While Noh drama was invented in the 700s, it was Zeami and Kan'ami who helped it become the traditional art form it still is today. Kan'ami's company got so popular that it was invited to perform in front of Japan's leader (called the "Shogun"), Ashikaga Yoshimitsu. The Shogun loved Zeami's performance so much that he gave Zeami a formal education and an acting job at his court.

When Kan'ami died, Zeami inherited the theater group, putting on plays and writing many of them himself. In fact, Zeami wrote many of the Noh plays that are still popular today. With the Shogun's support, Zeami's group eventually became the Kanze School of Noh Theater, which is one of five schools that you can still visit and see perform today. In fact, its long history helps make Noh the oldest form of theater still regularly performed. And because all of the Noh schools have carefully passed down their traditions for centuries, if you ever see one of Zeami's plays you will be seeing a piece of history come alive onstage.

In complete sentences, please use the text to answer the Two T's.

THEME—What is this passage about?

____

____

THESIS—What is the main point of the passage?

____

____

Practice 

Multiple Choice Questions

1. What is "Noh"?

   A. A theatrical way of saying "no."
   B. A Japanese form of theater that is circus-like.
   C. A Japanese form of traditional theater that is similar to opera.
   D. A Japanese word for "son."

2. What can be inferred from the fact that Shogun Yoshimitsu gave Zeami a formal education?

   A. The Shogun did not like Zeami's work so he wanted to help him make it better.
   B. The Shogun thought that it would make Zeami's acting even better.
   C. The Shogun disliked Kan'ami and wanted to help Zeami steal his role as leader of the theater troupe.
   D. The Shogun loved to sing and dance and wanted Zeami to teach him how.

3. Which of the following is NOT a feature of the Noh tradition?

   A. The actors improvised tricks and jokes made at the upper classes' expense.
   B. It contains many plays written by Zeami.
   C. It is still performed today, using many of the traditions used hundreds of years ago.
   D. It uses dance steps to convey emotions, since masks cover the actor's faces.

4. What does the author suggest allowed Zeami to lead his own Noh theater troupe?

   A. He used his popularity with the Shogun to leverage a takeover of the company.
   B. A theater troupe was the "family business" in Japan at that time, so the company was passed down to him upon his father's death.
   C. He was a shrewd businessman because of his formal education at the Shogun's court.
   D. He had written a lot of Noh plays.

5. Which of the following can be inferred from the text?

   A. Noh actors did not need to be very good dancers.
   B. Noh theater was an inspiration for European opera, invented in the 1600s.
   C. The author thinks that "joining the family business" is a silly thing to do.
   D. A Noh actor might play a character who was older or younger than he, or a female character when the actor was male.

Other Kinds of Reading

You may or may not be surprised to learn, just as you may or may not have been surprised to learn that you really didn't know how to read, that there are several different types of reading you didn't know how to do. Although you should always be reading the material closely, there are a few different angles from which you should closely review the material in front of you.

Fiction & Memoirs

Fiction

Most of your reading in school is either from textbooks or articles. These are usually written as straightforward essays. Essays are writings on a theme [a subject] that make a point about that theme using examples and specific facts. Essays can do a bunch of other things, but their main job is to make one point and make it clearly and well.

In school and at home, you probably also read fiction, but fiction is different from your other readings. For the most part, fiction has one job, too, but its job is to tell a story. By whatever means necessary, a work of fiction tells us about something that happened. That's pretty much it.

Memoirs

Memoirs are a lot like stories, but they are meant to be true stories. These are stories that are being recalled by the people whose story it is. In the old days, we called them autobiographies—life stories told in the first person. Memoirs are basically pieces of autobiographies. When reading memoirs we read them a little bit like nonfiction, looking for the Three T's, but mostly we read them like we read fiction.

Here's how we read fiction.

Fiction & Memoirs: STEW

Just as there are three main things to look for in most other kinds of prose passages, there are four main things to look for in fiction reading.

S—Subject
T—Tone
E—Eyesight
W—What Happened??

Let's start with a story most everyone knows.

Cinderella

Once upon a time, there was a beautiful girl named Cinderella. She lived with her wicked stepmother and two stepsisters. They treated Cinderella very badly. One day, they were invited for a grand ball in the king's palace. But Cinderella's stepmother would not let her go. Cinderella was made to sew new party gowns for her stepmother and stepsisters and curl their hair. They then went to the ball, leaving Cinderella alone at home.

Cinderella felt very sad and began to cry. Suddenly, a fairy godmother appeared and said,

"Don't cry, Cinderella! I will send you to the ball!" But Cinderella was sad. She said, "I don't have a gown to wear for the ball!" The fairy godmother waved her magic wand and changed Cinderella's old clothes into a beautiful new gown! The fairy godmother then touched Cinderella's feet with the magic wand. And lo! She had beautiful glass slippers! "How will I go to the grand ball?" asked Cinderella. The fairy godmother found six mice playing near a pumpkin in the kitchen. She touched them with her magic wand. The mice became four shiny black horses and two coachmen, and the pumpkin turned into a golden coach. Cinderella was overjoyed and set off for the ball in the coach drawn by the six black horses. Before leaving. the fairy godmother said, "Cinderella, this magic will only last until midnight! You must reach home by then!"

When Cinderella entered the palace, everybody was struck by her beauty. Nobody, not even Cinderella's stepmother or stepsisters, knew who she really was in her pretty clothes and shoes. The handsome prince also saw her and fell in love with Cinderella at once. He went to her and asked, "Do you want to dance?" And Cinderella said, "Yes!" The prince danced with her all night, and nobody recognized the beautiful dancer. Cinderella was so happy dancing with the prince that she almost forgot what the fairy godmother had said. At the last moment, Cinderella remembered her fairy godmother's words. "Oh! I must go!" she cried and ran out of the palace. One of her glass slippers came off, but Cinderella did not turn back for it. She reached home just as the clock struck twelve. Her coach turned back into a pumpkin, the horses into mice and her fine ball gown into rags. Her stepmother and stepsisters reached home shortly after that. They were talking about the beautiful lady who had been dancing with the prince.

The prince had fallen in love with Cinderella and wanted to find out who the beautiful girl was, but he did not even know her name. He found the glass slipper that had come off Cinderella's foot as she ran home. The prince said, "I will find her. The lady whose foot fits this slipper will be the one I marry!" The next day, the prince and his servants took the glass slipper and went to all the houses in the kingdom. They wanted to find the lady whose feet would fit in the slipper. All the women in the kingdom tried the slipper but it would not fit any of them. Cinderella's stepsisters also tried on the little glass slipper. They tried to squeeze their feet and push hard into the slipper, but the servant was afraid the slipper would break. Cinderella's stepmother would not let her try the slipper on, but the prince saw her and said, "Let her also try on the slipper!" The slipper fit her perfectly. The prince recognized her from the ball. He married Cinderella and together they lived happily ever after.

SUBJECT—What is the story about?

The story is about Cinderella, a girl who wants to go to a dance but is not allowed to by her mean stepmother.

TONE—How is the author telling the story?

The author of "Cinderella" uses a **light, descriptive tone** to tell the story.

To determine tone, it can be helpful to think about what the author's attitude is and to describe that attitude as a feeling. So an author may write in a reflective, wistful, regretful, affectionate or ________ tone. The list goes on.

If you are having a hard time figuring out tone, think of tone in terms of shading in pictures from dark to light. Something funny like *The Diary of a Wimpy Kid* might have a light tone, something scary or sad like a horror story might have a dark tone, while most articles and textbooks are written with a neutral [middle], gray tone.

In "Cinderella," the author uses a **light, descriptive storyteller tone** to tell the story.

The author is using a gray to light voice to describe the action and tell the story. He is not really showing too much opinion even when talking about the stepsisters.

But...

Be careful! Tone is different from Eyes.

EYES—Through whose EYES are we seeing the narrative unfold? Who's seeing the story?

In Cinderella we see the story through Cinderella's eyes.

To find the EYES, ask yourself:

Who is seeing the story?

- A character? (first person)
- An outside narrator? (third person limited)
- An all-knowing observer? (third person omniscient)
- What is THAT person's attitude toward the story?

Remember: Each character has his or her unique attitude [point of view], and each of these might be different from the narrator's attitude, and both of those might be different from what the author thinks. Got that? It's tough at first, but just try to notice who's telling the story, whose EYES we're seeing the story through, and what the author might be trying to tell us about what's going on.

WHAT HAPPENED & WHY?!

The What Happened is like the **THESIS** of a work of non-fiction—it's the point of the piece, which in this case is to tell us what happened and why. It's also the most IMPORTANT part of your reading.

Cinderella gets to the ball and meets the Prince who falls in love with her. All this happens because she is good, kind and hard-working.

When you read fiction, your job is to follow the narrative like a detective or a reporter. You must follow all the knots and loops of the thread of the story to make sure you notice EVERYTHING and how the EVERYTHING adds up to WHAT HAPPENED!

Come to think of it, that's not a bad way to read all kinds of writing!!

In fiction, this job can be a little tricky because the author is not always making it super clear what happened. Sometimes, because the author is telling the story through the EYES of a certain character, we can't always trust what that character is telling us. Then we have to interpret what that narrator is telling us to figure out what's really happening.

What does this mean?

Does your mom ever ask you a question like:

Are you going to eat your greens?

She isn't really asking you what your plans are and whether or not you really want to eat your greens. She's really TELLING you to EAT YOUR GREENS.

Or did you ever tell your dad:

I don't need the light on...

What you were really probably saying was, "I don't want you to think I need the light on, but I really, really hope you leave it on anyway!"

This is the same thing that happens in fiction. Depending on whose eyes you're seeing the story through, figuring out what's really happening can be tricky.

Like in this passage told through the eyes of a 6th grader:

I didn't care what the bully said. Big Alice didn't scare me. I wasn't leaving the playground because she told me to. Or because I was scared of her. It was just because I knew my grandma wanted me to take out the garbage, and it was probably getting stinky, so I thought it would be a good idea to hurry home. So, I ran out of the playground as fast as my feet could carry me. I was glad to be getting away; I mean getting home to help my grandma!

Can you figure out what's really happening here? How do you know?

Let's practice looking for STEW [Subject, Tone, Eyes, What/Why?] in the story below!

Visitors From Space

There were many electronic devices in the Mahoneys' den, and together they cast a gross blue glow over the four girls huddled together in sleeping bags on the den's floor. Most of the clocks said that it was just before two in the morning, but all the girls were still awake.

It was a Friday night, now Saturday morning, in the middle of January, just after the start of the new term at school. It was the girls' first sleepover of the new year. But, even for a sleepover, there was very little sleeping going on.

Agnes Mahoney, the host, had invited all three of her closest friends with a specific purpose in mind: they were going to make contact with aliens. She was in the Astronomy Club at school, and the day before she had seen through her telescope a strange, blinking object hurtling towards Earth. Obviously, aliens were coming, and she calculated that they would be arriving at 2:30 A.M. that Saturday.

So, when the majority of the clocks read 2:15, the girls bundled themselves up in their winter coats, scarves, hats, and mittens, and they tip-toed outside and up to the roof. A few miles away there was a big, motionless cloud, but from where they stood the air was clear, and the stars shone.

Agnes had already set up her telescope. She took off the lens cap and aimed it where her calculations said the alien ship should be. "Look!" she exclaimed to her friends.

The girls took turns looking through the telescope, each gasping and shrieking in fear and delight. Through the fuzzy round window of the lens they could see a round green ship, spinning in speedy circles that blurred its many lights together. The ship was coming their way! It was too exciting to be scary.

Agnes was prepared. She went over to a metal foot locker she had brought up to the roof that morning, and took out a bunch of glow sticks and a big flag she had painted. The flag showed the girls shaking hands with tall green aliens. She cracked the sticks so they would glow, and then she distributed them to each girl. "Wave them!" she shouted. "Wave them at the aliens!"

The girls began to jump up and down, making themselves as visible as possible. Agnes put the flag on a stick and waved it back and forth dramatically, as if she were about to lead them into heroic battle.

Within minutes the spaceship was visible without the telescope. With each passing second the ship swelled in size, gradually, until it plunged into the atmosphere and a big tail of white, green and yellow trailed the ship.

"It's working! They're coming our way!" shouted Agnes. But she was wrong! The ship flew right over their house and came to a stop five doors down where Beatrice, her rival in the Astronomy Club, lived.

"Dang!" shouted Agnes. "She's going to get all the attention at school on Monday! Just my luck!"

And the disappointed girls shuffled back to the den and their sleeping bags, hoping that maybe the next aliens would find them cool enough to pay them a visit.

Visitors from Space—STEW

In complete sentences, please use the text to answer the following questions.

What is the SUBJECT of the passage [what is it about]?

____

Describe the TONE of the passage [think of dark to light]:

____

The EYES of this passage belong to [whose eyes are we seeing the story through?]:

____

The WHAT HAPPENED & WHY of this passage are:

____

____

____

____

Multiple Choice Questions

1. Which of the following is the main reason the girls have a sleepover on this night?

   A. They have a day off from school the next day.
   B. They are best friends and have a sleepover every night they can.
   C. They want to make contact with aliens.
   D. They are completing a project for school.

2. What does "term" most closely mean as it is used in the second paragraph?

   A. A word or phrase to describe an idea.
   B. A semester of school.
   C. A rule.
   D. A subject.

3. What made the girls believe the aliens are coming?

   A. They received a message telling them the aliens were coming.
   B. Their teacher told them that he had seen the aliens approaching.
   C. Aliens come at this time every year.
   D. Agnes spotted a blinking object in her telescope and figured out when it would get to earth.

4. Why do the girls wave the glow sticks around?

   A. To catch the aliens' attention.
   B. To see the spaceship better.
   C. To send a message to the aliens.
   D. To imitate the spinning lights on the ship.

5. Why are the girls disappointed by the aliens?

   A. The aliens are not very interesting.
   B. The aliens don't like children.
   C. The aliens choose to visit Agnes's rival instead of them.
   D. They don't look like the aliens they'd seen in movies and on TV.

6. What reason does the author suggest for why the aliens don't visit Agnes?

   A. Agnes and her friends did something to make the aliens angry.
   B. Agnes and her friends do not speak the aliens' language.
   C. Agnes and her friends are not on the aliens' flight path.
   D. Agnes and her friends aren't cool enough.

If you're ever not sure — read some more

The nice thing about reading comprehension is that all the answers are in the text! In math or grammar, if you have forgotten a concept or approach, you may have no way of finding it out during the exam. In reading, however, if you're not sure of a detail, instead of staring off into space, look back to the text! It's all there!! It's the same for questions regarding specific lines. If you can't determine an answer from the specific lines given, read more before or after the lines to make better sense of them!

Poetry

Poetry can be imaginative, vivid, deeply felt and deeply thought. The words are usually arranged so that they have a pleasing sound or rhythm (sonnet, limerick, free verse, etc.) or in order to emphasize other particular qualities of the language.

Reading Poetry

Reading poetry even more, not less, than prose, is not about YOUR interpretation of it or what you think you see in the writing. Poetry involves a very precise use of language to make one or several points. Although it is often true that words and lines have more than one meaning, those meanings are what the author intended, NOT as readers may loosely guess at them. This is not to say that poets do not leave some things to a reader's imagination or interpretation, but that happens much less often than most students are led to believe and is only a piece of the poetry puzzle.

Once readers acknowledge that all the words count and that their meanings are intended by the poet, THEN the reader is free to delve into those meanings and to have a personal response to the material.

One nice thing about poems is that, for the most part, the entire piece is right in front of the reader, just as it is with a painting. Staying focused on the whole of the piece does not require flipping back and forth between pages but rather bearing down on what's immediately in front of you.

Don't worry about how hard it seems; just read it.

Many students are intimidated by poetry. Perhaps this is because there is more prose than poetry in the world. Perhaps this is because we don't read that much poetry in schools. Perhaps this is because poets use literary devices in their writing. Whatever the reason, poetry does not need to be difficult. Although poetry is often denser than prose with more meaning packed into fewer words, as with all complex readings the best way to handle it is to break it down to smaller and smaller pieces and process those! The good thing about most poems is that though they might be densely packed with meaning and images, they are usually much shorter than prose pieces, so you can feel comfortable taking your time to break them down. So when you see a poem on the Hunter Test, you need not get tripped up by it. You need to welcome it like an old friend. (Did you catch that simile? If not, keep reading!)

There are right and wrong ways to read and interpret poetry!

Some students think poetry is fluffy and silly and that there is no right way to decipher it, therefore anything they say about poetry is correct. Wrong! Poetry is full of meaning, plots [sometimes], characters [sometimes], imagery [often] and speakers [narrators]. And just like in your prose readings, poems make a point. All the clues are there. It's your job to pay close attention to the poem and figure out what the poet [or the speaker] is saying!

Reading Poetry Is not that Different from Reading Prose

Reading poetry is a lot like reading prose: we are still reading for the three T's. We are trying to figure out what the topic of the poem is, what the point the poet is trying to make about her topic and what tone the poet is using in order to get her point across.

Literary Devices

Some questions on the Hunter Test might ask you about the names of these literary devices, but even if they don't, it helps for us to know about them so that we can better decipher poetry. Also, fiction writers and nonfiction writers can use these literary devices too! It's just that they are especially crucial to understanding poetry.

1. Metaphor: comparing one thing to another thing not using "like" or "as" (The fog was a blanket; He was a gorilla on the basketball court). One thing actually BECOMES the other: "She was a pillar of strength."
2. Simile: comparing one thing to another thing using "like" or "as" (The fog was thick as a blanket; He was like a gorilla on the basketball court).
3. Personification: when an idea, object or animal is given human characteristics (The autumn leaves danced). Personification can also involve a person becoming the embodiment of something nonhuman (Kobe is the personification of evil; That nurse was kindness personified).
4. Hyperbole: obvious and extreme exaggeration that is intended for effect (I've been waiting here for an eternity).
5. Imagery: the use of sensory words (sight, sound, smell, taste, feel) to describe an object or person. Many of the poems you'll see on your state tests involve a lot of imagery. Understanding what these images stand for or are meant to convey is HUGE.
    a. a sky-blue blanket
    b. a freezing-cold greeting
6. Foreshadowing: the author's clues or hints to events that will follow.

7. Alliteration: repetition of initial sounds (usually, but not always, consonants) (Ask Adam for an apple; Several sweet sounds swooshed over the sea).
8. Rhyme: regular recurrence of corresponding sounds (The new plane flew into the deep blue).
9. Rhythm: the beat; the pattern of stressed and unstressed syllables
(da – dum – da – dum – da – dum = to be or not to be)
10. Onomatopoeia: words that imitate the sounds associated with them (buzz, beep, zoom).
11. Allusion: A reference to a real or imaginary story, event, character or person.

Which Literary Device?

Read each line, and then write which literary device is at play.

1. He was a monster on the football field. ____________________
2. The snow danced outside. ____________________
3. The baby's eyes were as blue as the sky. ____________________
4. The car honked its horn. ____________________
5. The mockingbird sang outside our window. ____________________
6. My grandma has been working here since the beginning of time. ____________
7. She had spiky green hair. ____________________
8. Betty baked bad brownies ____________________
9. She was so fast she was like a cheetah. ____________________

Example Poems

Read the following poems and try to answer these questions:

A) ***What is the poem about? What is the point of the poem?***
B) ***What is the tone of the poem?***
C) ***Do you notice any literary devices at play in this poem?***

First Day of School

Here I am in the hall of a new school,
swimming in a staring sea of unknown faces.
My parents, though not by nature very cruel,
move almost every year to new places.

My dad, you see, is a clerk in the military,
and my mom, my sister, my dog and me
follow him to this, that, and the other arbitrary
town all over this great, big, happy country.

Every time, like today, I get to make a new start,
to make a fresh identity for each school.
I can be the nerd, jock, clown, or fool,
or I can remain unnoticed, a useless part.

Everyone stares at me as if it's their right,
as if I've intruded into something I do not own.
Now all I want is to run away and get out of sight,
but the Army decides when I get a new home.

But what's this! "Hello!" says the girl in a yellow sweater.
Her name is Lydia, and she asks me to sit with her.
We talk and talk, and she tells me about herself,
and a new identity occurs to me for this school: myself.

1. What is the poem about? What is the point of the poem?

____

____

____

2. What is the tone of the poem?

____

3. Do you notice any literary devices at play in this poem? [Cite examples]

____

____

____

____

Multiple Choice Questions

1. Why does the narrator switch schools so often?

   A. He or she has behavior issues.
   B. He or she can't decide what kind of person to be.
   C. His or her father is in the armed forces.
   D. His or her family loves to travel.

2. What opportunity does changing schools offer the narrator?

   A. The chance to change identities.
   B. The chance to have friends all over the world.
   C. The chance to learn from really interesting teachers.
   D. The chance to get some distance from her family.

3. Which of the following literary devices is used in the poem:

   A. Simile
   B. Onomatopoeia
   C. Rhyme
   D. Foreshadowing

4. We can infer which of the following:

   A. That the speaker is a boy.
   B. That the speaker is a girl.
   C. That the speaker is lonely.
   D. That the speaker loves the army.

5. In the second stanza, the narrator mentions nerds, jocks, clowns, and fools. Mentioning these different kinds of people serves to:

   A. Show the different roles available to a new kid.
   B. Show the order of popularity of these different kinds of kids.
   C. Show the kinds of kids the narrator doesn't like.
   D. Show how all kinds of kids are basically the same.

Plays

Reading a play can be intimidating. There are capital letters and italics everywhere, and it's hard to tell where everybody is. The trick to remember is that plays aren't *really* meant to be read. Instead, they're guidelines for actors and directors to perform the play. Plays, like movies and TV shows, are meant to be seen!

But how helpful is that? You're stuck at a desk with sheets of paper and there's no way you can leave to go watch a play. So what do you do? **Imagine** the play in your head!

That's easier than it sounds because the playwright—the person who wrote the play—gives you clues about what the performance should look like.

The first clues to look for are called **stage directions**. Stage directions are written in *italics*. In these directions playwrights tell you where the scene takes place, who is involved, what the characters are wearing, what time of day it is and other important details about the setting and situation. Like all directions, do not ignore these! They tell a lot!

Try reading the scene below. Read the stage directions and try to imagine the setting and what's happening as you go. See the show in your head [close your eyes if you have to!]

Dramatic Text Example

from **<u>There's a Boy Under My Bed!</u>** by Stuart Servetar

The play opens on what looks like a child's room. It is dark in the room with just moonlight coming in the window and a nightlight by the door. Simon, a little creature with deep red fur and bright yellow spots, is sleeping in the bed.

There is no noise and nothing happens, but all of sudden SIMON sits straight up in his bed.

SIMON: Who's there?! What's happening??

He looks around his room. He's scared. There is no noise and nothing happens. SIMON turns on the lamp on his nightstand. Nothing.

SIMON creeps out of bed and looks around his room. SIMON is wearing bright footy pajamas with little fire trucks on them. He goes to open his closet but is too afraid. He hurries back to his bed. Sleep overtakes him. Without turning off the light, SIMON plops BACK down on his pillow asleep again.

Almost as soon as SIMON'S head hits the pillow, the bottom of his blanket flaps. And flaps again. A little hand reaches out from under the bed. The hand feels around the floor for a little while and then lifts the bottom of the blanket. A little boy crawls out from under the bed. He's wearing the same footy pajamas as SIMON. But he's a boy and not a furry creature.

The BOY stretches and shields his eyes from the lamp light. He snoops around the room a bit. Picks up a toy airplane and flies it for it a bit. Then the BOY walks back to the bed, turns off the lamp and scoots back under the bed.

The room goes dark and quiet. There is no noise and nothing happens, but all of sudden SIMON sits straight up in his bed.

SIMON: Mom? Mom? MOM!!!

A moment later the door to SIMON's room opens and a large, kind creature with yellow fur and red spots comes into the room.

SIMON: Mom!

MOM: Yes, dear?

SIMON: Did you turn off my light?

MOM: When you went to bed, dear.

SIMON: I mean just now.

MOM: No dear, I was trying to, you know, sleep!

SIMON: Oh....[pause]...Then I believe we have a problem.

MOM: What is that, dear?

SIMON: I think there's a boy under my bed.

MOM looks at SIMON. Looks around the room. Takes a long pause.

MOM: Oh no, dear. Not again!

Did you close your eyes? Did you see the little creature in his bed? Did you see the room? Could you imagine the boy crawling out from under the bed? The creature's mother hurrying to her son? If you did, then you just read a play!

Try it now with a slightly more complex scene and then answer the questions afterwards

Dramatic Text: PETER PAN Scene

(The nursery window is blown open, probably by the smallest and therefore most mischievous star, and PETER PAN flies into the room.)

PETER (*in a whisper*): Tinker Bell. Tink, are you there? (*A jug lights up.*) Oh, do come out of that jug. (*TINK flashes hither and thither.*) Do you know where they put it? (*The answer comes as of a tinkle of bells; it is the fairy language.*) Which big box? This one? But which drawer? Yes, do show me.

TINK pops into the drawer where the shadow is, but before PETER can reach it, WENDY moves in her sleep. He flies onto the mantel shelf and sits. Then, as she didn't wake, he flies to the drawer and scatters its contents to the floor. In his joy at finding his shadow, he forgets that he has closed TINK in the drawer. He sits on the floor with the shadow, confident that he and it will join like drops of water; they don't. Then he tries to stick it on with soap from the bathroom, and this failing also, he sits dejectedly on the floor. This wakes WENDY.

WENDY (*courteously*): Boy, why are you crying?

(*He jumps up and, crossing to the foot of the bed, bows. WENDY, impressed, bows to him from the bed.*)

PETER: What is your name?

WENDY (*pleased to be saying it*): Wendy Moira Angela Darling. What is yours?

PETER (*finding his own name too brief*): Peter Pan.

WENDY: Is that all?

PETER (*biting his lip*): Yes.

WENDY (*politely*): I am so sorry.

PETER: It doesn't matter.

WENDY: Where do you live?

PETER: Second star to the right and then straight on till morning.

WENDY: What a funny address!

PETER: No, it isn't.

WENDY: I mean, is that what they put on the letters?

PETER: Don't get any letters.

WENDY: But your mother gets letters?

PETER: Don't have a mother.

WENDY: No wonder you were crying.

PETER: I wasn't crying. But I can't get my shadow to stick on.

WENDY: It has come off! How awful. (*Looking at the spot where he had lain.*) Peter, you have been trying to stick it on with soap!

PETER (*snappily*): Well then?

WENDY: It must be sewn on.

PETER: What is 'sewn'?

WENDY: You are dreadfully ignorant.

PETER: No, I'm not.

WENDY: I will sew it on for you, my little man. But we must have more light. (*She touches something, and to his astonishment the room lights up.*) Sit here. I'm afraid it will hurt a little.

PETER (*a recent remark of hers bugging him*): I never cry. (*She seems to attach the shadow. He tests it.*) It isn't quite itself yet.

WENDY: Perhaps I should have ironed it.

The shadows wakes and is as glad to be back with Peter as he is to have it. He and his shadow dance together. He is showing off now. He crows like a rooster.

PETER: Wendy, look, look; oh the cleverness of me!

WENDY: You conceit. Of course I did nothing!

PETER: You did a little.

Multiple Choice Questions

1. Read the following sentence from the passage:

> He sits on the floor with the shadow, confident that he and it will join like drops of water. Then he tries to stick it on with soap from the bathroom, and this failing also, he sits dejectedly on the floor.

In the above stage direction, the word "dejectedly" most nearly means:

A. sleepily.
B. clumsily.
C. angrily.
D. sadly.

2. Peter is most likely feeling "astonishment" when the room lights up because:

A. He does not know how electricity works.
B. He is afraid he will be caught.
C. He needs the light to find his shadow.
D. He is jealous of Wendy.

3. Peter most likely cries because:

   A. He misses his mother.
   B. He is lonely.
   C. He wasn't crying.
   D. He can't get his shadow to stick on.

4. Read the following lines from the passage:

   PETER. Wendy, look, look; oh the cleverness of me!

   WENDY. You conceit. Of course I did nothing!

   PETER. You did a little.

   The word "conceit," as used in these lines, most nearly means:

   A. jerk.
   B. braggart.
   C. boy.
   D. thief.

5. Peter most likely sits on the mantel in order to:

   A. Survey the room.
   B. Find Tinkerbell.
   C. Hide from Wendy.
   D. Find some soap.

6. Peter most likely comes to the nursery to

   A. See it for the first time.
   B. Invite Wendy to come visit him where he lives.
   C. Find Tinkerbell.
   D. Ask Wendy to sew his shadow back on.

7. Through this scene, the author conveys which idea?

   A. Though Peter seems full of himself, he is actually insecure.
   B. Though Wendy is afraid of Peter, she conquers her fear.
   C. The Darling family should probably lock their windows.
   D. Though Peter and Wendy are different, they find a way to become friends.

Nuts & Bolts of Reading

1. Read the passage.
2. Keep reading until you've got your three T's. Usually you'll know your Theme and Thesis by the first few sentences of the **second** paragraph, but sometimes the author doesn't spit it out until much later. Hang in!
    a. Make sure you are clear on what the topic truly is [THEME]: just because they're talking about *bananas*, it doesn't mean that the topic is really *bananas*.
    b. Make sure you are clear on what the author's viewpoint is [THESIS]. Look out for the "but." Just because the author writes "most people think bananas," it doesn't mean the author thinks "bananas." In fact, he probably thinks "not bananas."
3. Once you've established what the "but" **and/or** author's point is, you will see that <u>every</u> body paragraph is designed to support that point.
4. Occasionally, authors will devote a body paragraph to an opposite example—something that seems to disagree with their point of view. Authors do this in order to:
    a. Seem fair—they want to create the appearance of examining all sides of an argument and of demonstrating their awareness of all sides of an argument or
    b. Strengthen their point—by raising and then ultimately rejecting opposing points of view, authors ultimately hope to make their own points of view look better.
5. Most passages make one and only one main point, and most of the questions depend on your being aware of what that point is.
6. Once you are done reading, follow this process for answering questions:
    a. Read the question,
    b. Paraphrase[10] the question so as to be sure you know what it's asking,
    c. Determine *your* answer to the question. If you don't have one, look back to the passage (especially and most definitely if the question is about a specific DETAIL). Don't flip back to the question until you've figured something out.
    d. Once you have an answer in mind:
        i. Read the answers given.
        ii. Eliminate any answers that seem wrong right off the bat.
        iii. If you find your answer during your first read-through of the answers—pick it.
        iv. If you don't find the answer you want but have one or two choices left, look closely at the remaining answers and try to find one or two words in an answer that would make it ***wrong***.
        v. If you are still left with more than one answer choice, pick the answer that seems the most limited [with words like *some*, *often*, *occasionally*, etc.] and the most like previous answers to other questions in the section. And then,

Move on! Remember, the longer you spend on a reading comprehension question the more likely you are to get the question wrong anyway, SO save time, energy and points and GTHOOT![11]

---

[10] put in your own words
[11] Get the Heck Out of There!

CHAPTER TWO

HOW TO WRITE

When we teach reading, we teach the ABCs; when we teach math, we teach the 1, 2, 3s; but when we teach writing, for some reason, we do not teach nouns, verbs and adjectives, or spelling, or how to make sentences connect to each other. Instead, we teach students how to say ABSOLUTELY NOTHING over the prescribed length of an assignment [which is really the only thing most kids end up caring about when they write: how long does it have to be?] Yuck.

Imagine a world in which students are taught certain rules about the words they are meant to write with and certain rules about how to put those words together! Imagine a world in which students are taught to mine their thoughts and lay them out in an ordered fashion!! Imagine. It's easy if you try.

Below, I will give you the benefit of our brief but extremely clear grammar recipe. If you learn and follow it, not only will you write better and with greater focus, not only will you learn to proofread your work for grammar and sense, but you will also end up having a better handle on English grammar than 92% of your fellow citizens, including the grown-ups [Stufact!].

How to Learn Grammar—It's WRITING, not SOUNDING

The thing to remember about grammar is that it is a measure of **WRITTEN** English, not **SPOKEN** English. Spoken English relies on a lot of implied meaning and, often, what sounds good or right. But since no one is around to explain what has just been said, **written** English needs to follow certain rules in order to be clear. As a result, what **sounds** right may be wrong, and what sounds weird or awkward may be 100% correct.

Which are correct?

- Beth is taller than her. / Beth is taller than she.
- I feel badly for you. / I feel bad for you.
- There is competition between the teams in the league. / There is competition among the teams in the league.
- Just between you and I, this test sucks. / Just between you and me, this test sucks.

If you go by how things sound on the questions above, you would probably be wrong every single time: the second option is the right one in each example! We explain below...

Before you learn the grammar of what is, for many of you, your native tongue [for heaven's sake!], you need to learn the basic building blocks of our grammar, the parts of speech.

Parts of Speech

Noun

- person, place, thing, idea:
  - chef, mall, bat, freedom

Proper Noun

- particular person, place, thing or idea:
  - George, Nevada, Coke, Communist

Verbs

- Action words [he **runs**, she **has**, they swam] **+**
- Being verbs and the verb "to be" [I **am** short]

	To Be	
	Singular	Plural
1	am/was	are/were
2	are/were	are/were
3	is/was	are/were

- Linking Verbs are verbs that describe how we notice things through our senses or how things change from one way of being to another....
  - appear, taste, smell, feel, look, sound, grow [when it means "become," not "get bigger"], seem, remain, become
  - I *remained* still while the nurse removed the splinter from my foot.
  - The jester *seemed* crazy.
  - The jester's laugh *sounds* creepy.
  - I *grow* tired of your whining.
- Verb Tenses
  - Agreement—when we say a verb "agrees" with its subject, we mean that it has the right "number" and tense —i.e., the verb is singular or plural if the subject is singular or plural, and the verb takes place in the right time period (past, present, future, etc.)
  - The basic verb tenses are fairly straightforward. You probably already knew that the verbs in the sentences below agree with their subjects.

The coat **hangs** in the closet.
The cats **played** with the mice.
The house of cards **shook**.

- Parallel Structure
  - This is one of the main concepts of grammar. Any time you have consecutive actions in a list, all the verbs must be in the same form and tense. Parallel structure also holds true for lists of nouns, adjectives or anything else—all items must be in the same form.

    YES: After school, I like to change my clothes, eat a snack and do my homework.
    NO: After school, I like to change my clothes, eat a snack and doing my homework.
    YES: I like swimming, fishing and singing.
    NO: I like swimming, fishing and to sing.

- Passive Voice
  - In English, we much prefer to have our subjects be the **active** partners, the nouns that are performing the verbs. We do not like passive constructions, where the subject is being acted upon, but they are not technically ungrammatical.

    YES: John Guare wrote *Six Degrees of Separation.*
    NO: *Six Degrees of Separation* was written by John Guare.

    YES: The dog was wagging its tail.
    NO: The tail was being wagged by the dog.

  When it comes to active voice, also definitely avoid having too many "ing" words [aka gerunds] lead off your sentences. Especially "being."

    NO: Being that we were hungry, we got pizza.
    YES: We were hungry, so we got pizza.

Adjectives

- Words that modify [describe] nouns:
  - The **blue** hat.
  - The **delicious** burger.
  - The **angry** leprechaun.

Adverbs

- Words that modify verbs, adjectives AND other adverbs.
  - The boy ran **quickly.**
  - She wore a **pale** blue hat. ["pale" modifies the adjective "blue"]
  - He ate a **red** hot chili pepper. ["red" modifies the adverb "hot" which is itself an adverb modifying "chili" which is an adjective describing "pepper"—whew!]

How do you know when it's an adverb modifying an adjective and not just two adjectives strung together? If you see a comma between the modifiers, they are distinct [separate] adjectives. If there's no comma, then the first word is the adverb modifying the following word. E.g.,

- *The still, dark night* means the night was still AND dark.
- *The still dark night* means the night continues to be dark.

WHY WE HATE GRAMMAR

One of the reasons teachers became loath [fearful, resistant to] to teach grammar was due to the weight of exceptions. Kids love rules/hate exceptions because they require thought. Ugh.

Luckily, there are far fewer exceptions of consequence in English grammar than there are in English spelling, which truly is bonkers and rule-resistant.

Exception #1: When We Don't Use Adverbs

There are times when we don't use adverbs. Pay attention to the following scenarios. **Linking verbs**, especially **sense verbs** [verbs dealing with the senses], **do not** take adverbs; they take adjectives instead.

Modifying Linking Verbs Especially the Five Senses [Especially Important for the Essays That Ask for *Sensory* Detail]

1. ***Feel:*** [emotions vs. touch] Mary feels **bad** about your pain.

   If Mary felt "badly," that would mean that there was something wrong with her fingers and she couldn't feel things properly when she touched them. In other words, "badly" used here would be referring to/modifying her ability to touch. If you're having trouble understanding this point, try replacing "badly" with another adverb. If you say, "I feel greatly," that doesn't really make sense, does it?

2. ***Smell:*** [scent vs. smelling] I just took a shower; I smell good. / The perfumer smells excellently; he can tell what kind of cologne you are wearing in an instant.
3. ***Look:*** [appearance vs. seeing] That piece of pizza sure looks good. / Make sure you look over the contract well.
4. ***Sounds/Hear:*** That song sounds good. / I haven't been able to hear well since touring with my band.
5. ***Taste:*** The rabbit stew tastes good. / The food critic accurately tastes all the spices in the dish

ADVERB ABUSE

Some people grow up not using adverbs too often in their everyday speech and writing. They get in the habit of saying things like: "I did good," "He eats fast," "She ran so quick..." Sometimes later in life [like in college], these people discover the beauty and purpose of adverbs. Often, like a cook who has just discovered spices, they then start sprinkling them on everything,

My favorite overuse of adverbs pertains to the word "feel," as in one's emotional state. A lot of late adverb learners love to say, "I feel badly about that." I feel bad that they feel compelled to do that. President Bill Clinton, who grew up in rural Arkansas [probably not a hotbed of adverb use], says, "I feel badly." No one has had the temerity [nerve, chutzpah, boldness] to tell him he's wrong, so please don't feel bad [and definitely don't feel badly] if you make the same mistake!

Exception #2: When We Don't Use Adverbs

The verb "to be" **does not** take adverbs; it takes adjectives instead. That's because the modifiers correspond to the subject, not the verb.

- I am fast [not "I am quickly"].
- He is loud.
- Those potato chips are excellent.

Pronouns

Pronouns are generic[19] words that take the place of specific nouns. The noun that a pronoun replaces is called its "antecedent." It is always important, as a reader, to be able to identify the antecedent of a pronoun; likewise, as a writer, it is your job to make sure your writing is free of ambiguity and that antecedents are easily identified. ("The novel's plot is tedious, as is the writing style. It could definitely use some improvement." What does "it" refer to? The novel's plot, or its writing style? Or the novel as a whole? Don't confuse your readers!)

There are many, many kinds of pronouns in the world of grammar, but the ones you most have to concern yourself with here are subject and object pronouns.

[19] universal, all-purpose

Subject Pronouns replace nouns that function as the subject.

Object Pronouns replace nouns that function as the object.

So what's a subject? A **subject** is the noun that performs the verb.

Examples:

The dog drove the bus. ("dog" is the subject)
Cats and dogs fight all the time. ("Cats and dogs" is the subject)
Pet ownership requires commitment. ("Pet ownership" is the subject)

So a **subject pronoun** is a pronoun that takes the place of one of these subjects. Here are the same sentences with subject pronouns.

It is a terrific movie.

They are happiest in the tropics.

They have strengths and weaknesses.

Simple enough. But what about objects? What are they? **Objects** are usually the nouns that receive an action from the subject. E.g.,

My grandmother and I went to a baseball game. (The object is "baseball game")

A player gave autographs to George and Tony. (The objects are "George and Tony")

So, with **object pronouns** taking the place of these nouns, we get:

My grandmother and I went to it.

A player gave autographs to them.

Here's a table of the subject and object pronouns for you to learn.

Subject Pronouns:		Object Pronouns:	
I	We	Me	Us
You	You	You	You
He/She/It/Who	They	Him/Her/It/Whom	Them

Special Singular Pronouns—Be on the Lookout!

Singular pronouns such as *everyone, no one, none* and *one* all take singular pronouns. That means if you want to write:

Everyone knows _________ *must learn how to write better,*

the pronoun in the blank must be *one, he, she* or *he or she*, NOT *they*. No matter how much sense *they* makes [it maintains gender neutrality for everyone and is so much less clumsy], *everyone* is singular, so the pronoun replacing it must also be singular. If you catch this in your writing, it will signal serious grammar chops!

How to Find Subjects

With all this talk of subjects, how do we know how to find them? The subject of a sentence is the noun that is performing the action. Usually in English, the subject comes before its verb and is toward the beginning of the sentence.

Betty eats cake for breakfast. / **Lou** likes toad racing. / **We** are family.

Occasionally in English, however, the subject comes after its verb, and of course tests love to exploit this fact:

There are three **things** that I like. / Here are **a key and a hat** for you. / [Weird, huh?]

Sentences can contain more than one verb and so can have more than one subject [each verb gets a subject even if it's just implied: Get over here! [the subject is whoever is getting bossed around]. When there's more than one verb in a sentence, get in the habit of determining the subject for each one. As for objects, they're easy: whatever nouns aren't subjects are objects!

Comparison

Pronouns are especially difficult to use when we're making comparisons. Consider which of the following two sentences is right:

I am cooler than he. OR **I am cooler than him.**

In normal speech, most people would say, "I am cooler than him." Again, if this were the Sounding Section, they'd be right. However, this is GRAMMAR, and according to the rules of WRITTEN grammar, in a comparison, both nouns [things being compared] are considered **subject** nouns, so both take **subject pronouns**.

So...the correct answer is: **I am cooler than he!**

Here's a trick for understanding this odd rule. Because both "I" and "he" are subjects, they must both have verbs. But, you say, there's only one verb here, "am," and it definitely does not go with "he." That's true. But that's just because we cut off the second verb.

What we're really saying is this: **I am cooler than he [is]!**

You would never say, "I am cooler than him is," so that's why you do NOT say "I am cooler than him." Just put in that missing verb yourself, and you'll see that the subject actually sounds better than the object.!

DON'T ABUSE THE "I"

Another common error people make when they start wanting to use good grammar is overusing "I." People who grow up speaking with less than perfect grammar often underuse "I": "Me and mom went to the mall," "My friend and me ate pie"...you get the idea. Once these people find out that it's "My mom and I...," "My friend and I...," etc., they start sticking "I" in everywhere, including into prepositional phrases and the objects of the sentences where they don't belong!

YES: He gave the ball to my friend and me.
NO: He gave the ball to my friend and I.

YES: There are many differences between my twin and me.
NO: There are many differences between my twin and I

Phrases

A phrase is a group of words that contains **neither** a subject **nor** a verb. Phrases provide additional information about the material in the sentence but have no overall impact on the rest of the sentence they live in.

My brother, by the way, is an idiot.

"By the way" is a phrase that tells you this is incidental[19] info about my brother. If you get rid of that phrase, you still have a fine [if troubling] sentence:

My brother is an idiot.

- NOTE: Sometimes students write in PHRASES rather than COMPLETE SENTENCES. This is when you end up writing INCOMPLETE SENTENCES. Don't do this! Remember: Each sentence must contain a SUBJECT and a VERB.

[19] Less important

Prepositions

Prepositions are words that describe the relationship between a subject and an object. The relation generally refers to location, direction or time.

The dog is **under** the tree.

"Under" tells us where the dog is in relation to the tree.

The cat came **from** the house.

Conjunctions

There are a lot of different kinds of conjunctions out there. The main ones we are interested in are called *coordinating conjunctions*—these are your basic conjunctions:

For, And, Nor, But, Or, Yet, So—aka FANBOYS! But remember—

- ***And, Nor, Or*** are NOT conjunctions when they are part of a list or grouping—Jack ***and*** Jill / beer, wine ***and*** sangria / neither Jack ***nor*** Jill / either beer ***or*** wine.
- ***For*** is a conjunction when it means **because.** It is not a conjunction when it's acting like a preposition.

  Conjunction: I went to the store, for the books were on sale.

  Preposition: I went to the bookstore for the book sale.
- ***Yet*** is not a conjunction when it means, "now" or "at this time."

Interrupters

What the heck is an interrupter? An interrupter interrupts!

- All of you, *by all means*, eat more cheese!
- *Heck*, we all want more cheese!
- *Sammy*, did you like that meme?
- All of a sudden, *bam*, it hit me!

Classify Parts of Speech Practice

Part A: Please classify each of the following as a noun, proper noun, verb, adjective, or adverb.

1. game ______________________
2. Apples to Apples ______________________
3. whale ______________________
4. funny ______________________
5. play ______________________
6. am ______________________
7. quickly ______________________
8. slowly ______________________
9. slow ______________________
10. correct ______________________
11. Thomas ______________________
12. doctor ______________________

Part B: Please list the conjunctions in FANBOYS:

F ______________________

A ______________________

N ______________________

B ______________________

O ______________________

Y ______________________

S ______________________

Punctuation

Commas

At last the secrets are revealed!

Let's be honest. Besides using commas to separate items in a list, most of us have NO idea when to use them. Most students drop them into a sentence whenever they feel it may have gone on too long or where they feel a breath should be taken or just 'cause! Wrong, wrong and wrong.

If you were marking a speech you were giving, you might put a comma in to remind yourself where to pause for breath. But again, reading isn't writing, and you don't need to tell your reader when to breathe. She can figure that out all by herself.

Here Is a List of What Commas Are For:

1. To separate a dependent clause at the start of a sentence from the rest of the sentence: While waking up this morning, I heard the phone ring.

2. To separate a long prepositional phrase or phrases at the start of sentence from the rest of the sentence: After a night of dancing, Cinderella needed a rest.

3. To separate items in a list of nouns, verbs, or adjectives:
   a. The hats, coats and scarves were in a pile on the bed.
   b. After school I like to change clothes, eat a snack and draw stuff.
   c. It was a cold, dark, stormy, scary, dread-filled night.

   You may also put a comma before the "and" in a list, but I prefer not to because that confuses things with number 4.

4. To separate independent clauses linked by conjunctions:
   a. I like cake, and I like soda.
   b. I like cake, but I hate pudding.

5. To set off appositive [descriptive] phrases within or at the end of sentences:
   a. My brother, the one in Boulder, likes rocks.
   b. Genie, the devil, loves grammar.
   c. There's nothing better than sleep-away camp, Let's review which is usually a bug-infested swamp of adolescent and pre-adolescent angst[20].

6. To separate out interrupters or exclamations:
   a. **However,** I disagree.
   b. There are, **nevertheless,** many things still to learn.
   c. **Holy guacamole,** Batman is in trouble!

[20] Anxiety; unease

7. To set off what a quotation:
   a. John said, "I do not want to go school today."
   b. "But you must," answered his mother, "because an education is a wonderful thing."

Here Is a List of What Commas Are Not For:

8. Don't add a comma before a conjunction when you are NOT adding a new subject or repeating the old one.

> **Yes**: I ate lunch with my friends and worked on my book all afternoon.
>
> **No**: I ate lunch with my friends, and worked on my book all afternoon.
>
> **Yes**: I ate lunch with my friend, and I worked on my book all afternoon.

9. Don't add a comma just because you've been writing for a while and haven't used one.

10. Don't add a comma where you think the reader might want to pause or catch her breath.

11. Joining two independent clauses by themselves. This is called a **comma splice** and it is wrong.

> **NO:** I like to eat hoagies, you like to eat subs.
>
> **YES:** I like to eat hoagies, and you like to eat subs.
>
> **YES:** I like to eat hoagies. You like to eat subs.

12. You don't have to add a comma before the "and" in a list. That's just what British people do.

> **GOOD**: Bobo likes to eat, run, and poop.
>
> **BETTER**: Bobo likes to eat, run and poop.

All of the commas in the following paragraph have been removed. Read through it and insert commas where they are needed based on the rules you just read.

> *Did you notice the title of this book? Did you notice what was wrong with it? Or did you think the title was* **Remain Calm***? Don't be embarrassed if you did. MANY people grown-ups and kids alike make the same mistake. Why? Well the brain wants the title to make sense. Remain Calm makes sense; Remain Clam doesn't. Also most of us only glance or skim things like titles instructions or epigraphs [which is what this paragraph is]. If we do read more closely we might read too quickly or too anxiously and flip letters automatically. This is what some dyslexic people do and when we're stressed we all become a little bit dyslexic: letters switch negatives and positives flip and up becomes down. So? Why does this matter? It matters because test makers on every level are all too aware of this tendency which is especially common in young minds. They know if you feel rushed stressed or distracted that you'll be prone to miss details get thin gs backwards or answer the question you imagine rather than the one on the page. That means it is VERY important that you find a way to quiet your mind focus on ALL the words and by all means no matter what Remain Clam!*

Done? Check your commas against the epigraph on the first page of this book!

Practice 

Comma Practice

Write each sentence correctly adding commas as needed.

1. Darrin likes to eat to drink and to fly kites.
2. The way Bobby my brother talks you would think he's from a different country.
3. Tomorrow will be July 4 2020.
4. My favorite date is Wednesday November 22 1961.
5. Mr. Getz my principal also teaches math science and gym.
6. Noah shine the light over here so I can see you better.
7. The kids were wearing fuzzy wool hats over their big round heads.
8. Even though you saved your money you still do not have enough for a bicycle.
9. Since you are late we had to start without you.
10. If you don't finish the project by tomorrow you won't get a good grade on it.
11. Before we moved to the city we had many animals on our farm.
12. Providing that you study for the test I am sure you will do well.
13. No there is not enough time to play a game of Monopoly before we leave.
14. Before we leave we need to turn off all the lights.
15. Well if you must choose the red dress I guess that is all right with me.
16. The light fluffy lemon cake was the hit of the party.
17. A new highway was built so motorists can move around the city more smoothly.
18. However we have tried to find our dog for two days.
19. Well do you want to be a squirrel instead?
20. The last time you told me a lie I believed you but not this time.

Apostrophes

An **apostrophe** is a punctuation mark that has two main uses: to show **possession** [this belongs to...] and to make **contractions** [combine two words into one].

Contractions

We use contractions to combine two words. **Use an apostrophe to show where a letter or letters have been removed (a contraction).**

Examples:

it is	**it's**	**class of 1987**	**class of '87**
does not	**doesn't**	**who is**	**who's**
they are	**they're**	**cannot**	**can't**
were not	**weren't**	**will not**	**won't**
you are	**you're**		

Examples:

Why didn't you answer the phone?

She hasn't received her paycheck yet.

Contraction Practice 1

Add apostrophes where necessary.

1. Sam isnt coming to the library with us.
2. Dont you want something to eat?
3. Weve been working on this project all month.
4. Its starting to feel like spring.

Practice 

Contraction Practice 2

Write the contraction form of the following words.

1. She would ________
2. Could not ________
3. Will not ________
4. He is ________
5. We would ________
6. I have ________
7. You are ________
8. We will ________
9. Should not ________
10. She is ________
11. It is ________
12. I would ________
13. That will ________
14. Who is ________
15. Did not ________
16. They are ________
17. He would ________
18. We are ________
19. Would not ________
20. They would ________
21. I am ________
22. You will ________
23. That would ________
24. She will ________
25. You would ________
26. That is ________
27. What are ________
28. He will ________
29. It would ________
30. I will ________

Possession

Use an apostrophe to indicate possession by adding ' or 's to the end of the word. But how we do this depends on if the word is singular, plural, ends in s or does not end in s!

Add ***'s*** to the singular form of a word (even if it ends in s)

Jason's car
James's cat
The printing press's pages

Add ***'s*** to plural forms that do not end in s.

The children's museum
The geese's food

Add ***'*** to plural forms that end in s.

Three friends' letters
Two cats' toys

If something belongs to two nouns, just make the second one possessive.

Tom and Jerry's apartment.
Jim and Jess's cake.

Examples:

All the players' uniforms are blue. (uniforms belonging to all the players)
The player's uniforms are blue. (uniforms belonging to one player)
A child's ball was kicked into our yard. (ball belonging to the child)
The men's department is on the second floor. (department for men)

Possessive Pronouns

Possessive pronouns confuse most kids because, right after we tell them that possessive nouns do take apostrophes, we tell them that possessive pronouns **don't**.

Remember, a pronoun takes the place of a noun and stands in for all nouns of that type.

"He" takes the place of all males

"She" takes the place of all females

"It" takes the place of all things [including animals unless a gender has been specified]

So,

Instead of writing:

This is Jack's boomerang.

With pronouns, we write:

This is his boomerang.

Notice that "his" takes the place of "Jack's" and the word tells us that the boomerang belongs to some dude.

Also notice also the we don't write "hi's" because possessive pronouns don't take apostrophes.

Similarly, we write "hers" not "her's," "yours" not "your's," "ours" not "our's," "theirs" not "their's" and, most importantly, we write "its" not "it's"!

If I had a glass of water for every time students wrote "it's" when they meant "its," I'd have my own ocean and a lot of glasses.

The reason students write "it's" is because English grammar is frying their circuits. There is a word "it's" which is a contraction of "it is." There are apostrophes in all possessive nouns, so...it seems only logical to write:

NO: This is it's last chance to shine.

But that is WRONG, WRONG, WRONG!

Below you see what's RIGHT, RIGHT, RIGHT:

YES: This is its last chance.

YES: Its coat was shiny.

YES: The sword comes in its own case.

YES: The spaceship blew out its engines.

YES: Sugar has its benefits.

YES: It's hard to get this straight!

Possessive Pronouns and Adjectives

Pronoun	Possessive pronouns	Possessive adjectives
I/me	Mine	My
You	Yours	Your
He/him	His	His
She/her	Hers	Her
It	Its	Its
We/us	Ours	Our
You (plural)	Yours	Your
They/them	Theirs	Their

Possessive pronouns in a sentence:

The ball is mine.

Is this doll yours or his?

That red car is theirs.

He likes store-bought macaroni and cheese, but dislikes ours.

Possessive adjectives in a sentence:

The ball landed in my yard.

Can I go to her house?

Their pool is the biggest.

When will our car be ready?

Possession

Please put in apostrophes as needed.

1. All the boys bicycles are gone.
2. The dancers dress was made of silk.
3. Did the cat eat the Smith familys food off of the table?
4. Marta plays on the girls basketball team.
5. Matthews and Marshas toys are all over the floor.
6. The heros arrows aimed for the villains heart.
7. The family of dragons breathed fire on the heroes shields.
8. The heroes horses heads were covered in flameproof armor.
9. The boys went to the girls party and danced with her friends.
10. Some of the girls friends danced while her other friends played Frisbee.
11. Unfortunately, it was the girls dogs Frisbee.
12. The girls dog chased its Frisbee, much to all her friends fear.

Possessive Pronoun / Adjective Practice

Write the correct possessive pronoun OR possessive adjective in the blank. Look to the underlined word for help.

1. When I got in the car, I saw that ____________ seatbelt was broken.
2. The house down the street is brand new, and the Smiths just bought it. Now the house is ____________
3. If your computer is broken, would you like to borrow ____________? I would be happy to loan it to you.
4. Sandra told me I could keep ____________ sweater since it no longer fit her.
5. I remember you left some books around here. Are those books ____________?
6. Peter ate ____________ sandwich while I ate ____________.
7. When it got dark, they went back inside ____________ house.
8. Yesterday I found a bird on the side of the roa____________ wing was broken.

Practice

9. You go __________ way and we'll go __________.

10. Even though we fight sometimes, I love __________ brother and sister.

11. That's a great basketball! __________ logo says "NBA" on it.

12. As soon as we got home, I went to my bedroom and my sister went to __________

13. I need to call the Johnson family and Dr. Chavez. Can you look up __________ phone numbers for me?

14. My mom and I went to a baseball game over the weekend; it's one of __________ favorite activities to do together.

15. Have you been to __________ house? They have a pool and a diving board!

16. After Becky made it clear that she had done all the work, she received the credit that was properly __________.

17. The soccer game should be canceled, but __________ referee does not care that it's raining.

18. Do you have a favorite color? I know what __________ is.

19. When you get to the apartment building, you can ring __________ buzzer and we'll let you in!

20. Danny, __________ backpack is unzipped.

21. When I went to __________ house, Zach showed me how to bake chocolate chip cookies.

22. If you want to use the watercolors, you need to ask Mrs. Straw; they are __________.

23. Did you know that the jacket Andy wears isn't actually __________?

24. I wish we could use our chimney, but __________ flue is broken.

Apostrophe and Possession Practice

1. Whos the partys candidate for vice president this year?

2. The fox had its right foreleg caught securely in the traps jaws.

3. Our neighbors car is an old Chrysler, and its just about to fall apart.

4. In three weeks time well have to begin school again.

5. Didnt you hear that theyre leaving tomorrow?

6. Whenever I think of the stories I read as a child, I remember Cinderellas glass slipper and Snow Whites wicked stepmother.

7. We claimed the picnic table was ours, but the Smiths children looked so disappointed that we found another spot.

8. Its important that the kitten learns to find its way home.

9. She did not hear her childrens cries.

10. My address has three 7s, and Tims phone number has four 2s.

11. Didnt he say when he would arrive at Arnies house?

12. Its such a beautiful day that Ive decided to take a sun bath.

13. She said the watch Jack found was hers, but she couldnt identify the manufacturers name on it.

14. Girls clothing is on the first floor, and the mens department is on the second.

15. The dogs bark was far worse than its bite.

16. The moons rays shone feebly on the path, and I heard the insects chirpings and whistlings.

17. Theyre not afraid to go ahead with the plans, though the choice is not theirs.

18. The man whose face was tan said that he had spent his two weeks vacation in the mountains.

19. I found myself constantly putting two cs in the word process.

20. Johns 69 Ford is his proudest possession.

Quotation Marks

Quotation marks are used to indicate that words are:

- being spoken
    - "I really like clams!" said the clown.
- copied from somewhere else
    - My recipe says, "Add garlic and butter to your clams."
- being used as titles of stories, articles or poems.
    - "Death Be Not Proud" is a brilliant sonnet, but "Batter My Heart" is better.
- referring to words in order to define them or single them out
    - Some people think "disinterested" means "not interested," but it really means "impartial."
- to indicate that the words being used have different or opposite meanings from the ones intended
    - Congress is supposed to be a "working" part of government.

For a lot of us, quotations marks can be tricky to use. Mostly because there is often a lot of punctuation and capitalization to keep straight. Let us help you keep things straight!

Spoken Quotes

Bill's mom barged into his room and said, "Clean up this pigsty!"

As is often the case with grammar, more than just quotation marks are involved here.

Capitalization In Quotes

Whatever is between the quotation marks is what Bill's mom said; everything else is what the narrator says. Because what Bill's mom says begins a new sentence, the first word in her quote is capitalized.

*Bill's mom barged into his room and said, "**C**lean up this pigsty!"*

Commas In Quotes

Commas ALWAYS come after the last word the narrator said and before the quotation marks. Like so:

Bill's mom barged into his room and said, "Clean up this pigsty!"

So I shouted back, "Well, I don't remember asking you to come in my room!"

And so on. It doesn't matter what word comes before the first quotation mark; it is always followed by a comma.

Punctuation in Quotes

At the end of the quotes, we often have another punctuation mark. In the examples above, we have periods and exclamation points. If the punctuation is in the original quote, it always comes inside the quotation marks.

When We Don't Capitalize

If a sentence starts with a quotation, do NOT capitalize the first word **after** the quotation.

> *"I don't care. You must clean it up before you go out to play,"* ***m****y mom said, angrier than ever.*

Or:

> *"Fine, ruin my life, why don't you?"* ***s****obbed her sulky son.*

Don't let the question mark throw you: "sobbed" is still part of the sentence and therefore **not** capitalized.

But:

> *"Oh, it's hardly as bad as that." My mom examined the mess on my dresser and laughed at how thick the dust was.*

My is capitalized in this sentence because it has begun a new sentence that is separate from what has been said, and we *always* capitalize the beginnings of those. So, unless the first word after the quotation is a proper noun or the beginning of a new sentence, **DO NOT** capitalize it.

This same rule holds for a quote that has been broken up mid-statement:

> *"Oh, come on," I said, "this will take all afternoon."*

We do **not** capitalize *this* because it is a continuation of the quoted sentence that started with *Oh, come on*.

When you're trying to figure out whether or not to capitalize something, just ask yourself two questions:

- Is it the start of a new sentence [either the narrator's or the speaker's]?
- Is it a proper noun?

Unless the answer to one of those is "yes," don't capitalize it!

Practice 

Capitalization Practice

Practice: Correct the capitalization errors in the following sentences.

1. i like to go to mcdonald's on tuesdays after Soccer Practice.

2. meredith says it is Silly for me to go to mcdonald's after Soccer because Fast Food is not healthy.

3. my Mom said after i finished my homework i could watch spongebob.

4. at Soccer practice, I hurt my Ankle, so i am going to see the Doctor on wednesday Morning.

5. I go to sunshine elementary school and my teacher's name is Mr. oliver.

6. my favorite Book is the star-bellied Sneeches by doctor Seuss.

7. one day I want to go to africa and see a real Tiger.

8. for dinner last night i ate Pizza from domino's.

9. this weekend I need to study for my Spelling Test before I play Video Games.

10. i made my Favorite stuffed animal at build a bear, and I named her daisy.

Usage

Usage is all about how words are used or misused.

Confusing Words

English is a mutt language; it is formed from a number of different languages, so not everything makes sense. Sometimes words that seem like they should be related to one another are not at all. Worse, words that seem like they should be spelled one way are really spelled another way—or are actually different words if spelled the other way! Therefore, it is very important to be aware of the confusing words and try to keep them straight!!

Unfortunately, there is no magic bullet when it comes to spelling. There is no trick we can tell you that will show you how to spell every word. Even professional writers have trouble with spelling, so don't feel bad if you struggle with it.

However, there are certain words that you absolutely must know how to spell by heart. Why? Because if you get them wrong you will spell a *different* word and change the meaning of your sentence. That's a whole additional level of spelling something wrong! Below are some of the trickier words.

Homophones, Homographs and Compound Words

Homophones

As if writing weren't hard enough already, now you've got to be on the lookout for something new: **homophones**! Homophones are words that *sound* the same but are spelled in different ways and mean different things.

You probably already know a few of them. The two most common sets of homophones are made up of three words that sound the same. They are *there, their* and *they're* and *to, too,* and *two*. Here's how you use them:

There/they're/their:

There: this one is talking about a place. *Please take this book to the table over **there.***

Their: this one shows that people own something. *The family took **their** dog to the park to play.*

They're: this one is a contraction that means "they are." If you can substitute "they are" and the sentence still makes sense, you need to use *they're*: *Many schools are in my hometown, but **they're** not all very good.*

To/too/two:

To: this one talks about direction or is used with verbs: *It is important **to** do your homework before you go **to** the park.*

Too: this one means *also*, or it means excessively: ***Too** many people are in the stadium for me to enter, **too**.*

Two: this one is simply the number 2. It's really simple: *There are **two** kinds of people: those who understand grammar and those who don't.*

These two sets of homophones are the most common, but there are many, many more. Here are a few more common ones that you should know.

Which/witch: A *witch* is a person who casts spells on you; use *which* for everything else! (*Which* book did you read? The book, *which* is 300 pages long, is on fire.)

Rose/rows: A *rose* is a flower and the past tense of rise (I *rose* from my chair); *rows* are the lines of seats at the movie theater.

Right/write: *Right* means to be correct, and it is also a direction (turn *right* up ahead); *write* is what you do with your pencil in class.

It's/its: *It's* is a contraction that means "it is," so if you can substitute "it is," you know you need to use *it's*. On the other hand, *its* is a word that shows possession: a dog licks *its* tail. This pair is a big one, so make sure you get it straight!

Your/you're: *Your* is used to show that you own something: you clean *your* room. *You're* is a contraction that means "you are," so you have to be able to substitute "you are" in order to use this one: *You're* going to get in trouble if you do that.

Our/Are: These aren't strictly homophones, but kids (and grown-ups) still get them confused. *Our* is another word that shows ownership, and it means "belongs to us": *Our* house is in a nice part of town. *Are* is a verb that means "to be": Those men *are* all over six feet tall.

Weather/whether: These are important ones to get right. *Weather* refers to what goes on outside—rain, wind, the sun, etc. *Whether* is the word we use to signal that there's a choice: I don't know *whether* or not I'll go to the beach today. It depends on the *weather*.

Addition/edition: *Addition*, with an "a," is what you do in math class; that's why it has "add" in it. *Edition* with an "e," is a version of something: first *edition* copies of the book are quite rare and therefore worth a lot of money.

Flower/flour: *Flower*, with a "w," is something you pick from a plant to give to your valentine; *flour*, with a "u," is what you bake a cake with.

Soar/sore: *Soar*, with an "a," is what an eagle does when it flies above you. *Sore*, with an "e," is how you might feel after an injury playing sports.

Then/than: *Then* is used to talk about time: I went to the mall, and *then* I went home. *Than* is the word we use to compare things: My brother is much taller *than* I am.

Whole/hole: *Whole* is used to talk about the entire something: I can't believe I ate the *whole* thing. *Hole* is what we use to talk about a big gap: the dog was walking along and suddenly fell in a big *hole* in the construction site.

Common Homophone Pairs and Triples

are	our	
be	bee	
bare	bear	
brake	break	
buy	by	bye
cent	scent	sent
coarse	course	
dear	deer	
die	dye	
eye	I	
for	fore	four
hair	hare	
heal	heel	he'll

hear	here	
it's	its	
in	inn	
knot	not	
know	no	
mail	male	
marry	Mary	merry
son	sun	
steal	steel	
tail	tale	
way	weigh	
weak	week	
wear	where	

Practice

Homophone Practice—1

Choose the right homophones in each sentence.

1. Which/witch woman was accused of being a which/witch?
2. In New York City, there/their/they're are many museums that are world-famous for the quality of there/their/they're collections. There/Their/They're an important part of New York's international appeal.
3. To/Too/Two many people these days struggle when they try to/too/two choose among their homophones. But hey, if there are only to/too/two choices, at least the odds of getting it right are pretty good.
4. If it's important to you that you right/write well, you'll have to develop the right/write editing habits.
5. It's/Its always funny to watch a dog chase it's/its tail.
6. Do you know weather/whether or not the weather/whether is suitable for a ski trip?

Homophone Practice—2

Fill in the blank with the correct homophone. Choose your words from the table and explanations on the previous page.

1. I have __________ (2) sisters but only __________ (1) brother.
2. The bottom of my shoe, its __________, is about to come off.
3. Do you know ____________________ or not we have a test in math on Friday?
4. I hope _____________ okay that I borrowed your pen!
5. I do not believe that _______________ going to the concert! My parents would never let me.
6. This restaurant is supposed to be great. Have you come ________________ before?
7. You can come to ________________ house if you want. My parents can make us dinner.
8. I have seven books in my bag. That's two more ________________ you have in yours.
9. Put the ______________ to the metal, drive faster!
10. I have way more Oreos than I can eat. Please, have ________________!
11. I want to ________________ my hair pink next year.
12. I hear that Bosc ________________ are ripe this season. We should go order a dozen from Harry & David.

Homographs

Now for another confusing set of words: **homographs**. Homographs are words that are spelled the same (though sometimes pronounced differently in different situations) and have different meanings. Huh? Here's an example.

*I **live** in a big house on Montague Street.*
*I went downtown to see my favorite band **live** in concert.*

Live is spelled the same way in these two sentences, but it is pronounced in two different ways and means two different things. In the first sentence, *live* means where you and your family spend all your time, but in the second *live* means that the music was not a recording.

There are many homographs in English, but the only way you can learn them is by hearing people speak and being a careful reader. Just be on the lookout for them.

Compound Words

The final kind of word to look out for is the **compound word**. As you might guess, a compound word is a word that is made up of two other words stuck together. *Lighthouse*, *doorknob* and *shoelace* are common compound words you probably already know.

However, there are some compound words that are not so straightforward (see? Another compound word). Here are two of them that might be confusing.

Someone. This is a compound word. It is NOT two words. *Someone* is calling me on the phone. I need *someone* to help me with this.

Sometimes. This is also a compound word. It is NOT two words. *Sometimes*, I feel like winter will last forever. I get to go visit my family in California, but only *sometimes*.

Here are some more:

A lot NOT Alot

"A lot" means "very much."—Thanks a lot, Goober!
"Alot," is not a word. Don't use it. EVER.

All together v. Altogether

"All together" means "as a group."—We succeed or fail all together.
"Altogether" means "completely" or "entirely."—I find lumpy oatmeal altogether revolting.

Every day v. Everyday

"Everyday" means "ordinary" or "usual."—These are my everyday kicks.
"Every day" means a "period of time."—I like to eat food every day.

All right v. Alright

They both mean the same thing: "okay," "satisfactory," "certainty," or "safe."—Everything is all right, and that's alright by me!

Some Time v. Sometime

"Some time" means "a considerable period of time." –For some time, the world has been turning.

"Sometime" means "a vague time in the future."—I'll call you sometime.

Cannot NOT Can Not

"Cannot" means "unable."

"Can not" means "this is not a can."

Compound Word Questions

Choose the right word to fit the sentence.

1. A lot/Alot of people like ice cream.
2. Some people would eat it every day/everyday.
3. Celery can not/cannot make people fat.
4. Altogether/All together, the team must decide if the sacrifice is worth the risk.
5. Booboo went some time/sometime without blinking his eyes.
6. Everyday/every day thoughts usually include imagining sometime/some time when everything will be perfect.

WEIRD ISN'T WRONG, AND AWKWARD ISN'T WRONG

As a young person, you've probably had days in which you've felt as if you were all feet and elbows, a gangly duckling struggling to turn into a swan. In spite of the direction to find sentences "without awkwardness," occasionally you will run into sentences that seem awkwardly phrased or oddly constructed to you. That oddness, however, is not enough to make it incorrect. Some of the sentences you will face may make use of slightly odd constructions with which you might not be familiar but are perfectly acceptable English. Remember, whatever error you pick must have a grammatical reason behind it. "It sounds weird" is not a reason. You're weird, but that doesn't make you wrong!

How To Write
Short and Extended Answers

In the 4th Grade State tests you will be called on to write short and extended essays in response to questions comparing reading passages.

Attacking Essay Questions

1. As you read the passages you will be given, make sure you pay attention to the Three T's. Make extra sure you know the THESIS [nonfiction point of the piece] or WHAT HAPPENED [fiction].
2. Once you've finished breaking down the passage, read the question.
   - **Make sure you read the question carefully and process it before going forward.**
   - **Make sure you answer the question the *test* is asking and not one you've assumed by skimming.**
   - **If some part of the question is unclear, read it again and try to decipher it as best you can.**
   - **If you still cannot precisely understand the question, suggest your best understanding of the question instead. Make sure you clearly explain your understanding and remain consistent with it. For example:**
     - If by nature the question is referring to the outdoors, then...
     - If by nature we mean the force of life...
3. Once you have an understanding of the question, determine your answer to the question based on the THESIS or WHAT HAPPENED.
4. If the question refers to a specific point or section within the piece, make sure you reread that part of the passage and break down that segment in detail.
5. Once you've determined your answer, write it down and pick out your examples [underline them in text].
6. In forming your answer, think of it as your own thesis. It could still be as simple as:
   - "The author discusses how to hunt for deer in two specific ways," or
   - "The author wrote this piece in order to show how difficult it is to hunt. He demonstrates that in lines..."
7. As you construct your answer to the question, BE SURE you respond to all parts of the question.

Now you're ready to write a short [one or two paragraph] essay!

Short Answer Form

Below are sample questions for short essays.

Short Answer Sample Question

In the passage, the author states that ducks do not necessarily make the best pets. Give at

least two details from the passage that support this idea.

Short Answer [One Paragraph]

1. WHAT YOU THINK—Answer the question.

   According to the passage, ducks are bad pets.

2. WHY YOU BELIEVE IT—

   Ducks are horrible pets because they bite, poop everywhere and are hard to pet.

3. PROVE YOUR WHY.

   In his story, the author shows us just how bad a pet a duck can be. In lines XX – XX he writes, "Whenever I tried to cuddle with the duck, he nipped at me or pooped all over the place." He also says, "Petting a duck, or anything with feathers, can go wrong quickly if you pet them the wrong way."

4. CONCLUDE—Sum up your point and add to it if you like!

   Overall, because of their messy and bad behavior, ducks make terrible pets. However, they do make great meals!

Now try one of your own!

How to compare passages

Same THEME/Different but related THESES (The plural of thesis!)

Often, there will be not one but two passages for you to read. Do not fret! Double the number of passages does not mean double the trouble. Indeed, the process we've learned still applies. You should read each passage using the ibidPREP method: finding the theme, thesis and tone for each.

As you will soon realize, the passages almost always have the same theme. What does often differ, however, are the passages' theses. The authors may hold different views on an issue, may agree on an issue but disagree about its causes or effects, or may agree on an issue but disagree about the action that should be taken. Lastly, one passage may be an example or the subject of another. Therefore, your objective for dual reading passages is to first read each passage independently. Then, after doing so, figure out the key differences in the passages' theses and how they relate to each other.

Practice Short Answer from Two Readings

The two narrators below are mother and son. They each wrote about the same experience.

Worst Saturday Ever!

I hate having to go shopping. Every year my mom tells me I need a new nice shirt for Christmas, and new shoes, and new dress pants. They're so ugly, itchy and stiff! I just wish I could wear what I wanted to family gatherings. But if I didn't agree to go to the mall with Mom on Saturday, she wouldn't let me play Xbox for like a month. So I went with her, and once we got there it was so boring! I wanted to wander into other stores, and I wanted to get a pretzel at the food court. I wasn't hungry, necessarily, but didn't I deserve a treat for agreeing to this? When we finally got to Macy's, I wanted to get in and out as soon as possible. But my mom took forever! Even worse, once we found a shirt and stuff that worked fine, Mom was all, "Maybe you need a tie, maybe you're old enough, let's see what colors they have here," so we spent even more time in the store just walking around. She asked me if I liked a tie and I said "Fine" without really looking, and I was disgusted to see it was purple! She should know purple is a dumb color and I hate it. So basically, this shopping trip did not change how I feel about them.

That Time of Year Again?

Time goes so fast now that my three children are all in school! Before I know it, it feels like another whole year has passed, and each of my kids has outgrown all her party dresses or all his dress shirts. My eldest son has always loved to go shopping with me, and my daughter will wear pretty much anything I get her. But Timmy, the youngest—it's almost like he enjoys being a pain in my rear! Every year I try so hard to make him feel special, by taking him to the mall all by himself, and every year he still rails against having to do something as simple as try on some clothes so his mom can pay for them. Such a hard life he has! He drags his heels and walks as slowly as possible throughout the entire mall, begs for all sorts of treats and toys, and refuses to try on more than two options for every item of clothing he needs. And even then, he only agrees when I threaten to take away his video game privileges for a week. I tried to get through the whole ordeal as fast as possible, and found some things that fit him and didn't look horrible on him, and then I thought how nice it would be for him to wear a purple tie, to complement his sweet light brown eyes. I got him to wander over to the tie selection, asked him if he liked a nice lavender one, and he said he did! So I bought it, and felt like maybe we made some progress on the shopping front.

Practice 

In a short, well-written answer, please compare and contrast Timmy and his mom. What do they share in their telling of their experience, and how are they different? Be sure to mention details from their pieces and describe not just what they are saying but how they are saying it.

Extended Essay

The extended essay will also ask you to answer questions about your passages. For this it will be very important to put together a strong thesis [your "why"] and have all your details collected to prove your "why".

The author believes that the sea otters are not really endangered because he[21]*...*

Set about reading, processing and finding an answer to your question in the same way as in Attacking Essay Questions above.

If the essay involves two passages, the question will focus on a common THEME in both. See how they compare regarding that THEME [subject] and try to come up with a point that characterizes both passages in terms of the THEME.

The Rise of the Machines!

Machines are everywhere in our daily lives. They're in our kitchens, our living rooms, our bedrooms and even in our bathrooms! Not only are machines everywhere in our homes they are in our schools, workplaces and, if you're old enough, in your pocket [a cell phone]. Cell phones have done great things for us and many machines have too—they've made a lot of work and tasks easier and more efficient. However, sometimes machines have unintended consequences—impacts that weren't planned for. Not all of these consequences are good.

When we think of tablets or cell phones or computers we often think of how much fun they are and how great they are for communicating, looking up things or sharing things like pictures and ideas. Unfortunately, some of these devices are so good at what they do that some people use them too much! You may sometimes see people looking at their phones while they are driving or crossing the street. That is super dangerous. You may also know people who spend all day on their computers. You may even see little children using tablets at the dinner table. So much overuse of even the best machines can be bad for people's attention, safety and their interactions with real people in front of them.

From an economic sense, the way people earn money, machines can also be destructive. Many machines have begun to take over jobs that used to belong to people. Have you noticed that there are fewer and fewer toll booths on your highways and bridges? Fewer subway token clerks in their booths in the subway? In factories now, robots do a lot of the jobs that people used to do to put together things like cars and other machines. Maybe one day, a machine will even take this writer's job!

So, when you wish for a cell phone or the latest video game console, be careful! You might actually be taking someone's job away or distracting yourself from the important things in life. Machines, like everything else, should be used thoughtfully and with great care.

[21] Remember, always check the author's name at the beginning of a passage to determine his or her gender!

Extended Answer Sample Question

The passage explores the ideas that machines have both positive and negative impacts on society. How are these ideas developed over the course of the passage? Which impact seems greater?

In your answer, be sure to do the following:

- explain how the idea that machines can have a positive impact is developed over the course of the passage
- state which impact seems greater and explain why
- use details from the passage in your answer

How to Structure Extended Essay

1. **Intro Paragraph**
   a. WHAT YOU BELIEVE—
   The passage suggests that although machines can be very helpful, they do not solve all our problems
   b. WHY YOU BELIEVE IT—
   Machinery does not solve all our problems because it often causes new problems even as it eliminates others.
   c. HOW YOU WILL SET ABOUT PROVING YOUR WHY.
   Numerous examples in the passage demonstrate the limits and negative impacts of machines among all the good they do.
   d. BRIEFLY MENTION YOUR EXAMPLES
   Among these, the discussions of robots and cell phones show how machines often do more harm than good.

—Everything after your intro is meant to prove your WHY—

2. **Body Paragraphs**
   a. Paragraph 2 — Example 1—Robots
      i. Topic sentence—
      Robots are the perfect example of machines not solving problems.
      ii. Cite SPECIFIC details from the passage and quote them appropriately
         a. As the author says in line 8, "Many robots...
         b. The author also adds in line 16, "Not only do robots harm humans, but..."
      iii. Conclude—Though robots can be threatening there are other more dangerous machines out there.
   b. Paragraph 3 — Example 2—Cell Phones
      i. Topic sentence—
      Cell phones contribute to users' distraction problems.
      ii. Cite SPECIFIC details from the passage and quote them appropriately
         a. As the author says in line 32, "Many cell phones..
         b. The author adds in line 48, "Not only do cell phones do everything for us..."
      iii. Conclude—Though cell phones make our lives easier, they make it harder for us to

solve problems ourselves.

c. Paragraph 3a – Example 3 [if you have a good 3rd example and time, use it. If not, just mention it as additional proof in conclusion along with any other possible examples you might have.]

3. **Conclusion**—Recap your WHAT and WHY and then add in any extra observations you may have on thetopic.

As shown above through the author's mention of robots and cellphones, machines do not always make life better or easier.

It is obviously false because of the "because" stated above [Paragraph 1, Sentence 2] and proved with the examples above.

Although some may say it is true because of "some contrary reason," this reason only serves to make topic even more false because "some reason of your own to contradict the contrary."

4. **Over-read**—Re-read what you've written.
   a. Make sure there are no blatant grammatical errors.
   b. Make sure that the essay is reasonably legible.
   c. Make sure that paragraphs are clearly delineated.

How to Write the Essay

Now that we've tackled the topic, come up with an answer and planned it, let's write.

The Bare Bones

Everything you write should have a beginning, a middle and an end—from the shortest sentence to the longest essay. It all starts with the sentence.

Bad Rules

Most students we work with recall very few writing guidelines, and the ones they do recall are often wrong, unimportant or misguided.

Don't use "I"—It's not great to start every sentence with the pronoun "I," but if you use "I" sparingly and correctly, then it's not really a problem. [Remember that I told you this.] **Length matters**—Most students spend more time worrying about how long their essays are than actually writing them. Longer essays are not better, nor are short essays necessarily bad or good. Your one and only job in an essay is to answer the question in front of you completely, make one point, and support it with examples in a clear, well-reasoned and structured essay.

Sentences

Every sentence must contain a verb and a subject. That's it!

I ran home.

In fact, with English sentences, the shorter the better. Some sentences may even have only one word. When the verb is a command, the subject is implied in the verb:

Stop! [It is implied that someone, YOU, should stop.]

If, in your writing, you find yourself sticking together clause upon clause with lots of phrases sprinkled in your sentence, START ANOTHER SENTENCE. They're free!

NO: *I ran home, and then I got a drink of water because I was thirsty from running but the water was warm, so I spit it out!*
YES: *I ran home and got a drink of water. Unfortunately, the water was warm, so I spit it out! Yuck.*

Paragraphs

Paragraphs—the Beginning

The seond brick in the wall of the essay is the paragraph. The beginning of the paragraph may be called the TOPIC SENTENCE. This sentence usually connects to the previous paragraph (unless it's the first sentence of the first paragraph) and advances the essay (or story) to its next step. Here's an example:

> *Just as cotton was king in the South, manufacturing ruled the North.*

After the TOPIC SENTENCE of a paragraph, the next sentence generally begins to explain the point of the TOPIC SENTENCE—we'll call it the POINT SENTENCE.

> *The Northern states did not have the best land for large-scale farming, but they did have many of the features needed to become strong manufacturing centers.*

See? This second sentence explains and elaborates the TOPIC SENTENCE.

Paragraphs—The Middle

Now we're off to the races! Everything from here to the END of the paragraph is meant to provide specific examples to support the POINT SENTENCE.

> *Many of the Northern states had excellent harbors like New York and Boston harbors, which made it easier to sell their products. The Northern states also had larger city populations in which to find workers, such as those in New York, Boston and Philadelphia. Another common feature of the people of the Northern states was a strong belief in the value of work that came in part from their Puritan ancestors.*

Paragraphs—The End

The thing to remember about all endings: conclusions conclude. The CONCLUDING SENTENCE should do what all endings do—wrap things up and leave us pointed toward the future.

> *All of these things made the North a strong manufacturing power and helped lead to the conflict of the Civil War.*

All Together

> *Just as cotton was king in the South, manufacturing ruled the North. The Northern states did not have the best land for large-scale farming, but they did have many of the features needed to become strong manufacturing centers. Many of the Northern states had excellent harbors like New York and Boston harbors, which made it easier to sell their products. The Northern states also had larger city populations in which to find workers, such as those in New York, Boston and Philadelphia. Another common feature of the people of the Northern states was a deep belief in the value of work that came in part from their Puritan ancestors. All of these things made the North a strong manufacturing power and helped lead to the conflicts of the Civil War.*

Good Rules

Good Rule #1

Use paragraphs. Indent. Line up your margins! These are relatively simple tasks that some young students simply whiff on.

Use paragraphs to break up your essay into some semblance (shape, form) of intro, body, conclusion. Delineate (define) those paragraphs by moving the first word of the paragraph in about the width of your finger. Lastly, make sure the rest of your lines make it all the way to the outer right margin of the page and then all the way back to the left side margin. Keep an eye on your lines and make them stack neatly on top of each other.

Why do all this? For the same reason we use proper grammar and proof read our work: To make our essay accessible to our reader and get our point accross as clearly as possible.

Good Rule #2

"Would" is future not past...

A lot of students write in a weird tense. I'll call it the conditional past. Instead of using the simple past and writing "I went to school," many often write "I would go to school." It's not necessary. When telling a story the simple past:

Yes "I went," "We ate," "We see"

No "I would go," "We would eat," "We would see."

Use "would" only for truly conditional formulations such as "I would eat if you were going to," "We would go if they let us." Note that the conditional tense is based on situations that hinge on something else that has happened or might happen.

How to Edit [the soul of writing!]

Many students look at writing essays the way most people would look at swimming through a lake of acid without goggles; the sooner they can get to the other side, the better.

Here's the problem though. Writing an essay is actually more like cooking a delicious meal. You have to take the right amount of time that each part requires in order for it to come out correctly.

Read it

First, do your paragraphs and sentences have clear beginnings, middles and ends?

Are you repeating yourself and being repetitive and redundant, like this sentence?

Do your ideas build upon and flow into each other? What does that mean...

Build And Follow

As the cars of a train go, so do your ideas. Each must **follow** the one before it. [See below.]

It does not crash into the idea ahead of it, nor does it **disconnect** from the one before it. [See below.]

Think of your sentences as being made of two parts, a first idea and a second idea. As you write, the second idea of your previous sentence becomes the first idea of the next sentence, and so on. This way, like the cars of a train, your ideas build upon and follow each other. By connecting sentences in this way, you ensure that you are not confusing [or boring] your reader [or accidentally crashing into them].

Here's how this might work:

- The man went to the store.
    - The store was crowded.
        - Crowds had formed because a storm was coming.
            - **The storm was going to be bad.**
                - **Because it was going to be so bad, everyone went to the store to stock up.**
                    - **Try writing something this way, and then go read one of the proofreading paragraphs (pg. <?>). It helps!**

Segues

Nope, not those weird people-mover things you see all over Washington, D.C., and other touristy towns. We mean the **words that connect** your ideas. Don't just start your sentences with "One example is..." and "Another example is..." [although that's better than just starting to talk about things out of the blue].

NO: *Idea 1: One example of an evil animal is the American housecat.*
Idea 2: Another example of an evil animal is the Canadian mongoose.

YES: *Idea 1: American housecats are widely considered to be evil. Canadian mongooses are pretty awful too.*

Some Useful Segues...

Because	Therefore	Although	While	Similarly	Further-more
Thus	As a result	However	First of all	Conse-quently	Alternatively

Stop Repeating Yourself, Stop Saying the Same Things Over and Over, & Don't Be So Repetitive and Redundant

What makes English such a fabulous language in which to communicate [and American English especially] is that it favors conciseness and clarity. You can get to the point really quickly. When you reread your work, watch for any sentences that do not move your argument forward at all. You want each sentence or idea to move forward from the previous one, even if that progress is only a centimeter or so.

Zero Sentences

Zero sentences are those bad sentences many students are so fond of; they simply restate the previous sentence. Students usually resort to zero sentences in order to fill space or because they can't think of anything else to say or to point out things that are insanely obvious. In other words, these sentences say nothing. If you are repeating yourself to fill space, stop it—your readers aren't idiots; they will notice. If you are repeating yourself because you can't think of what to say next, look to the end of your last sentence. For example:

A. [Sentence 1] All cats are evil.

B. [Sentence 2 – Zero sentence – BAD] The American housecat is evil

C. [Sentence 2 – Point Sentence – GOOD] Perhaps the most evil member of the feline family is the American housecat.

The Over-Read

The most important part of writing is re-writing. The first time we put down our thoughts, we are trying to get our ideas on paper as directly as possible and connect our examples while they're fresh in our minds. But, the second (and third, fourth, fifth...) times we go over our words, we are shaping and honing our message to be clear, concise and engaging to our readers. If you can communicate this way, you are writing!

So, once you have finished writing your piece, make sure you have left yourself a few minutes in which to read it over. When you read it over, you are no longer the writer of the piece, you are an **editor**, and you are reading for:

- **BEGINNINGS**, **MIDDLES** AND **ENDS**.
- **BUILD** & **FLOW** OF IDEAS.
- **SPELLING** AND **GRAMMAR**.
- **REPITITION** & **REDUNDANCY** & **REPEATING** YOURSELF!

Proofreading

Test your new grammar and over-reading skills here! Mark each paragraph with your pencil to make it right!

Reading 1

Proofread this story. Correct any errors.

The little old lady lived by the river. She had many friends among the animals in the woods. The came to her house every morning and every morning She fed them. One day the animals came to the little old ladys' house, but she wasnt there. The bird tapped on the window pane, but no one answered. the deer knocked on her door with their hoof , but still she did not answer. What had happened to the old lady. All the animals were deep Concerned.

Reading 2

Proofread this story. Correct any errors.

Goober is my worst student. She wears too sock. Goobers Brain is filled with too many thing . Some of the things in Goobers' brain is: dust bunnies, pillows, candles, and smelly socks. I also think that Goober is too big to Fit in my office.

Reading 3

Proofread this story. Correct any errors.

Poppa wasnot like other Grandpas. He didn't live in florida or play Golf or visit us at regular times like thanksgiving or the 4th of july. Like our Dad he traveled all around the world had amazing adventures and told us all about they. he didnot give us presents at regular times either like on us birthdays or at christmas. He had poppas holidays

Some times he would just show up in the middle of the week and announce happy February 17th Day! Noone else knew that february 17 was a holiday- so we had it's all to ourselves. My brother simon and me loved it. Are mom was not so thrilled. Most of the time mom loved Pops like crazy, but some times she wished her dad be a teeny bit more like the other Grandpas who reads the paper sat on benches and celebrated regular holidays like labor day.

Reading 4

Are you ready for the EDITING CHALLENGE? ***REVISE, EDIT*** *&* ***IMPROVE*** *the following:*

There are so many fun subject in school. It is so hard to pick a favorite subject. However, overall my absolute favorite subject is reading.

Why is reading my favorite subject? Well, that is because one, it is fun to do. Two, what do I do when I am sad, read! Someone should write a song about that. And lastly, three, I love to get rapped up in a good story.

It is fun for your mom and dad to read to you once in a while. Also, at school we have litaracher groups (book clubs). However, there is homework. Our teacher reads to us too, but after that we discuss it.

Reading in the ela in my opinion doesn't count as real reading. Neither do practice tests. That is because they have questions about them. Also, there aren't chapters or polt twists, and worst of all, no cliffhangers! Information book sort of count as real books. Also, in my opinion, picture books don't really count as real books. Biographys such as the Who Was... books do count as real books. They may picuters but it's ok.

In conclusion, reading is my favorite subject. It is fun for the whole family (and class).

NO MORE—Mommy, Daddy, Grandma, Grandpa, Uncle, Aunt and/or Caretaker Writing

As a child you live in a world in which the people around you know you very well. In fact, often they provide the entire structure for your existence. Because they help form the structure of your life, they know most everything about you and understand what you're talking about without your having to explain it. The rest of the world is not like this. Please think of your readers as intelligent people who are interested in what you say, but know very little about you or your topic.

So, when you write essays and if you want your reader to understand what it is you're talking about, be sure to introduce your subject AND be very clear about what that subject is even once you have introduced it. Be extra careful to make sure your reader knows to what or whom your pronouns are referring! Ambiguous pronouns are the death of essays and storytelling.

No more of this:

Yes, it's true. When we go to the house, we are more free. They tell us we can go where we want because it's safer than home. Even though we have to be very careful of the riptide.

More of this:

Vacations are usually freer times for my siblings and me. We usually go on vacation to a house by the beach. Our parents feel comfortable letting us go where we want there because they feel it's safer by the beach than in our neighborhood in New York City. Of course, we still have to be very careful when we swim because of the riptide!

CHAPTER THREE

READING AND WRITING

Reading and Writing—Putting It All Together!

Let's try practicing How to Read, the Three T's and How to Answer on the readings below. Please find the theme, thesis and tone of the pieces.

Blood

Anyone can recognize blood on sight. A drop of it across the room is enough to make you forget whatever you're doing. Blood is a magnet for human attention.

There is good reason for this. Long ago, if people saw blood it meant that a terrible injury had occurred, a creature was very sick, or a creature was doing violence to another creature. For prehistoric man, then, blood was a sure sign that he probably needed to stop what he was doing and do something else instead. Probably that something else was to run away.

Most advanced creatures have blood in their bodies. Fish, mammals and birds all have it, and some insects have something very similar called "hemolymphs." Clearly, blood must be important, but what does it do?

Simply put, blood is the body's transport system. It is how your body gets essential nutrients from the food you eat to your muscles, and oxygen from your lungs to the rest of your body. Carrying oxygen is your blood's most important job because a human can live for only a couple of minutes without oxygen.

Your blood also helps keep you from getting sick. There is a type of cell within the blood called "white blood cells," and they are part of the immune system. That means these are the cells that travel around your body attacking bacteria and germs that might make you sick.

Another type of cell is the red blood cell. Unsurprisingly, these are the cells that make your blood look red, because they contain high levels of iron (think of rust). These are the cells that carry oxygen.

Amazingly, some other species do not have red blood. Lobsters have blue blood, and lizards have green blood! Additionally, even though all humans have red blood, there is some variation in our blood as well. Human blood comes in eight common types, which differ from each other in how they respond to germs and viruses.

It is actually important to know which type of blood you have because someday you may need to receive blood, or somebody important to you may need to receive blood. Some people can receive only certain kinds of blood. Receiving someone else's blood is called "getting a transfusion," and transfusions are essential for people with certain illnesses and people who are injured. That is why in times of war or great natural disasters, charities usually sponsor blood drives during which they try to get as many people as possible to donate blood.

Fortunately, most people now come into contact with large amounts of blood only at these blood drives or when they watch horror movies. All the same, a drop of blood out in the open grabs human attention as strongly as ever.

THEME—What is this passage about?

___

___

THESIS—What is the main point of the passage?

___

___

Multiple Choice Questions

1. Which of the following is **NOT** offered as a reason prehistoric man would need to pay attention to blood?
   A. The presence of blood could mean he was seriously hurt.
   B. The presence of blood could mean creatures were hurting one another.
   C. The presence of blood could mean food was present.
   D. The presence of blood could mean an animal was very sick.

2. What does the author suggest is blood's most important function?
   A. To fight disease.
   B. To carry nutrients around the body.
   C. To store the necessary iron in the human diet.
   D. To carry oxygen to all parts of the body.

3. What do white blood cells do?
   A. Carry oxygen.
   B. Fight bacteria and germs that might make you sick.
   C. Determine which blood a person can receive through a transfusion.
   D. Coordinate the efforts of the red blood cell.

4. Why does the author mention the existence of blood in other creatures?
   A. The author thinks other creatures are more interesting than humans.
   B. To suggest that something so common must be important.
   C. The only way to learn about human blood is to study other kinds of blood.
   D. To show that all blood is basically the same.

5. Why does the author think it is important for you to know what kind of blood you have?
   A. To know the people from whom you can receive transfusions and to whom you can give them.
   B. To discover if you have any illnesses of the blood.
   C. Charities want you to know which kind of blood you have.
   D. The kind of blood you have can influence your personality.

Short Answer

Using the text as evidence, explain a situation when you may need to know which kind of blood you have.

Short Answer

How does the author suggest blood's role in human lives has changed since prehistoric times?

Short Answer
The author discusses the many purposes blood serves in the body. Explain and describe these purposes using the text as evidence.

CHAPTER I. Murder at the Manor

Lightning struck the shining weather vane poking out of the Sturgess mansion. The thunder sounded immediately after and rattled the fine china and silver spread out in Jim Hancock Sturgess's luxurious dining room. Jim's guests, a dull crowd of rich people whose comments that evening had not yet gotten beyond the weather and the quality of the soup, shouted in alarm, "The power is out!"

"Not to worry!" shouted Jim over the strained voices. "Not to worry! We have a generator ready for just such an emergency, and I'll go switch it on. Harrison will be fetching candles for us in the meantime. Stay calm and hold still!"

In the perfect darkness within the dining room, Jim's steady steps could be heard making their way toward the basement.

"Harrison? Harrison, where are you?" called out a female voice in great fear. "Are those candles nearly ready?"

"No need to be frightened," a man answered, slurping his soup. "Can't let a little bit of weather hold you back from a good meal. Why, when I was in India—"

"You're not in India, I'm sure," a different woman answered. "So why don't you be quiet? We have every reason to be scared of the dark."

"Don't you tell me to be quiet!"

"I will if I want!"

"Shut up!"

"Don't talk to my wife that way!"

"I'm not your wife!"

"Look! Over there!" shouted a new voice.

The sound of a man running was echoing up the tiled hallway. Shaky candlelight was getting nearer and nearer, nearly blowing out as a gust of wet wind spun through the house. Harrison burst through holding a candlestick, his white butler shirt untucked from his belt and his hair standing on end.

"Come quickly everyone! Now!" All the guests ran after Harrison, bunching close near him to be within the light. They went down stone steps into the basement and suddenly a horrible scene fell within the rim of the candle's light.

Hanging limp and grossly bent around the generator was Jim Hancock Sturgess. You didn't have to have fought in India or have attended medical school to see that he was dead.

"Murder!" shouted Harrison, "and someone here has done it! Not one of you will leave until there's a confession."

Murder at the Manor – STEW

In complete sentences, please use the text to answer the following questions.

What is the SUBJECT of the passage [what is it about]?

____

____

Describe the TONE of the passage [think of dark to light]:

____

The EYES of this passage belong to [whose eyes are we seeing the story through?]

____

The WHAT HAPPENED & WHY of this passage are [in other words, WHY is this story worth telling?]

____

____

Multiple Choice Questions

1. What causes the alarm at the beginning of the story?

   A. The food isn't very good.
   B. The conversation isn't very good.
   C. The power goes out.
   D. Jim Sturgess is a bad host.

2. What do the guests do when the power goes out?

   A. They bond together as the stress brings out the best in them.
   B. They immediately begin to quarrel.
   C. They help Harrison to get the candles.
   D. At least one of them sneaks off to murder Jim Sturgess.

3. What is the big crisis?

   A. Harrison may be a murderer.
   B. Sturgess can't get the power back on.
   C. The meal can't be eaten in the dark.
   D. Sturgess is dead.

4. What does the story suggest is most likely to happen next?

   A. The guests and the butler will all try to figure out who among them is the murderer.
   B. The guests and the butler will work together to fix the generator.
   C. The guests and the butler will finish their supper.
   D. It will turn out that Sturgess is just pretending to be dead as a practical joke.

Extended Response

The situation inside the Sturgess mansion is very different at the beginning of the story compared to what it is at the end. Describe how this change occurred, using specific details from the story to support your answer

In your answer, be sure to do the following:

1. Describe what is going on at the beginning
2. Describe what is going on at the end
3. Explain what caused the change
4. Include specific details from the text to support your answer

Rock Climbing

I remember the first time I saw my older brother Sam go rock climbing; I was only four years old. Uncle Bill drove us to the climbing gym, which looked like a regular building from the outside. But as soon as we got inside, it was like we were in a huge cave! There was a big difference though: this cave had lots of brightly colored polka dots all over bumpy walls. The ceiling was the highest I've ever seen, and all the bumpy walls had more bumps sticking out of them. These were, as you might have guessed, the climbing walls. As we walked closer, I saw the ground was covered with big, squishy blue mats and that there were long ropes dangling down from the tops of the enormous walls. The polka dots I saw turned out to be hand and foot holds.

I was so excited to start climbing, but I soon found out you had to be at least five years old to climb, and my birthday wasn't until that October. Sam was seven years old then, so he got to climb. I was so jealous. First, Sam had to get weird-looking rubber shoes because his own shoes wouldn't fit on the tiny holds. Then, they gave him a funny thing that kind of looked like a seatbelt—his harness—and he had to put it on over his shorts. There was a hole for each leg, and his instructor tightened it around Sam's waist. It looked like a weird diaper!

Now Sam was ready to get tied in. The instructor helped him, but he had to learn how to tie all the knots. I didn't know their names then, but first Sam had to make a figure-eight loop on the rope, loop it through his harness, and then follow through the figure-eight again to tie himself in. Lastly, there was one more safety knot: a half hitch.

Once Sam was ready, his instructor told him to say, "On belay?" You pronounce it like "delay," and it's the word that tells your climbing partner to keep your safety rope tight in case you fall. Sam said, "On belay?" and the teacher said, "Belay on." After that Sam said, "Climbing," and his teacher said, "Climb on."

And he was off! Slowly Sam made his way up the tall wall, grabbing at any hold he could. Some were really big and had great little pits for a hand to grab onto, but some were as small as a golf ball and not even half as round. One time Sam thought he had a firm grip, but his hand slipped—I thought he was going to die! Fortunately, his instructor had his rope tight, so Sam just swung in the air from his rope until he could grab onto the wall again.

When Sam reached the top of his climb, he found a bell there and rang it. He had made it! A second later, he let go of the wall and dangled off it as his instructor lowered him down slowly. As soon as Sam touched down on the floor, I knew I would go rock climbing the minute I was old enough.

Since this is a MEMOIR, in complete sentences, please use info from the text to find the STEW in the passage.

What is the SUBJECT of the passage [what is it about]?

____

____

Describe the TONE of the passage [think of dark to light]:

____

The EYES of this passage belong to [whose eyes are we seeing the story through?]

____

The WHAT HAPPENED & WHY of this passage are [in other words, WHY is this story worth telling?]

____

____

Multiple Choice Questions

1. The author describes the climbing gym as having a large, soft mat on the floor. What can we infer is the reason for this mat?

   A. The climbing gym also hosts gymnastics classes.
   B. People like to take naps when they are tired of climbing.
   C. Part of rock climbing includes intentionally falling onto the floor.
   D. The mat is a safety precaution just in case the ropes fail.

2. What is the reason the author gives for not climbing himself?

   A. The author is afraid of heights.
   B. The author's uncle wouldn't allow it.
   C. The author does not meet the gym's age requirement.
   D. The author has no interest because it seems boring.

3. Which of the following did Sam **not** use to rock climb?

   A. a safety harness
   B. a helmet
   C. special shoes
   D. a rope

4. Why does the author tell you that "belay" rhymes with "delay"?

A. Because the author anticipates you might not have heard the word before.
B. Because the author wants to write a poem about this experience.
C. Because the two words also happen to be synonyms.
D. Because the author wants to make sure you will be safe if you ever go rock climbing.

5. What does the comparison between a hold and a golf ball do in the passage?

A. It tells us that rock climbing and golf are similar sports.
B. It provides an interesting subplot to the story.
C. It helps us visualize the way a rock wall looks.
D. It discusses the way in which the two are different.

6. How might this passage be different if told from Sam's point of view? Choose the best answer.

A. It would spend a lot more time talking about how annoying the author is.
B. We would read about what it is like to be a great height above the ground.
C. The passage would be longer.
D. It would go into detail about how uncomforta ble it is to wear a harness.

Short Answer

Using the text as evidence, explain at least two of the safety precautions that the rock climbing gym has put in place.

Short Answer

Why do you think the author tells us about the jealousy he or she feels towards Sam (in the second paragraph)?

Short Answer

The author does not come out and say that he or she has gone rock climbing since this experience of watching Sam rock climb. Do you think the author has now gone climbing? What are some clues that he or she might have? Use the text to make your argument.

Ski Trip

When Dad and I saw my aunts and uncles at Thanksgiving last year, they told us about their idea to go on a family ski trip to Tahoe. I thought it sounded like a great idea, since I hadn't even seen snow since I was five years old!

So on a cold morning in February, my dad and I left our quiet home in San Francisco at six o'clock. I took my pillow with me, so I could fall right back asleep in the car, which is exactly what I did. I woke up from time to time and saw different landscapes go by: first the familiar strip malls of my hometown, then light brown rolling hills with occasional cows, then rocky crags with little creeks and streams running parallel to the highway. We were getting closer!

It was also getting colder too. I was amazed to find that even though we had only driven a couple of hours, we were already in a place where frost was still on the ground. When we stopped to get gas and stretch our legs, I could instantly see my breath and started shivering in my pajamas. I would need to break out my snow pants soon!

The gas station had a diner, and we stopped for lunch. We had also agreed to meet here with the rest of our traveling crew. Altogether we made a caravan of four cars: Uncle Phil's SUV, Aunt Colleen's Subaru, my cousin Katie's little white Camry, and my dad's rented Ford Explorer.

After eating, we filled up the four cars with gas and went on our way, keeping each other's cars in sight as much as possible. My cousins Nathaniel and Matthew moved into our car, so we could play car games and not get bored.

After a little while, we saw a stream of winding red brake lights ahead and slowed to a standstill. Because we were stopped, I looked down at the ground and realized what I thought had been more frost was actually a little layer of old, hard snow. Were we already that high up the mountain? We were on the El Dorado Highway and crawling towards its highest point, Echo Summit. We wondered what caused the traffic jam, but after turning on the radio we found out: there was fresh snow ahead. Not just on the side of the road, on the road. It had snowed just that morning, and more snow was coming!

We were all nervous because none of the aunts and uncles had driven in snow before, or not for a long time. Uncle Phil and Aunt Colleen felt okay with their cars because they had four-wheel drive. But Katie and my dad hadn't expected there to be so much snow, and they only had two-wheel drive plus chains for their tires in their trunks. Dad didn't know if he should put on the chains, but his question was soon answered when we saw highway patrolmen parked on the side of the road, lights flashing. They told us that unless we had four-wheel drive we would have to put on chains. Finding a safe place to pull over, my dad put on his gloves and quickly hopped out of the car. He got the chains out of the trunk and got to work, moving quickly so we wouldn't all freeze!

He got the chains on quickly, and soon we were off again. Because we had to stop, though, we got separated from Uncle Phil and Aunt Colleen, who had continued with the flow of traffic. It was just us and cousin Katie in her Camry behind us, and she later said she thought she would never make it up that mountain! We all felt like we were walking on eggshells as we rode on the chains, but they ultimately helped us get to safety.

By the time we reached our cabin that night, we were all too exhausted to even think about skiing! But the next morning we were ready to go and have a good time. Still, I don't think any of us want to relive that especially scary drive to Tahoe in Februaryagain.

Since this is a MEMOIR, in complete sentences, please use info from the text to find the STEW in the passage.

What is the SUBJECT of the passage [what is it about]?

____

____

Describe the TONE of the passage [think of dark to light]:

____

The EYES of this passage belong to [whose eyes are we seeing the story through?]

____

The WHAT HAPPENED & WHY of this passage are [in other words, WHY is this story worth telling?]

____

____

Multiple Choice Questions

1. When did the narrator take the ski trip?

   A. Last Thanksgiving.
   B. When the narrator was five years old.
   C. April.
   D. February.

2. Why does the narrator talk about putting on snow overalls?

   A. To talk about what you have to wear when you go skiing.
   B. To illustrate how he or she likes to dress.
   C. To indicate how cold it's gotten so quickly.
   D. No reason; snow overalls should not be mentioned at all.

3. What can be inferred about Aunt Colleen? Choose the best answer.

   A. She likes being prepared for all weather when traveling.
   B. She is Matthew's mom.
   C. Subaru is her favorite car brand.
   D. She feels unsafe driving without all-wheel drive.

4. What does the curved line of red lights on the highway indicate?

   A. That there are dangerous weather conditions ahead.
   B. That the highway patrol is nearby.
   C. That there are weird red streetlights up ahead.
   D. That there is a traffic jam on the highway.

5. Why does cousin Katie think she will never make it up the mountain alive?

   A. Driving in the snow was an unusually scary event for her.
   B. She thinks there are wild animals in the mountains.
   C. There have been reports on the radio about car accidents.
   D. She didn't know how to put chains on her car.

Short Answer

Using the text as evidence, explain how the narrator demonstrates the passage of time and distance in the second paragraph.

Short Answer
In your own words, explain why the snow in the story is dangerous.

Extended Response

The narrator suggests that he/she feels regret about making the trip to Tahoe. Use the text to explain why the narrator feels this way, and make an argument about why you agree or disagree with the narrator about this.

Barber Surgeons

Can you imagine going to your local hair salon to get your wisdom teeth taken out? Well, if you lived in Europe in the Middle Ages, this might have been your reality! Barber surgeons were some of the most common European medical people of the Middle Ages. They usually took care of soldiers during or after battles.

The first barber surgeons, however, worked in monasteries. Around 1000 A.D., religious rules required monks to keep the top of their heads shaved and to have their blood withdrawn regularly. At the time, "bloodletting" was thought to cure or prevent illness and disease.

Bloodletting was based on an ancient system of medicine made up of four different bodily fluids "humours." To be healthy, they thought these humors had to be in balance. The humors were black bile, yellow bile, blood, and phlegm. Though modern medicine has since disproven this theory of humours and the practice of bloodletting, it was the most common medical practice performed by surgeons for almost 2,0 00 years.

So, because monks were bled every so often, each monastery had to train or hire a barber. And, over time, barbers expanded their practice from merely head-shaving and bloodletting to other minor surgeries as well.

Another factor that contributed to this odd job is that, in this era, surgery was not generally conducted by doctors. Doctors tended to be academics: they worked in universities and mostly just observed or consulted patients. Doctors considered surgery to be beneath them, and so were initially content to let barbers do the dirty work.

Barbers, on the other hand, already worked with the body. Since they had sharp razors for shaving and cutting hair, it made sense that they would use them for other purposes, especially when there wasn't an official title for a person who performed surgery. After the role was established, barber surgeons could be expected to do anything from cutting hair to amputating, cutting off, limbs.

Deaths from surgery in these times were quite high, often from loss of blood and infection. People then lacked so many of the methods we have now to ensure safety. Tourniquets—devices to stop blood flow—were still very basic, and the idea of infection was unknown until relatively modern times.

In fact, before the mid- to late-1800s, surgeons did not even wash their hands before performing surgery or delivering infants. Doctors at the time believed that infections were chemical damage, caused by exposure to bad air. They called this air "miasma," and thought it was a substance that came from rotting bodies. *Eww*. The theory held that the origin of plagues and epidemics was due to a miasma, and that a smaller miasma could cause an infection during surgery. They also thought that little could be done to predict or prevent a miasma from entering the wound. Surgeons also thought it made them weak to wash their hands before surgery; "tough men" were not afraid of getting dirty.

As time went on, however, the role of barber surgeon started to fade. From 1210 to 1499, Paris barber surgeons partnered with doctors to learn human anatomy—the way the body is constructed. Doctors were beginning to practice surgery too, however, and eventually the barbers recognized that licensed doctors had better qualifications for the potentially life-threatening operations. Italy chose to give barbers an inferior legal status compared to physician-surgeons in 1349. In England, two groups merged to form the official Company of Barber-Surgeons in 1540, but they split apart once more in 1745 creating the Barbers' Company and the Company of Surgeons.

At least officially, there are few traces of barbers' links with the surgical side of the medical profession anymore. However, one interesting remainder is the barber's red and white pole. It is said to represent the blood and bandages associated with surgery. Next time you get a haircut, think of how lucky you are that you're not going in for an operation instead!

In complete sentences, please use the text to answer the following questions.

What is this passage about?

____

____

What is the main point of the passage?

____

____

Multiple Choice Questions

1. What is not a reason that barber surgeons emerged in the Middle Ages?

   A. Monasteries needed someone to cut hair and draw blood.
   B. Surgery was usually not done by trained doctors.
   C. Shaving heads and cutting hair dealt with bodies, as did surgery.
   D. Surgery was highly dangerous and often life-threatening.

2. What is the difference between "humours" and "miasma"?

   A. Humours were considered dangerous and miasma a natural part of human life.
   B. Miasma was considered dangerous and humours a natural part of human life.
   C. Humours were thought to be what resulted when a miasma passed over an open wound.
   D. Miasma was considered to be a specific type of humour.

3. Based on the information in the passage, which of the following is an example of a procedure a barber surgeon might perform?

   A. Helping a mother give birth.
   B. Complex neurosurgery (surgery of the brain).
   C. Cutting off an unsaveable limb.
   D. Doing an autopsy on a cadaver.

4. According to the passage, why might people get their blood drawn in the Middle Ages?

   A. Their doctor told them their black bile, yellow bile, and phlegm levels were lower than their blood level.
   B. Their priest told them they needed to so they could make up for their sins.
   C. They had surgery done in which the tourniquet stopped working.
   D. They had the common cold.

5. Which of the following does the text suggest is true?

   A. Doctors did not know how to perform surgery.
   B. Patients preferred to see barber surgeons instead of doctors.
   C. Because methods were less developed at the time, surgery used to seem like a relatively simple skill.
   D. Barber surgeons had greater talent at performing surgery than most doctors.

Short Answer

Using the text as evidence, describe what people thought "miasma" could do. Provide at least one specific example.

___

___

___

___

___

___

___

___

Short Answer

What did doctors do in the Middle Ages? Be sure to give examples of which specific activities they spent their time doing.

Short Answer

The author suggests that the role of barber surgeon gradually became less popular over time. Use the text to explain some reasons why, and some examples of different countries who replaced barber surgeons.

Serena Williams

Serena Jameka Williams grew up in a small town outside of Los Angeles, California in 1981. She started playing tennis at three years old, after watching her older sister Venus play. Before long, both girls caught the attention of coaches and local tennis players for their talents, and both wanted to pursue tennis more seriously. Venus and Serena's dad Richard homeschooled them both, and both their parents coached them and helped them learn the game.

When Serena was nine, her parents moved the whole family from California to Florida, so that the girls could work with a famous tennis instructor named Rick Macci. However, because their dad wanted them to have time to be like regular kids, he stopped sending Venus and Serena to national junior tennis tournaments. Both sisters developed well under Macci's training, but their father pulled them out of Macci's academy when Serena was in ninth grade.He believed that he could bring them to even higher levels if he coached them himself.

Richard taking over coaching seems to have been a shrewd move: Serena and, to a lesser extent, Venus seemed unstoppable in their rises to the top. Serena saw her sister turn professional at 14 years old, so she did the same, even though her parents wanted her to wait until she was 16. Then, at the age of 18, Serena won the U.S. Open, becoming just the second African American in history to do so. Serena finished that year ranked fourth in the entire world. In this year, 1999, her sister Venus was one slot ahead of her at number 3.

While Venus stayed in third place for another two years, Serena dropped to 6th place, also for another two years. This would all change in 2002, when Serena reached her peak. At 21 years old, she jumped all the way up from the number six to the number one ranking, winning six singles tournaments. She also became the sixth woman in history to win the Grand Slam, which means that she won the four biggest international tournaments: Wimbledon, the French Open, the U.S. Open and the Australian Open.

Venus was close behind at spot number two, but this was a sign of a general shift: Serena continued to break world records and remained one of tennis's best women players while Venus continued to fall. While still an incredible player, Venus dropped to 11th place in 2003 (Serena dropped to 3rd).

All of these successes, pressures and high expectations came with a cost to Serena. In late 2003, after returning from an injury, she failed to live up to expectations. She was still doing better than most players but not as well as people thought she should. People in the media criticized her and questioned her dedication to tennis.

In 2007, Serena returned to tennis with new dedication, vowing to become number one once again. She accomplished this in 2008, ultimately ranking number two worldwide and then climbing to number one in 2009.

Though she is still an active player and, as of 2016, the number two player in the world, Serena already has a career for the record books: She is the only female player to win over $50 million in prizes; she has won more titles than any other active player (seventh-most all-time); and she has won a record-setting four Olympic gold medals. Serena and her sister have remained close throughout, despite having a bit of a rivalry—Serena has won 17 of their 28 face-offs over their careers. The sisters have also won 22 doubles titles together, including 3

Olympic gold medals.

Amazingly, they still aren't done. Serena Williams continues to play and continues to win. Who knows what other records she may set?

In complete sentences, please use info from the text to answer the following questions.

What is this passage about?

____

____

What is the main point of the passage?

____

____

What is the tone of the piece and what type of writing is this, most probably?

____

____

Multiple Choice Questions

1. Why did the Williams family move from Lynwood to Florida?

   A. The most important tennis tournaments are on the East Coast.
   B. Tennis is more popular in Florida than in California.
   C. The Williams parents wanted Venus and Serena to work with a particular coach.
   D. They did not like Los Angeles.

2. Why did Richard Williams begin coaching his daughters?

   A. He wanted to spend more time with them.
   B. He was dissatisfied with the level of coaching they were getting.
   C. Rick Macci did not like the Williams.
   D. Venus and Serena would only listen to their dad.

3. Serena achieved which of the following successes in 2002?

   A. She earned more money than any other player.
   B. She became the first African American to win the US Open.
   C. She was ranked number one in the world.
   D. She turned pro.

4. Which of the following is NOT something Serena Williams accomplished in her career?

   A. Earning more than any other tennis player in history.
   B. Becoming the oldest number one tennis player in history.
   C. Winning more tournaments than any other active player.
   D. Winning more Olympic gold medals than any other tennis player.

5. Which of the following can be inferred from the text?

   A. The best tennis players turn pro while still in their teens.
   B. Tennis is most popular in countries that host a Grand Slam tournament.
   C. Tennis players make more than players in other sports.
   D. Male tennis players on average earn more than female tennis players.

Short Answer

Using the text as evidence, explain how we can infer that tennis was very important to Serena and Venus' parents.

Short Answer

What can be inferred about African Americans in tennis from the line, “At the age of eighteen, Serena won the U.S. Open, becoming just the second African American in history ever to do so”?

Extended Response

The author spends some time comparing Serena to her sister Venus's tennis career. Using the text as evidence, what is the arc of their careers in relation to one another? How has it changed over time? What effect has it had on their bond as sisters?

Video Games as Art

The history of video games goes as far back as the early 1950s, when computer scientists designed simple games as part of their research. By the 1970s and 80s, video arcade games and gaming consoles using joysticks, buttons, and other controllers, along with images on computer screens and home computer games were introduced to the general public. Since the 1980s, video gaming has become a popular form of entertainment and a part of modern pop culture in most parts of the world.

Now, games can be played in many different places: on our computers, on special consoles like Xbox and PlayStation, in arcades and on our phones. There are many, many different categories of games too, like action, adventure, role-playing, simulation, strategy and sports. Of these many types of video games, a new sort has recently emerged—one that is centered on telling a story, instead of the idea of winning or losing. In other words, a video game designed to show something dramatic like a play or a movie, rather than just to achieve a goal. These games are not only changing what video games can look like, but they are also making games more interesting to different kinds of people.

Life Is Strange is one of these story games. Gamers play as Max Caulfield, a photography student who discovers that she has the ability to rewind time at any moment. After having a vision of an approaching storm, Max must try to prevent it from destroying her town. A player's actions shape the story as it unfolds and can reshape it by traveling back in time. There are problems and goals players must work towards, like finding certain objects or asking particular questions in conversation with other characters. The emphasis of the game, however, is the story which unfolds differently depending upon how player choose to play it.

In another example, Gone Home, gamers take on the role of a girl returning to Portland after traveling in Europe. Her family is gone from her house, and she has to figure out what has happened in her absence. It is set in 1995, and players must examine common household objects within the home to unlock journal entries and discover the events that took place there. There are no set goals in the game; however, the game rewards players when they explore new areas of the house and search for new messages. Much of the gameplay involves looking at objects and notes within the house. While players may finish the game without finding all the parts of the story, the story does not change no matter how it is played.

A game called Journey, is the most like a piece of art of our examples. While there does seem to be a story, much of it is mysterious. In Journey, the player controls a robed figure in a huge desert traveling towards a mountain in the distance. The path towards this mountain, the final destination of the game, is divided into several sections players can travel through one at a time. The only form of communication the robed figure has is a musical chime. This chime also transforms dull, stiff pieces of cloth found throughout the levels into vibrant red, affecting the game world and allowing players to progress through the levels. The robed figure wears a trailing scarf which when charged by approaching floating pieces of cloth briefly allows players to float through the air.

More so than both Gone Home and Life is Strange, Journey emphasizes the beauty that players experience while playing. The game has picturesque scenery, and the soundtrack is an important and beautiful part of the game. People who play it call it a moving and emotional experience, and the idea of winning is probably the least thing on gamers' minds when they play.

In complete sentences, please use info from the text to answer the following questions.

What is this passage about?

____

____

What is the main point of the passage?

____

____

What is the tone of the piece and what type of writing is this, most probably?

____

____

1. Which of the following is a good description of the earliest video games?

   A. Games were in video arcades that you had to visit in order to play them.
   B. Games were on handheld consoles you could take with you anywhere, but had to have the special handheld machine.
   C. Games were made primarily to conduct psychological tests on children.
   D. Games were made by computer scientists to understand computer technology.

2. What aspects of a video game, according to the article, would NOT lead it to be seen as art?

   A. A beautiful soundtrack and well-designed scenery.
   B. A design that provokes feelings instead of requires you to solve a problem.
   C. A very realistic simulation of an athletic sporting event.
   D. A story that is given more importance than the game's puzzles or tasks.

3. Why does the game Gone Home require you to examine household objects?

   A. Because part of the game is about cleaning as many objects as you can.
   B. To get the full story that the game is trying to tell.
   C. Many household objects unlock secret passageways in the home.
   D. They allow you to go backwards in time within the game.

4. The author suggests that the game Journey uses music as a way to make the game's experience more moving. What else about the game contributes to its emotional experience?

A. The scenic backdrop as you move through the game from scene to scene.
B. The dull, stiff pieces of cloth throughout the game.
C. The fact that it does not have obstacles like a regular game.
D. Having conversations with other characters.

Short Answer

What are some of the ways you can play video games? What are some of the different categories?

Short Answer

Describe how the game Life is Strange is played.

Extended Response

The author suggests many reasons a video game can be a work of art. Write an essay in which you identify and explain these reasons. Be sure to quote the text to make your case.

Practice

COMPARING TWO PASSAGES

Read the two passages. Then answer the questions that follow.

The *Titanic's* Only Voyage

Today, it is difficult to imagine traveling without airplanes. But planes were not ready to carry passengers until the 1940s. So, before this, traveling across the ocean had to happen by ship. There were many ships that people used for travel, but one ship drew a lot of attention: the *Titanic*.

In 1912, the *Titanic* was the largest ship that had ever been built, and it was about to go on its first trip. The huge ship could fit 3,000 people and was almost three football fields long (100 yards each). For its first voyage, the *Titanic* carried 2,224 people including first class, second class, third class and crewmembers. It departed from England on April 10, planning to arrive in New York City seven days later.

Unfortunately, on the fifth day of its journey, the *Titanic* received warnings from other ships. The night lookout spotted an iceberg near midnight, but the crew could not steer around it in time. The berg scraped the ship's starboard (right) side, and its compartments began to fill with water.

Everyone thought the *Titanic* was "unsinkable," so it did not have enough lifeboats for every person onboard. As it became clear the *Titanic* would sink, people started to panic, and many lifeboats left the ship only half full. By the time the ship sank, more than 1,500 of the 2,224 aboard did not make it to safety. The lifeboats saved fewer than half of the passengers and crew.

A ship nearby, the *Carpathia*, rescued the people in lifeboats early on the morning of April 15, but it could not reverse the tragedy that had already happened. As a result of this terrible accident, it soon became international law for all ships to have enough lifeboats for every person onboard.

A Close Shave

Sally was always excited when summer came. Not only was she happy for the break from school, she also looked forward to so many things that came with it: swimming, going to summer camp, eating popsicles, and other summery activities. But, above all these things, she loved going on board the *Serendipity* the most.

The *Serendipity* was her dad's sailboat. Her dad had had it since before she was even born. His dad had taught him to sail when he was little, and her dad had carried on that tradition with Sally and her brother Bobby. She got to spend lots of time with her dad on the boat, and she could stare out at the ocean from its cozy seats for hours. She was also always learning new things, like how to adjust the sails and how to steer with the rudder.

Every summer Sally's family rented a house near the beach, so they could sail to their hearts' content. The first day her family got to the beach, Sally insisted they go to the harbor. She missed sailing so much! The whole family got aboard the *Serendipity*, her dad adjusted the sail, and they were off. As soon as she felt the wind in her hair, Sally knew summer had arrived.

Quickly, however, a wind picked up. The day had been completely sunny, but now it looked stormy and overcast. Her dad was having trouble keeping control of the boat, and, after a huge gust of wind, the boat swerved wildly. Sally heard a splash. She looked to where her brother had been sitting; he was no longer there! She soon heard his shouts for help from the choppy water. She started to jump in after him, but her dad quickly stopped her.

"You hold the rudder!" he shouted, before jumping in after Bobby. For a moment her father and brother disappeared underwater, and she thought she'd lost them both forever.

After what seemed like hours but was only moments, both heads began bobbing. Finally her brother and father started to make their ways towards the boat. Sally held onto the rudder as tightly as she could, and kept it in one place as her dad got Bobby and himself back into the boat. Sally learned that day that as much as she loved sailing, she also had to be very careful whenever she went out to sea.

Short Answer

In "The Titanic's Only Voyage," ships are described as the main form of transportation in the early 1900s. Why was this the case? What made the Titanic such a special ship?

Short Answer

In "The Titanic's Only Voyage," a very impressive ship fails when no one thought it would. What causes the ship to fail, and why do so many people die as a result? What could have been done differently to save more people's lives?

Short Answer

In "A Close Shave," Sally gets excited about many things about summer. Using one detail from the story, tell what she liked about summer. Using another detail from the story, tell why sailing was particularly special to her.

Extended Response

"The *Titanic's* only Voyage" and "A Close Shave" are stories about boats and the ocean. Both stories show how risky ocean travel can be, yet each does so in a different way. How are these stories the same and how are they different? Use details from both stories to support your answer.

- Describe how "The *Titanic's* Only Voyage" and "A Close Shave" show the dangers of sea travel.
- Include details from both stories to support your answer.
- Compare and contrast the two explanations.

The Little Ghost

By Edna St. Vincent Millay

I knew her for a little ghost
That in my garden walked;
The wall is high—higher than most—
And the green gate was locked.

And yet I did not think of that
Till after she was gone—
I knew her by the broad white hat,
All ruffled, she had on.

By the dear ruffles round her feet,
By her small hands that hung
In their lace mitts, austere and sweet,
Her gown's white folds among.

I watched to see if she would stay,
What she would do—and oh!
She looked as if she liked the way
I let my garden grow!

She bent above my favorite mint
With conscious garden grace,
She smiled and smiled—there was no hint
Of sadness in her face.

She held her gown on either side
To let her slippers show,
And up the walk she went with pride,
The way great ladies go.

And where the wall is built in new
And is of ivy bare
She paused—then opened and passed through
A gate that once was there.

Multiple Choice Questions

1. What does the speaker notice first about the ghost in her garden?

A. The ghost wore a broad white hat.
B. The ghost is happy to be in the garden.
C. The ghost is there even though the gate is locked.
D. The speaker is afraid of the ghost.

2. What can be inferred about the speaker's garden?

   A. It is a garden composed entirely of mint and other herbs.
   B. There is a wall that goes around the entire garden.
   C. The garden has been there for many centuries.
   D. It is a place where the speaker spends the majority of his/her time.

3. Which of the following literary devices is used in the poem?

   A. Simile
   B. Rhyme
   C. Onomatopoeia
   D. Foreshadowing

4. We can infer which of the following?

   A. That the speaker is old.
   B. That the speaker is young.
   C. That the speaker is afraid of ghosts.
   D. That the speaker believes in ghosts.

5. In the 7th stanza, the speaker mentions a wall that has no ivy. This mainly serves to:

   A. Emphasize the newness of that particular wall.
   B. Imply what the ghost is thinking about.
   C. Show why the speaker is not afraid of the ghost.
   D. More th soroughly illustrate the poem's setting.

Shadwell Stair

By Wilfred Owen

I am the ghost of Shadwell Stair.
    Along the wharves by the water-house,
    And through the cavernous slaughter-house,
I am the shadow that walks there.

Yet I have flesh both firm and cool,
    And eyes tumultuous as the gems
    Of moons and lamps in the full Thames
When dusk sails wavering down the pool.

Shuddering the purple street-arc burns
    Where I watch always; from the banks
    Dolorously the shipping clanks
And after me a strange tide turns.

I walk till the stars of London wane
    And dawn creeps up the Shadwell Stair.
    But when the crowing sirens blare
I with the other ghosts am lain.

1. The 1st and 2nd stanzas are different from each other in what way?

   A. They have different rhyme patterns.
   B. The first describes an action and the second describes the speaker.
   C. The first is happy and the second is sad.
   D. The first is more confident than the second.

2. Why does the speaker describe the reflection of moons and lamps at dusk?

   A. Because the image is a simile for what the speaker's eyes look like.
   B. Because the image is a further description of the poem's setting.
   C. Because the image contrasts with the rest of the poem.
   D. To express how much the speaker enjoys looking at them.

3. What can we infer about the events in the 3rd stanza?

   A. They cause the speaker's mood to vastly improve.
   B. They seem to mirror what the speaker is feeling.
   C. They give the speaker a reason to turn back from ghost into human.
   D. They are described by a different speaker than in the previous two stanzas.

4. During which time of the day does the poem take place?

   A. Late morning.
   B. Afternoon.
   C. Twilight.
   D. The middle of the night.

5. When the speaker lies down at the end of the poem, which has NOT happened?

   A. The sun has risen.
   B. The speaker spent time with many other ghosts.
   C. The stars have disappeared.
   D. The birds have started to chirp.

Extended Response

"The Little Ghost" and "Shadwell Stair" are poems that have very different descriptions about ghosts. How are the portrayals of the two ghosts similar, and how are they different? Use details from both poems to support your answer.

- Explain the perspective towards ghosts that is in "The Little Ghost."
- Explain the perspective towards ghosts that is in "Shadwell Stair."
- Include details from both poems to support your answer.
- Compare and contrast the two explanations.

Planning Page

You may PLAN your writing for the next question here if you wish, but do NOT write your final answer on this page. Write your final answer on the NEXT two pages.

Practice

ELA Strategy—Scoring on the ELA

On the short response questions in the ELA section, there are two possible points available for each one. Here's what you need to know about scoring.

2 Points.

- Your conclusions and interpretations about the passage you just read are valid. This means NOT arguing that the pretty poem about ballet is actually about how Keith Hernandez was a great ballplayer, or how Xbox is better than Playstation. So stay on topic!
- Your conclusions and interpretations of the text will be interesting. This may be the hardest point to manage, but it's not too difficult. It means that they want you to think critically about what you're reading, so this is the point to talk about what you think it's really about, what the tone is, and what the main point is.
- Mention examples from the text. This is so easy, so important, and yet so many kids have trouble with it. Show us that whatever you're saying about the story, essay, poem, play, etc. is correct by quoting parts of it and referring to examples. BE SPECIFIC.
- Use complete, grammatical sentences. This doesn't mean that you can't make some spelling mistakes or some small errors, but you have to be close enough that the reader can understand you.

1 Point

- A response to the text that is mostly a summary of what you just read. This means that you are NOT thinking critically about what you read, but at least you're able to tell us what happened.
- You cite the text at least a little bit, giving us some information relevant to what you're telling us about the text.
- Your sentences are incomplete.

No Points

- A response that does not address the prompt. This means that you could write the best piece of writing ever seen in the western world, but if it's off-subject you get a zero.
- Your response is wrong. If you don't understand what you just read, no points for you.
- A response that is in some language that is not English. This is a no-brainer. I shouldn't even have to tell you this. Answer in the same language the question was asked in!
- A response that cannot be understood because it is ungrammatical or illegible. That means that if they can't read your handwriting, you get a zero.

Here's what you need to know for the extended response questions. They're graded on a four-point scale along four different areas:

- **Content and Analysis**. This is a measure of how clearly and persuasively you present a claim or argument based on the text.
    - 4 Points. Clearly introduce your topic that fits the prompt. Write insightfully about the text.
    - 3 Points. Clearly introduce your topic that fits the prompt. Write an average level analysis about the text.
    - 2 Points. Introduce your topic that more or less fits the prompt, and give only a summary of the text.
    - 1 Point. Write on a topic that does not fit the prompt, and show little understanding of the text.
    - 0 Points. Show no understanding of the text at all.

- **Command of Evidence**. This is a measure of how well you use the text to make your case.
    - 4 Points. Make your argument with varied, persuasive, and specific examples and information from the text.
    - 3 Points. Make your argument with persuasive and specific examples, but with little variety of evidence.
    - 2 Points. Make only part of your argument with persuasive and specific examples, with some evidence from the text not fitting your case.
    - 1 Point. Try to use evidence from the text to make your case, but generally fail and use evidence that does not fit your topic.
    - 0 Points. Use no evidence at all.

- **Organization and Style**. This is a measure of how clearly your essay is organized, how logically you present your evidence and ideas, and how clearly your sentences and paragraphs are written.
    - 4 Points. Organize your essay clearly; connect your sentences with correct words and phrases; use words appropriate to an intelligent 4th grader; and conclude your essay with a sentence that fits your topic and essay.
    - 3 Points. Do all the things required for 4 points, but just do them less well.
    - 2 Points. Attempt organization, but without much success; use links and phrases without much success; use vocabulary that is not at grade level; provide a conclusion statement that fits the essay.
    - 1 Point. Little to no effort in organization; absence of connecting words; use vague words or wrong words; and use a concluding statement that does not fit your essay.
    - 0 Points. None of the traits of a 4 point essay.

- **Grammar and Spelling**. Here they will grade your ability to use English grammar, the correct words, capitalization, punctuation, and even spelling.
    - 4 Points. Make few if any errors.
    - 3 Points. Make some errors, but none that get in the way of understanding the essay.
    - 2 Points. Some errors that make the essay difficult to understand.

- 1 Point. Frequent errors that make the essay hard to understand.
- 0 Points. Errors that make comprehension of much of the essay impossible.

This may all seem complicated, but just keep these four things in mind and you'll do great.

- **Active Sentences**. We like it when our sentences are active because it makes them more interesting to read. What is an active sentence? It is when the subject does the verb.
  Good: The player hit the ball into the outfield.
  Bad: The ball was hit into the outfield by the player.
- **No Zero Sentences**. Every sentence you write should tell us something new. If you are repeating yourself, either find something else to say or consider yourself done with the question.
- **Use the Text to Support Your Answer**. This is crucial. If you are going to tell us something about what you've just read, you must tell us why what you say is correct. Be specific.
- **Use Proper Grammar**. This is an English test. Not all of your answers have to be poetry, but at least follow the rules of grammar.

ELA Strategy Questions

Now that you've read lots of different passages, please try to answer the following questions in complete sentences.

1. What are the Three T's that you are looking for when you first read the passage?

____

____

2. What does reading for details mean?

____

____

3. What is an inference?

____

____

4. Please define the following literary devices. Even better if you can think of an example.

    - Metaphor _______________________
    - Simile _______________________
    - Personification _______________________
    - Foreshadowing _______________________
    - Rhyme _______________________
    - Hyperbole _______________________
    - Imagery _______________________
    - Onomatopoeia _______________________
    - Alliteration _______________________

5. What is the best way to go about answering questions on the reading comprehension?

____

____

6. How do you tackle questions that ask you the meaning of a vocabulary word? What if you do not already know the meaning of the word? What are some ways you can figure out the meaning of the word? What are context clues?

____

____

7. For an extended response question, what should you include in an introduction?

____

____

8. For an extended response question, what should you include in a conclusion?

____

____

9. For an extended response question, what should you include in a body paragraph?

____

____

10. What is a run-on sentence? How can you avoid them?

____

____

Practice

11. What is an incomplete sentence? How can you avoid them?

____

____

12. How do you know you need to start a new paragraph?

____

____

13. How do you know you need to start a new sentence?

____

____

14. What does it mean to plan your extended response? What should you include in your planning?

____

____

15. What does it mean to proofread? What should you be looking for? How long should you take to proofread?

____

____

____

____

____

HOW TO AVOID

Part II—

Time & the Student Mind

1 TIME IS AN ILLUSION REALLY

Students are fascinating creatures. They are a hybrid blend of child and adult, and you seldom know which you're going to get when—except when it comes to matters of time. When it comes to matters of time, students are infants. Even after working with thousands of students, I have yet to come across a teenager who had an accurate sense of time when it came to tests. Most students are freaked out about time from the start, so they rush—really, really psychotically and brutally rush. I have seen some kids so spooked about time they won't even take the time to work out 2 + 2 or read through to the end of a simple sentence.

Often kids have received these notions of time through their parents, who have told them, "You read too slowly." BAD PARENT! Most students who think they read too slowly actually read too quickly and don't have any idea what the heck it is they just supposedly read. So, when they get to the questions they have NO IDEA how to answer them, and that is where they lose time and points! All because of NOT, NOT, NOT reading slowly and carefully.

2 INDECISION IS THE ULTIMATE TIME SUCK

While it is true that time is an illusion and that attempting to save time results in loss of time or points and usually both [rushing wastes time], still it is possible to save time [life is a paradox[22]—get over it]. Students waste more time resisting doing the thing than doing the thing itself would take. When students give me the "Oh, I knew how to do it, but it would have taken too much time" line, that is when I feel myself growing older and when that small vein on my temple begins to throb. DO NOT MAKE DECISIONS BASED ON HOW LONG YOU THINK SOMETHING IS GOING TO TAKE. IF YOU HAVE ANY IDEA HOW TO SOLVE A PROBLEM, START DOING IT. JUST GETTING GOING WILL SAVE YOU ALL THE TIME YOU'LL NEED TO SOLVE IT. TRUST ME ON THIS. REALLY!

[22] something that seems to be a contradiction but is still true

EXAMICIDE

YOU CAN GET FASTER AT GOING SLOWER–THE SLOWER YOU GO THE FASTER YOU GO

This is another one of those time paradoxes that I spend an inordinate amount of time trying to prove to my students. First, I need to slow my students down enough for them to do the thing the right way. Then I really, really have to convince them to write everything out and not skip steps. Once they get used to not rushing and being thorough, they're amazed: most problems take no time at all!

It is like learning to play a piece of music. You don't begin at full speed. First you learn the notes and the phrasing and then, as you become familiar with playing the song, you get up to speed. If you try to play a piece quickly from the outset, you'll never learn it properly. If you rush through every math problem and every reading passage, you will never learn how to read or do the math properly. Once you know how to do a thing right, you will begin to go quickly naturally and it will never feel rushed. It will feel smooth, efficient and right. As Goethe[23] said, "Never rush; never rest."

See next Examicide on Page pg. 272→

[22] old, dead German writer, thinker, colorist

CHAPTER FOUR

MATH

MUST KNOW MATH—ARITHMETIC

Must Know Terms

It's easy to speak any language if you know a few key basics. Learn these essential terms in order to start speaking better math:

- **Sum:** The result of addition.
- **Difference:** The result of subtraction.
- **Product:** The result of multiplication.
- **Quotient:** The result of division.
- **Even Numbers:**
  - Any whole number that can be divided by 2 without a remainder.
  - N.B.: When an odd number is divided by 2, the whole number remainder can only ever be 1.
- **Zero**: Zero is an integer and it's even [when zero is divided by two the remainder is zero!] However, it is neither positive nor negative, and although you may divide zero by any number, you CANNOT divide any number by zero.
- **Prime Numbers:**
  - Positive numbers that have only two distinct [different] factors: 1 and itself.
    2, 3, 5, 7, 11, 13, 17, 19, 23, 29, 31,etc....
  - 1 is NOT a prime number. [It only has one distinct factor {itself}, not two.]
  - All primes are odd numbers except 2, which for obvious reasons can be divided only by itself and **one** (there are no other numbers between them).
- **Multiples**
  The whole number products of a number.
  E.g., the multiples of 12 are: 12, 24, 36, 48, 60, 72, 84, 96, etc.
  N.B.: The first multiple of every number is itself.
- **Factors**
  The factors of a number are those integers that can be multiplied with other integers to form that number.
  E.g., the FACTORS of 6 are 1, 2, 3 and 6.
- **Distinct**
  This simply means "different." As in, in the set {1, 2, 3, 3, 4}, there are five terms but only four DISTINCT numbers.
- **Digits**
  These are the individual numbers that compose bigger numbers—think of them as the letters that form bigger words or numbers. In other words, in the number 1,234 the digits are 1, 2, 3, and 4. The digit 1 is in the thousands place, the digit 2 is the hundreds place, and so on.
- **Consecutive**
  This simply means "in a row" or "one after the other." As in, the first five consecutive positive numbers are 1, 2, 3, 4, 5. Be careful, though; sometimes "one after the other" could mean different things. As in, the first five *consecutive* even numbers are 2, 4, 6, 8, 10.
- **Inclusive**
  A series of numbers is said to be inclusive if the first and last terms in the series are part of the list.

Addition

The first step in math is to have a solid grip on adding. I can't tell you how many times I've even seen students use their fingers to add 9 + 4. Don't get me wrong, using your fingers is far superior to saying "12." However, better still is KNOWING that 9 + 4 = 13.

The tricky ones to remember are the ones that go "around the bend"—i.e. from single digits over ten from the teens over twenty, and so on.

Adding Pairs to Lock In—[No more fingers]

2 + 7 = 9	2 + 8 = 10	2 + 9 = 11
3 + 7 = 10	3 + 8 = 11	3 + 9 = 12
4 + 7 = 11	4 + 8 = 12	4 + 9 = 13
5 + 7 = 12	5 + 8 = 13	5 + 9 = 14
6 + 7 = 13	6 + 8 = 14	6 + 9 = 15
7 + 7 = 14	7 + 8 = 15	7 + 9 = 16
8 + 7 = 15	8 + 8 = 16	8 + 9 = 17
9 + 7 = 16	9 + 8 = 17	9 + 9 = 18

Subtraction Pairs to Lock In—[No more fingers]

18–9 = 9	14–7 = 7	12–5 = 7
17–9 = 8	14–8 = 6	12–4 = 8
17–8 = 9	13–9 = 4	12–3 = 9
16–9 = 7	13–8 = 5	11–9 = 2
16–8 = 8	13–7 = 6	11–8 = 3
16–7 = 9	13–6 = 7	11–7 = 4
15–9 = 6	13–5 = 8	11–6 = 5
15–8 = 7	13–4 = 9	11–5 = 6
15–7 = 8	12–9 = 3	11–4 = 7
15–6 = 9	12–8 = 4	11–3 = 8
14–9 = 5	12–7 = 5	11–9 = 2
14–8 = 6	12–6 = 6	

Adding and Subtracting—The Basics

Adding is easier if you locate yourself around 5's and 10's.

If you're having trouble learning what 5 + 8 is, just think of it as:

5 + (5 + 3) which=

(5 + 5) + 3 which=

10 + 3 which=

13!

Adding with 9 is easy. Just think of adding with 10 and take away 1!

9 + 8 = 10 + 8 – 1 = 18 –1 = 17!

Once you have figured a way to learn all your figure pairs by heart [more tips in back], then you can use your knowledge of adding pairs to go around the bend when adding higher numbers.

28 + 7 is the same as 20 + 8 + 7,

and since you know that 8 + 7 = 15,

then you know that 28 + 7 = 20 + 15 = 35!

Now try some of your own:

Addition

1. 54 + 12 =
2. 79 + 7 =
3. 13 + 8 =
4. 23 + 7 =
5. 49 + 14 =
6. 88 + 7 =
7. 94 + 4 =
8. 165 + 6 =
9. 24 + 9 =

The same game works for subtraction. Try to get yourself down to the nearest multiple of ten [10,20,30,40,etc...] and then take away what's left!

54 – 8 = (54 – 4) – 4 = 50 – 4 = 46

or

Try to see 54 – 8 as 14 – 8; 14 – 8 = 6, so 54 – 8 = 46.

Now try some of your own:

Subtraction

1. 117 – 9 =	3. 451 – 16 =
2. 224 – 8 =	4. 818 – 9 =

Stack and Add

When we get to adding bigger numbers to bigger numbers, we build our answers by doing some heavy lifting. The first things to lift are the heaviest things: put the bigger number on top of the littler number!

When you do this, you need to line your numbers up in columns the same way you build a building with columns. These columns are the ones, tens, hundreds, thousands places, and so on.....when you fill one up you add it to the other.

We'll start with the ONEs—we always start with the ONEs [every journey begins with the first step!].

$$\begin{array}{r} 879 \\ \underline{+368} \end{array}$$

9 + 8 = 17. The 17 won't fit into the ONES column, but 7 will. Seven is the ONEs part of the number 17, so that's where the seven belongs. The 1 from 17 will go into the TEN's column because that's where it belongs. Then add up that 1 with all the other TENs. If those add up to a number greater than 9, do the same with the sum and you get.

$$\begin{array}{r} 8^{1}79 \\ \underline{+3\ 68} \\ 7 \end{array}$$

1 + 7 + 6 = 14 , so now leave the 4 in the TENs place and carry the 1 to the HUNDREDs place.

$$\begin{array}{r} 8^{1}79 \\ \underline{+3\ 68} \\ 47 \end{array}$$

Now do the same thing with the HUNDREDS place: add 'em up!

1 + 8 + 3 = 12; now simply leave the 2 from the 12 in the HUNDREDs place, but where do we put the 1? Since there are no more columns to put it on top of, make one of your own! Drop it at the bottom and your answer is built!

$$\begin{array}{r} 8^{1}79 \\ \underline{+3\,68} \\ 1{,}247 \end{array}$$

This method can be used to add stacks of numbers as tall as the Empire State Building! If you are adding a stack of three or more numbers, the number you will carry may be 1, 2, 3 or more. The size doesn't matter, just lift the digit over to the next column.

$$\begin{array}{r} 45{,}873 \\ 1{,}687 \\ +\quad \underline{245} \end{array}$$

$$\begin{array}{r} 4^{1}5,^{2}8^{1}73 \\ 1,\,6\,87 \\ \underline{+\quad 2\,45} \\ 47,\,8\,05 \end{array}$$

Try some!

Stack and Add

1. $\begin{array}{r} 542 \\ \underline{+\,239} \end{array}$

2. $\begin{array}{r} 116 \\ \underline{+\,172} \end{array}$

3. $\begin{array}{r} 1{,}342 \\ 429 \\ \underline{+576} \end{array}$

4. $\begin{array}{r} 95 \\ 74 \\ 56 \\ \underline{+63} \end{array}$

5. $\begin{array}{r} 38{,}362 \\ 7{,}415 \\ 6{,}089 \\ \underline{+4{,}715} \end{array}$

6. $\begin{array}{r} 9{,}876 \\ 5{,}432 \\ \underline{+1{,}987} \end{array}$

Stack and Subtract

74 – 31

To stack and subtract, start the same way you stack and add. Put the bigger number on top of the smaller number, and then subtract each number in a lower column from the number above it.

$$\begin{array}{r} 74 \\ \underline{-31} \\ 43 \end{array}$$ because 4 – 1 = 3 and 7 – 3 = 4

We start subtracting as we did adding [and as we will multiply] in the ones place. This time though, we're moving down the number line instead of up, so now instead of carrying when our sum goes over ten, we're borrowing when the number we want to subtract is bigger than the number above it.

264 – 79=

$$\begin{array}{r} 264 \\ \underline{-79} \end{array}$$

We are always going to borrow one and only one from the digit to the left. Borrowing makes the number to the left one less than it was.

$$\begin{array}{r} {}^{5}\not{6}\ {}^{1}4 \\ -3\ \ 9 \\ \hline 2\ \ 5 \end{array}$$

If the next top number to the left is also less than the number you are subtracting from it, you simply borrow one from the number to its left and combine it with the amount left in the column, so...

$$\begin{array}{r} {}^{1}\not{2}\ {}^{15}\not{6}\ {}^{1}4 \\ -7\ \ 9 \\ \hline \end{array}$$

Note: If there is nothing below a number on top, you are subtracting zero.

$$\begin{array}{r} {}^{1}\not{2}\ {}^{15}\not{6}\ {}^{1}4 \\ -0\ \ 7\ \ 9 \\ \hline 1\ \ 8\ \ 5 \end{array}$$

If a top digit in a number is zero, then we need to go one more place to the left to borrow the one...that will make the zero = ten, and we can borrow from that ten and make the ten = nine.

$$\begin{array}{r} 2\ {}^{9}\not{0}\ {}^{1}4 \\ -0\ \ 7\ \ 9 \\ \hline 1\ \ 2\ \ 5 \end{array}$$

And that's the deal.

Try it!

Stack and Subtract

1. $\begin{array}{r} 681 \\ -598 \\ \hline \end{array}$

2. $\begin{array}{r} 2{,}032 \\ -1{,}841 \\ \hline \end{array}$

3. $\begin{array}{r} 10{,}002 \\ -7{,}390 \\ \hline \end{array}$

4. $\begin{array}{r} 6{,}387 \\ -721 \\ \hline \end{array}$

5. $\begin{array}{r} 10{,}209 \\ -10{,}186 \\ \hline \end{array}$

MULTIPLICATION TABLES
Know:
Multiplication Tables through 12s

Especially your 9s and 12s tables.There are ways to make the multiplication tables easier. First, it helps to have a solid grip on adding. I can't tell you how many times I've seen students use their fingers to add 9 + 4. Don't get me wrong, using your fingers is far superior to saying "12." However, better still is KNOWING that 9 + 4 = 13.

Once you're comfortable with adding, let's go to the multiplication tables and start with the ONES [always start everything at ONE].

	1	**2**	**3**	**4**	**5**	**6**	**7**	**8**	**9**	**10**	**11**	**12**
1	1	2	3	4	5	6	7	8	9	10	11	12
2	2	4	6	8	10	12	14	16	18	20	22	24
3	3	6	9	12	15	18	21	24	27	30	33	36
4	4	8	12	16	20	24	28	32	36	40	44	48
5	5	10	15	20	25	30	35	40	45	50	55	60
6	6	12	18	24	30	36	42	48	54	60	66	72
7	7	14	21	28	35	42	49	56	63	70	77	84
8	8	16	24	32	40	48	56	64	72	80	88	96
9	9	18	27	36	45	54	63	72	81	90	99	108
10	10	20	30	40	50	60	70	80	90	100	110	120
11	11	22	33	44	55	66	77	88	99	110	121	132
12	12	24	36	48	60	72	84	96	108	120	132	144

Stacking

The multiplication tables go only so far: what do we do with the really big numbers?!

The way to multiply big numbers is by stacking. You may have been taught some other methods, such as lattice, but you shouldn't use these methods on the test. You need to use **stacking**. Just in case you forgot how to stack, since you've been doing lattice for so long, here's a review!

Stacking is kind of like carrying in addition. Say you need to multiply 24 × 6.

$$\begin{array}{r} 24 \\ \underline{\times\ 6} \end{array}$$

We need to multiply 6 x 4 and also 6 x 2. We do 6 x 4 first [BEGIN ALL MULTIPLICATION AND ADDING IN THE ONES COLUMN], which equals 24. But where do we put the 2 and where do we put the 4? We put the **ones** number (in this case, the 4) under the TOTAL line into the ones column, and we "carry" the **tens** place number (in this case, the 2).

Now we have this:

$$\begin{array}{r} {}^{2} \\ 24 \\ \times\ 6 \\ \hline 4 \end{array}$$

The next step is to multiply 6 x 2. We know that 6 x 2 is 12. Great. But what do we do with the 2 sitting on top of the other 2? We **add** it to the 12! So 12 + 2 = 14! What do we do with the 14? We put it under the line in front of what's already there.

Now we have:

$$\begin{array}{r} {}^{2} \\ 24 \\ \times\ 6 \\ \hline 144 \end{array}$$

And that's our answer! 144!

Let's try stacking one when we have two two-digit numbers.

$$\begin{array}{r} 72 \\ \times\ 96 \\ \hline \end{array}$$

We need to multiply 2 x 6 first. That's 12.

$$\begin{array}{r} {}^{1} \\ 72 \\ \times\ 96 \\ \hline 2 \end{array}$$

Next, we multiply 6 x 7. That's 42. Then we add the 1 to 42, and we get 43. We put everything in the right place just as we learned above.

$$\begin{array}{r} {}^{1} \\ 72 \\ \times\ 96 \\ \hline 432 \end{array}$$

Now we are all done with the 6, and we need to move on to the **9.** Before we do anything, we put a **0** underneath the 2 because we're really multiplying by 90 not 9—so we add a zero to our answer.

$$\begin{array}{r} {}^{1} \\ 72 \\ \times\ 96 \\ \hline 432 \\ 0 \end{array}$$

Next, we multiply the 9 by the 2 and be sure to carry the 1 in 18.

$$\begin{array}{r} {}^{1} \\ 72 \\ \times\ 96 \\ \hline 432 \\ 80 \end{array}$$

Then we multiply the 9 by the 7, which is 63, and then we add the 1: 63 + 1 = 64, so:

$$\begin{array}{r} {}^{1} \\ 72 \\ \times\ 96 \\ \hline 432 \\ 6480 \end{array}$$

Now we need to add this all together, so we put in another SUM [total] line.

$$\begin{array}{r} {}^{1} \\ 72 \\ \times\ \ 96 \\ \hline 432 \\ +\ 6480 \\ \hline 6912 \end{array}$$

And that's our answer! **6,912!**

So

FUN MATH FACT

If you are picking through a bunch of numbers for an answer to a multiplication problem, you can always sort through the units digits first.

$$\text{E.g., } \begin{array}{r} 4{,}382 \\ \times\ 17 \\ \hline \end{array}$$

A. 76,786 B. 76,494 C. 74,952 D. 74,494 E. 73,328

In other words, start by multiplying the units digits. Then you'll know that whatever the answer is its unit digit must be a 4. That narrows your options down to B and D.!

Stacking Practice

Do on a separate piece of papter as needed

7. 25×6

8. 42×7

9. 98×14

10. 27×79

11. 82×96

Division

Now that we're comfortable with multiplication and factoring, let's work on division. If you've mastered multiplication and addition, there's no part of division you can't handle.

What is division? Here's an example of a division problem written two different ways:

$$24 \div 8 \text{ and } 8\overline{)24}$$

In each case, 24 is the dividend and 8 is the divisor. The answer, which we haven't gotten to yet, is called the quotient.

So what is division asking us? It's asking us what number we'd have to multiply the *divisor* by in order to get the dividend or, as we say in English, how many times one number goes into another number.

In this case the answer is three: 8 times 3 equals 24. So three is the quotient.

But what do we do when we can't find the dividend or the divisor in our multiplication tables?? How can we divide then?

We do it step by step. Let's take the following problem:

$$693 \div 7$$

However, the best way to write this is the other way, like so:

$$7\overline{)693}$$

Why? Because this makes it easier to do the subtraction we'll have to do. You'll see.

It's important to know your digits when you do this and remember how to multiply by ten.

First, we see if seven goes into the **first** digit, which is six. It does not [bummer], so we see if it goes into the first **two** digits: 69. Of course seven goes into 69! It doesn't go in ***exactly***, but that doesn't matter: it just has to get close. Seven times nine gets us to 63 which is as close as we can get to 69 by sevens!

So we put a nine on the line above the nine in the TENs column. We put it there because we're really multiplying by 90. We then write 630 beneath 693, like so:

$$\begin{array}{r} \mathbf{9} \\ 7\overline{)693} \\ \underline{-630} \end{array}$$

Now we have a subtraction problem: 693 – 630. Which equals what? 63. So we write that down below our subtraction problem.

$$\begin{array}{r} \mathbf{9} \\ 7\overline{)693} \\ \underline{-630} \\ 63 \end{array}$$

Now we have a NEW division problem: 63 divided by 7. You know this—you just did it! 7 goes into 63 nine times. We put this nine above the three to give us a quotient of 99!

$$\begin{array}{r} \mathbf{99} \\ 7\overline{)693} \\ \underline{-630} \\ 63 \\ \underline{-63} \\ 0 \end{array}$$

Now there's one more step! We have to check to make sure we did our work correctly. The best way to check your math is to do the reverse operation. In this case, we will MULTIPLY.

$$\begin{array}{r} 99 \\ \underline{\times 7} \\ 693 \end{array}$$

But what about when it doesn't go into the number exactly any number of times? What do we do then? Then we have a remainder, which is explained below

Division Practice

Solve the following division problems using long division.

1. $369 \div 3 =$
2. $452 \div 4 =$
3. $612 \div 6 =$
4. $5{,}775 \div 5 =$
5. $897 \div 9 =$
6. $1213 \div 6 =$

Remainders

Remainder—the whole number amount left over when one number is divided by another.

Remainders are one of the first stops on the math highway. The point at which many students stop and say, "No thanks. I'm out." When you throw most kids 17 ÷ 4, the math gears grind to a halt and they look blankly at you and say, "You can't. It doesn't go in evenly."

While it is true that 17 ÷ 4 does not have a whole-number solution, 17 can absolutely be divided by 4. In fact, any number can be divided by any other number. The answer may not be pretty, but there will be an answer[33].

$$\begin{array}{r} 4\text{r}1 \\ 4\overline{)17} \\ -16 \\ \hline 1 \end{array}$$

Fun Facts about Remainders

1. If a number goes evenly into another, the remainder is zero.
2. The remainder can never be equal to or greater than the divisor.

3. If the number being divided is less than the divisor, the remainder is equal to the number being divided.

$$5 \div 7 = 0\text{ r}5$$

Remainders are **not** the same as quotients with decimals or fractions in their answers. The decimal or fractions are simply part of the answer.

For example: When 17 is divided by 4 the **ANSWER** is 4.25 or $4\frac{1}{4}$ Or you may say the answer is 4 remainder 1. To find out what the remainder would become as part of the answer just keep dividing it by the divisor 4 until you get to 0 or your answers repeat...And they always will!

$$4\overline{)17} = \overset{4}{4\overline{)17}} = \overset{4\frac{1}{4}}{4\overline{)17}} = \overset{4.25}{4\overline{)17.00}}$$

$$\begin{array}{r} \underline{-16} \\ 1 \end{array} \qquad\qquad \begin{array}{r} \underline{-16.00} \\ 1.00 \\ \underline{.80} \\ .20 \\ \underline{.20} \\ 0 \end{array}$$

Inequalities

What's an inequality? Easy. It's the opposite of an equality. So what's an equality? You don't realize it, but you already know what an equality is: it's what you have when you have an equal sign. Here are some equalities[34]:

$$3 = 3$$

$$7 - 3 = 4$$

$$5 \times 3 = 15$$

Those are called equalities because what's on the left side of the equal sign has the same value as what's on the right side of the equal sign.

Inequalities, on the other hand, are what you have when what's on the left side of the equal sign is NOT equal to what's on the right side of the equal sign. In that case, we can't use an equal sign; we use something else instead: < or >.

Those are the two inequality signs. When do you use which?

The big, open part of the sign faces the bigger value and the small, pointy side of the sign faces the smaller value. Simple as that.

So:

$$3 > 2$$

$$6 < 2 + 5$$

$$7 - 3 < 5$$

Got it? Now try these practice problems.

Inequality Practice Set

1. 8 _____ 9
2. 7×6 _____ 41
3. $\frac{1}{3}$ _____ $\frac{1}{2}$
4. $2 + 5 - 6$ _____ $24 \div 12$
5. $\frac{1}{2} + \frac{1}{4}$ _____ $\frac{2}{3} + \frac{1}{6}$
6. $2 \div \frac{1}{4}$ _____ $10 \div 2$
7. $30 - 2$ _____ $(100 \div 2) \div 2$
8. 1.98 _____ 1.979
9. $\frac{5}{6}$ _____ $\frac{5}{7}$
10. 1.74 _____ $\frac{7}{4}$
11. $10{,}872$ _____ $9{,}872 + 99.99$
12. The remainder when 27 is divided by 6 _____ The remainder when 15 is divided by 8

Factors, Multiples and Fractions

It is very easy to confuse factors and multiples. How do I know this? Because—

EVERY SINGLE STUDENT I'VE EVER HAD CONFUSES
FACTORS AND MULTIPLES!

Before we start getting fractions straight, let's make sure we can get factors and multiples straight.

Factors

A factor is a *cause*, something that makes something else happen.

Factors are parts of a number, generally ***smaller*** than the number...

*Icy roads are a **factor** in many auto accidents.*

*3 is a **factor** of 12.*

Multiples

A multiple is a repeated amount of something, a copy.

Multiples are generally ***bigger*** than the number...

*The designer made **multiples** of his original design to sell in department stores.*

*36 is a **multiple** of 12.*

One thing to keep in mind for factors and multiples is that the number you are considering is **ALWAYS** a factor and a multiple of itself.

12 is a **factor** of 12 [1 × 12 = 12]

and

12 is a **multiple** of 12 [12 × 1 = 12]

When we factor on most tests, we're looking for factor pairs of a number, so the best thing to do is use the factor rainbow, or do what I like to do which is play bouncy-bouncy. [see below]

Factors of 12

1, 2, 3, 4, 6, 12

Multiples of 12

12, 24, 36, 48, 60, 72, 84, 96, 108, 120, 132, 144...

Factors

The factors of a number are those numbers that can be multiplied by other numbers to form the original number.

E.g., the FACTORS of 6 are 1, 2, 3 and 6

Now that we know our times tables, we can start factoring. Factoring is an incredibly important skill for doing math. The best way to go about finding factors is to play bouncy-bouncy.

Place the number you want to factor [let's say 24] in the middle of the page or area you are writing in. Directly below that, on the left margin, write the number one [1] because 1 is a factor of all numbers.

24

1,

On the right margin, place the number you are factoring [24], it's partner [1 x 24 = 24].

24

1, 24

Then think of the next number after one that could go into your number. In this case 2 works. Just like when you write a list, write a comma after 1 and write 2.

24

1, 2, 24

Then, on the other side of the line, place a comma to the left of 24 and write 2s partner. In this case it's 12.

24

1, 2, 12, 24

Then you go up from 2 and keep seeing if each consecutive number is a factor of your number or not [check out our Multiplication Tips and Tricks to help you with that!] By the time you get to the middle you will have covered all the numbers!

24

1, 2, 3, 4, 6, 8, 12, 24

Note: Do not forget that the first factor pair of every number is itself and one!

Factoring Practice

Find all the distinct factors of the following numbers.

1. 24

_____ _____ _____ _____ _____ _____ _____ _____

2. 36

_____ _____ _____ _____ _____ _____ _____ _____ _____

3. 20

4. 15

5. 60

6. 72

What does all this have to do with fractions?

Factors and multiples come in very handy when we're working with fractions. We need factors to help us reduce fractions and in order to turn improper fractions into mixed numbers.

Let's read a little bit about fractions first, then we'll see how factors and multiples can help us with them.

Fractions

What pronouns are to grammar and experiments are to science, fractions are to most arithmetic, algebra and beyond. These simple little machines do a lot more than torture kids who just don't get them. They actually make all kinds of equations easier because, as I said above, they are actually little machines!

Everyone knows that the top of a fraction is called the numerator and most everyone knows that the bottom of the fraction is called the denominator. However, most people don't know what the little line between them means. Do you?

The line between the numerator and the denominator means per or divided by.

So in truth each fraction is *really* a tiny division problem.

$\frac{1}{1}=1\div 1=1$ $\frac{4}{2}=4\div 2=2$ $\frac{9}{3}=9\div 3=3$

And so on.

The trouble comes for kids when the numerator is smaller than the denominator. We call those fractions **proper fractions** and fractions with larger numerators than denominators **improper fractions** because they're bigger than one. However, calling those kinds of fractions "improper" is silly because there's no such thing as an improper division problem. You can put any number over any rational number, and, it's not only proper, it's totally kosher!

Examples

$\frac{17}{3}$ $\frac{15{,}000}{7}$ $\frac{1{,}234}{234}$

In lower grades, you're asked to make improper fractions into mixed numbers, but, as you get older, you'll have less and less use for mixed numbers and more and more use for messy, old improper fractions.

THE MAGIC OF ONE—FRACTIONS EDITION

Like zero, the number one has a lot of magical properties that allow us to do amazing things in math. Here's one property that will come in really helpful very shortly:
Any number divided by itself equals one.

$$8 \div 8 = 1$$
$$2{,}732 \div 2{,}732 = 1$$

Since we now know that a fraction is just a little division problem, then we also know that:

Any number over itself in a fraction equals one.

$\frac{☺}{☺} = ☺ \div ☺ = 1$ $\frac{2{,}372}{2{,}372} = 1$ $\frac{8}{8} = 1$

But back to ***proper*** fractions...

Proper Fractions

Another way to think of fractions is to see them as a number of pieces of a whole.

Let's say you and your friend Pooky each have a chocolate bar.

- If you cut yours into halves, you have two halves.
- If Pooky cuts her bar into fourths, she'll have four fourths.
- If you want to give your friend half of your chocolate bar, you give her $\frac{1}{2}$.
- If she wants to give you the same amount back, how much does she have to give you?
    - She has to give you $\frac{2}{4}$! That's because $\frac{1}{2}$ and $\frac{2}{4}$ are equivalent fractions—different sized pieces that add up to the same amount of chocolate.

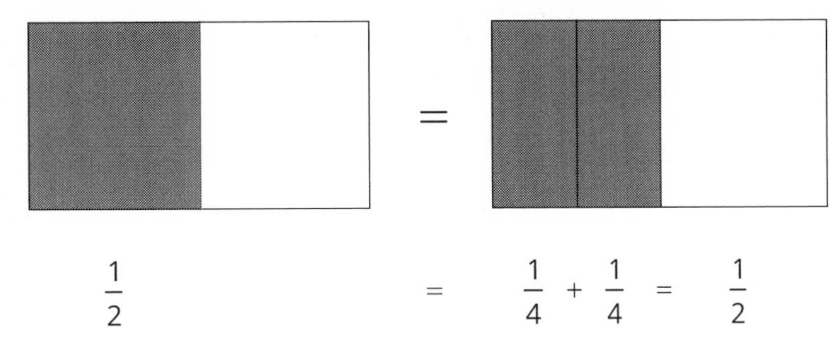

$\frac{1}{2} = \frac{1}{4} + \frac{1}{4} = \frac{1}{2}$

Now we could continue treating fractions as chocolate bars.

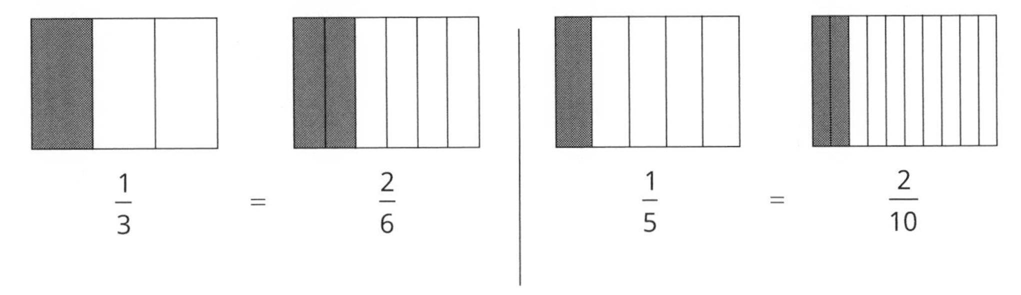

$\frac{1}{3} = \frac{2}{6}$ | $\frac{1}{5} = \frac{2}{10}$

Or...

We can start treating fractions like **numbers** and move them around like the tools they are...

Instead of drawing pictures every time we want to find equivalents, let's think back to our old friends multiples and factors [remember I told you they'd come in handy]. If you want to make **equivalents** of fractions, you can go up using multiples [easy] or go down using factors [harder but SO helpful in the long run]

Finding equivalents using multiples—Just multiply by one! Thanks to the Magic of One (See pg. 159) we can change the look of any fraction without changing its value if we multiply it by one—but one expressed as some equivalent of one like $\frac{2}{2}$, $\frac{3}{3}$, $\frac{4}{4}$, etc. Anything we want as long as it is equivalent to one!

What are some multiples/equivalents of $\frac{1}{2}$?

$\frac{1}{2} \times \frac{1}{1} = \frac{1}{2}$ $\quad \frac{1}{2} \times \frac{2}{2} = \frac{2}{4}$ $\quad \frac{1}{2} \times \frac{3}{3} = \frac{3}{6}$ $\quad \frac{1}{2} \times \frac{4}{4} = \frac{4}{8}$

Here are some more examples:

$\frac{1}{3} \times \frac{1}{1} = \frac{1}{3}$ $\quad \frac{1}{3} \times \frac{2}{2} = \frac{2}{6}$ $\quad \frac{1}{3} \times \frac{3}{3} = \frac{3}{9}$ $\quad \frac{1}{3} \times \frac{4}{4} = \frac{4}{12}$

$\frac{1}{4} \times \frac{1}{1} = \frac{1}{4}$ $\quad \frac{1}{4} \times \frac{2}{2} = \frac{2}{8}$ $\quad \frac{1}{4} \times \frac{3}{3} = \frac{3}{12}$ $\quad \frac{1}{4} \times \frac{4}{4} = \frac{4}{16}$

The same is true of we had more than one in the numerator:

$\frac{2}{5}\times\frac{1}{1}=\frac{2}{5}$ $\frac{2}{5}\times\frac{2}{2}=\frac{4}{10}$ $\frac{2}{5}\times\frac{3}{3}=\frac{6}{15}$ $\frac{2}{5}\times\frac{4}{4}=\frac{8}{20}$

Recognizing Equivalents

1. $\frac{1}{2}=\frac{\square}{8}$
2. $\frac{2}{3}=\frac{\square}{12}$
3. $\frac{3}{4}=\frac{\square}{20}$
4. $\frac{\square}{25}=\frac{2}{5}$
5. $\frac{1}{3}=\frac{\square}{21}$
6. $\frac{\square}{35}=\frac{1}{5}$
7. $\frac{4}{\square}=\frac{1}{4}$
8. $\frac{1}{3}=\frac{9}{\square}$
9. $\frac{1}{2}=\frac{8}{\square}$
10. $\frac{12}{\square}=\frac{3}{5}$
11. $\frac{3}{4}=\frac{6}{\square}$
12. $\frac{6}{\square}=\frac{1}{2}$

Fraction Modeling

1. The model below is shaded to represent a fraction.

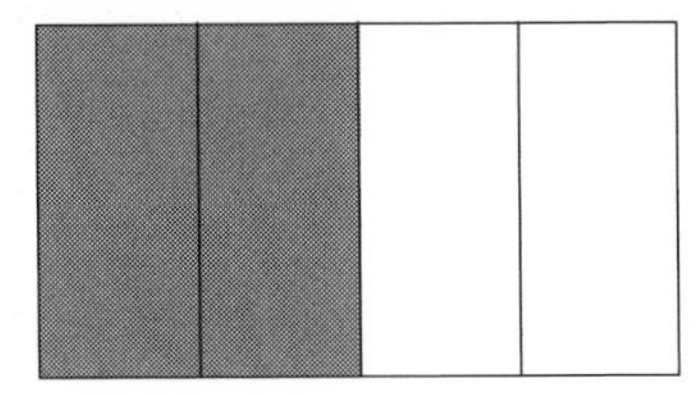

Which model shows an equivalent fraction?

A. 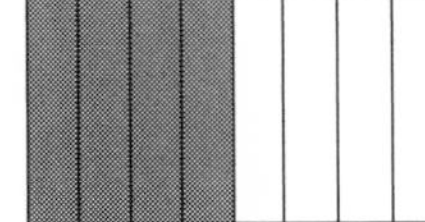

B. 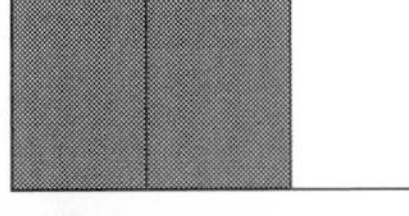

C. 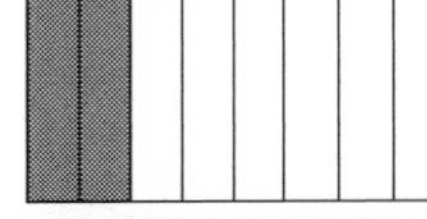

D.

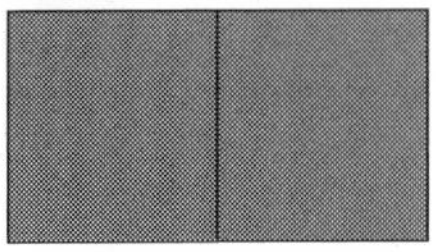

2. Julie is making posters for her class president campaign. The shaded part below represents the fraction of a meter of butcher paper she uses for each poster.

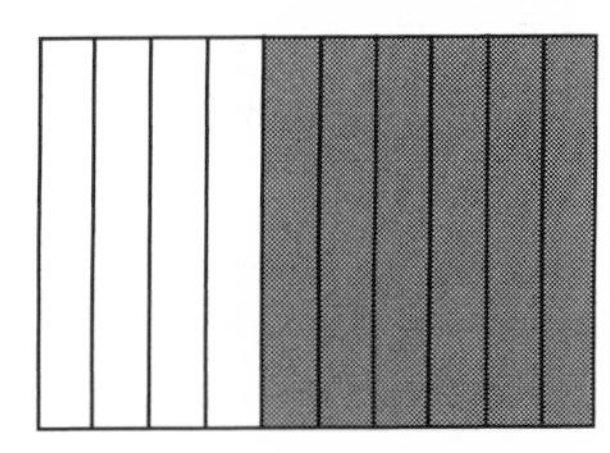

How many meters of paper, in all, will Julie need to make 5 posters?

A. $1\frac{1}{10}$

B. 3

C. $6\frac{2}{5}$

D. 30

3. Which set of models is equivalent to the expression $3 \times \frac{2}{6}$?

A. 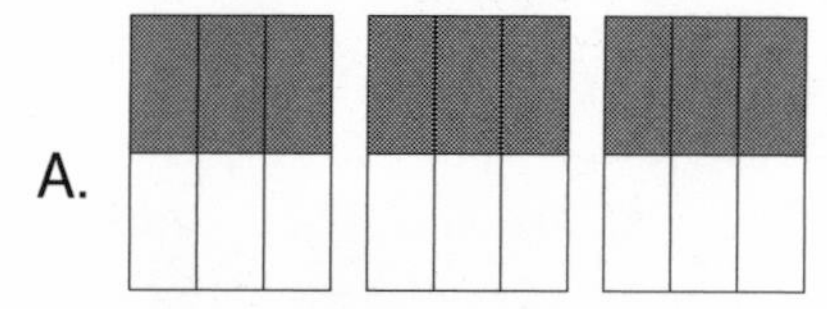

B. 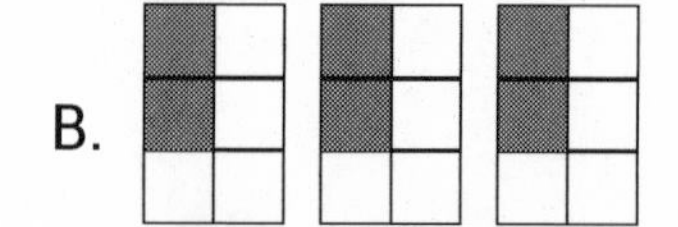

C. 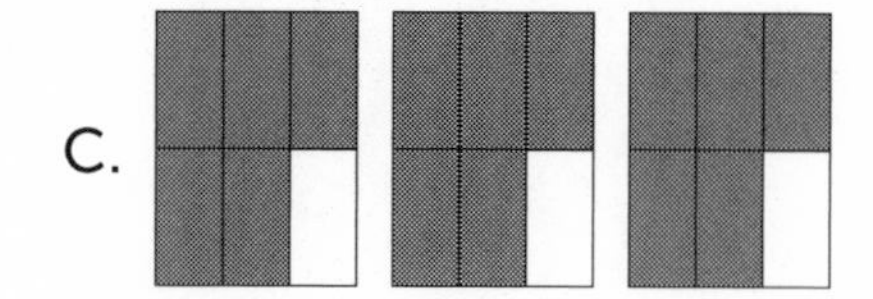

D. 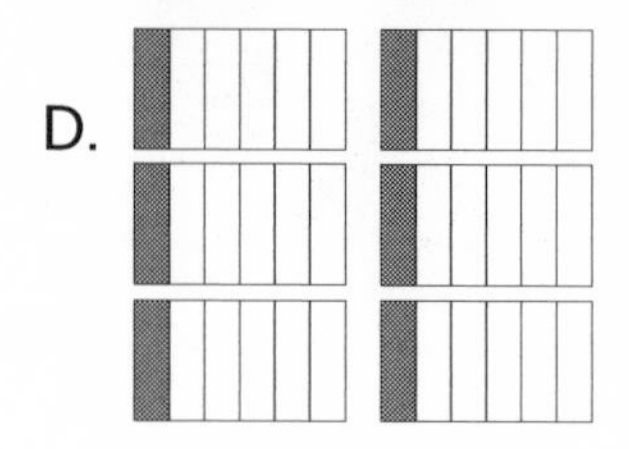

4. The model below is shaded to represent a fraction. If you were to draw a horizontal line in the middle of the model, what would be the unsimplified fraction of the shaded area?

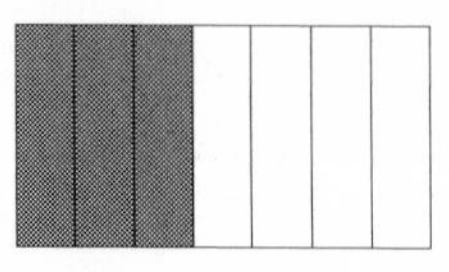

A. $\frac{14}{3}$

B. $\frac{6}{7}$

C. $\frac{6}{14}$

D. $\frac{3}{14}$

5. Jorge is building a table. The shaded part represents the fraction of a yard of wood he uses for each table.

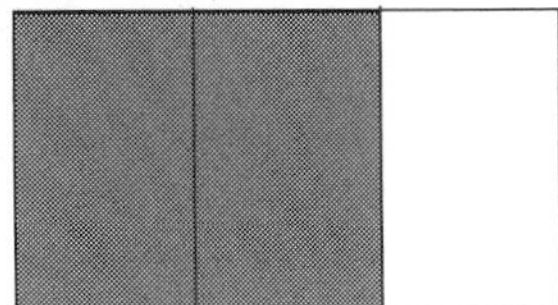

How many yards of wood, in all, will Jorge need to make 11 tables?

A. $11\frac{2}{3}$

B. $7\frac{1}{3}$

C. $3\frac{2}{3}$

D. $1\frac{1}{3}$

6. The model below is shaded to represent a fraction.

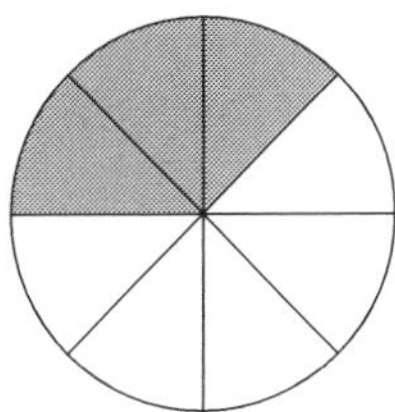

Which model shows an equivalent fraction?

A. 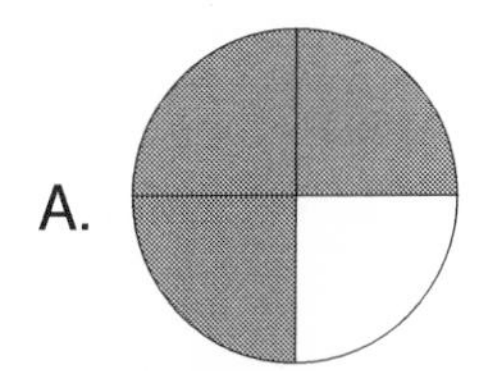

B. 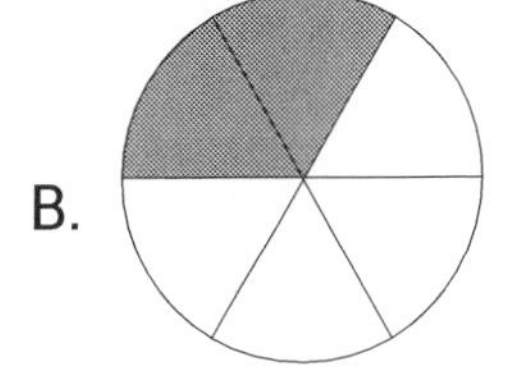

C. 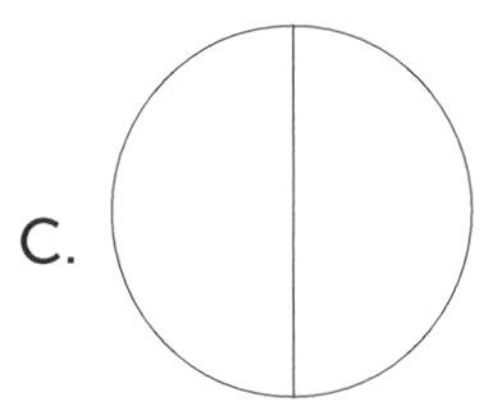

D. 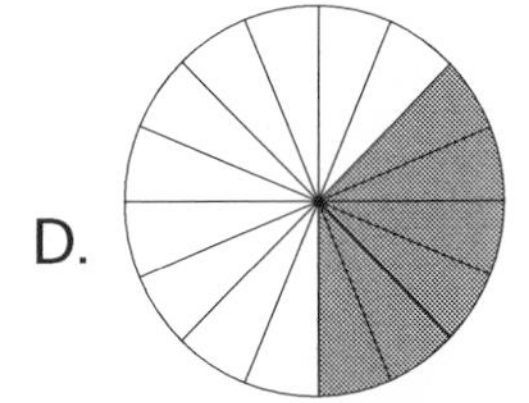

7. Which number line has the correct fraction marked to match the shaded model?

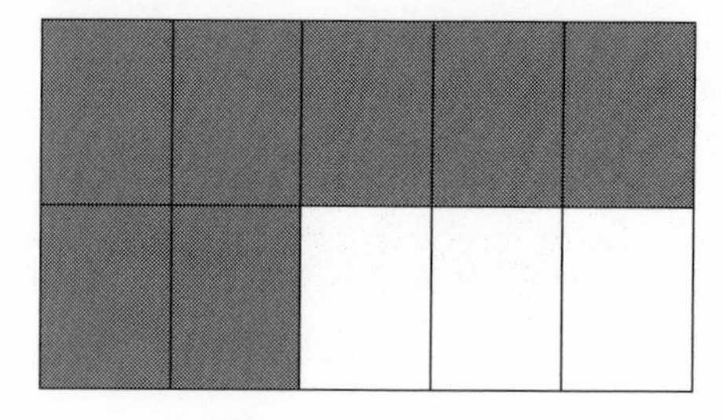

A. 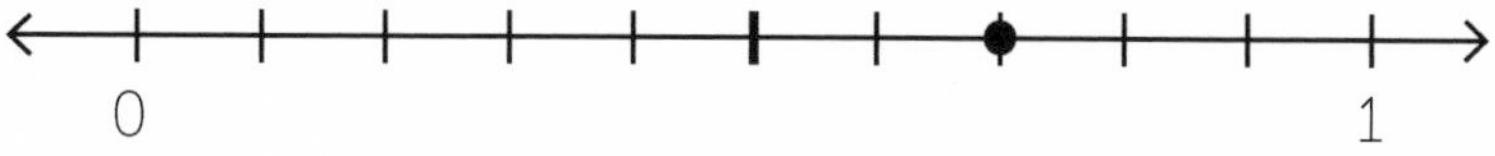 0 1

B. 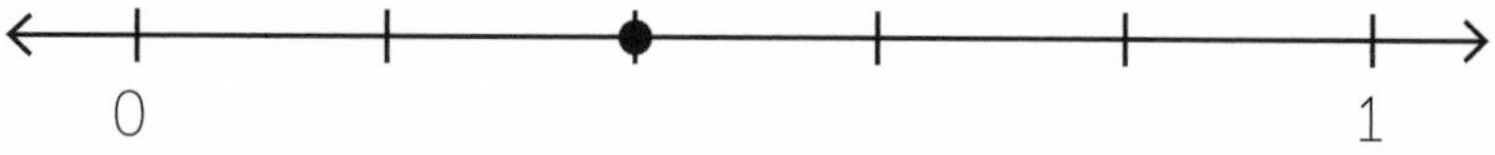 0 1

C. 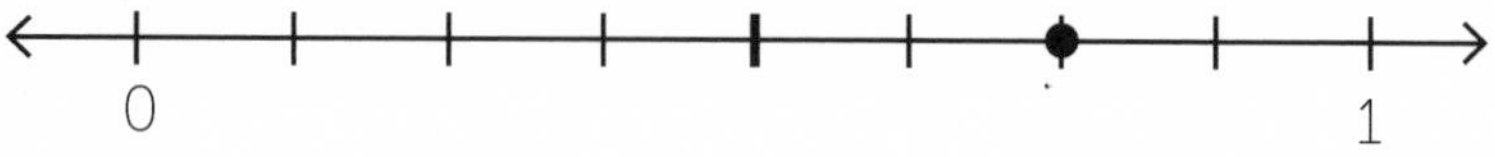 0 1

D. 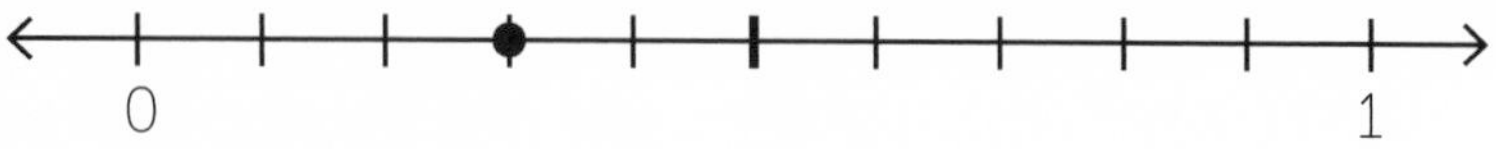 0 1

8. Cecily ate $\frac{5}{8}$ of a pizza, as shown in the model. What is the meaning of the denominator in this example?

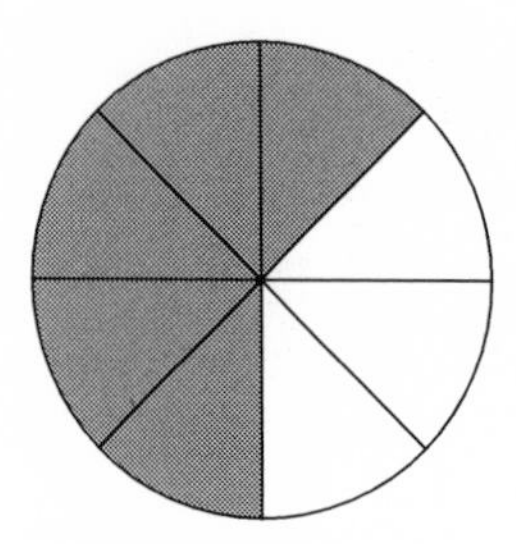

A. Cecily ate 5 slices.
B. Cecily ate 8 slices.
C. The pizza was cut into 5 slices.
D. The pizza was cut into 8 slices.

9. Which set of models is equivalent to the expression $6 \times \frac{1}{5}$?

A. 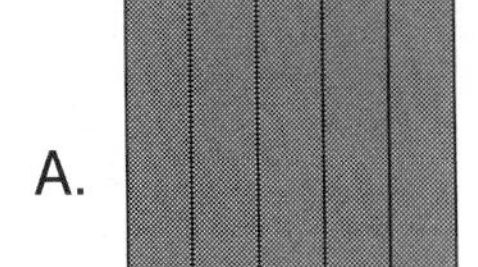

B. 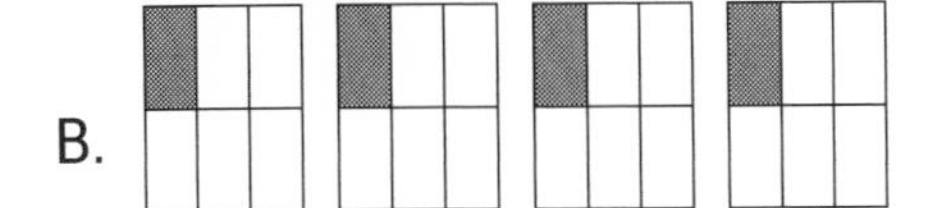

C. 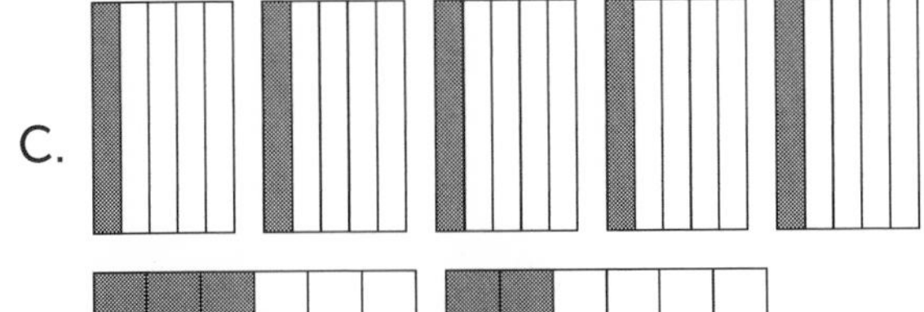

D. 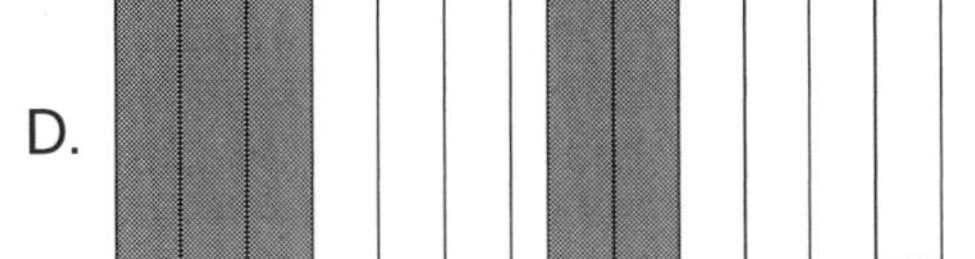

10. Ben is in charge of bringing birthday cake for his friend Doug's birthday. The shaded part below represents the fraction of a cake he anticipates each guest eating.

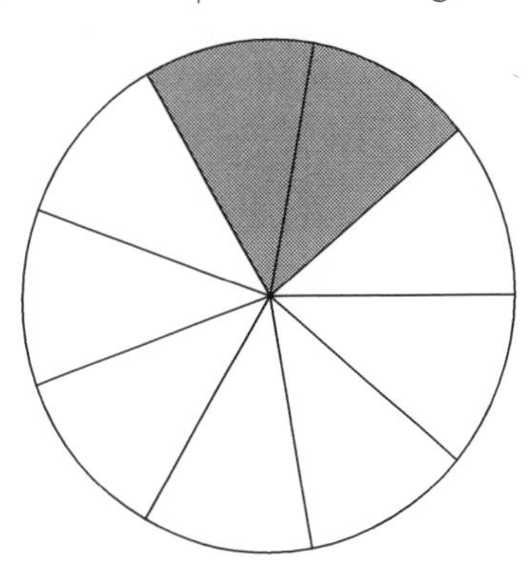

How many cakes, in all, will Ben need to feed 10 guests?

A. 1

B. $\frac{12}{9}$

C. 2

D. $\frac{20}{9}$

11. What decimal represents the shaded part?

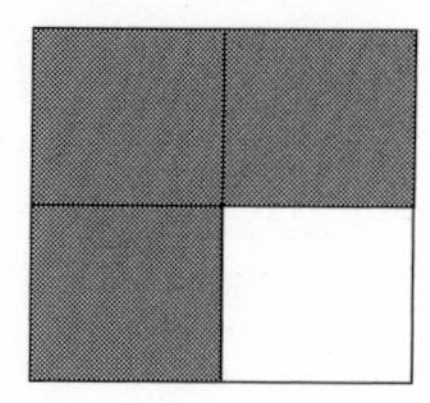

A. 0.75
B. 0.67
C. 0.34
D. 0.3

12. Which set of models is equivalent to $\frac{3}{7}$?

A. 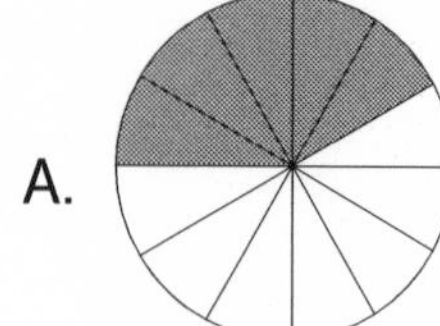

B. 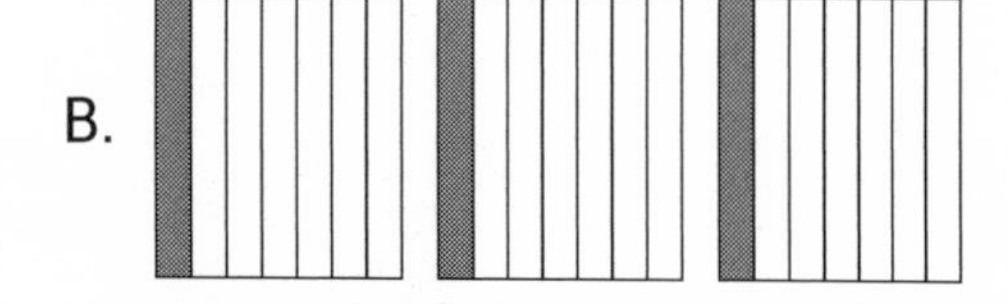

C. 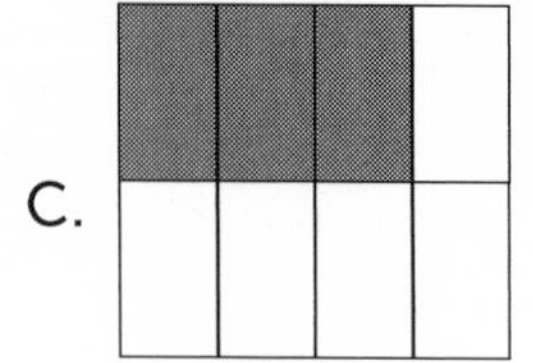

D.

Reducing

Now, however, let's say we have a bloated looking fraction made up of two big-looking numbers, and we want to find simpler equivalents of that fraction by making the numbers smaller. To simplify a fraction [reduce it], we don't try to find multiples of the numbers that compose [make up] the fraction. Instead, we try to find common factors: numbers that go into both the numerator and the denominator.

The easiest number to "see" inside other numbers is 2.

$$\frac{12}{24}$$

both 12 and 24 have 2 inside them, so to reduce the fraction instead of multiplying the top and bottom by a common multiplier as we did to find equivalents above, here we DIVIDE the top and bottom numbers by the common factor, in this case 2.

$\frac{12}{24}$ divided by 2 = $\frac{6}{12}$, but wait a minute, $\frac{6}{12}$ also have a common factor of two,

$\frac{6}{12} = \frac{3}{6}$ but wait one more time!! 3 and 6 share a common factor as well....not two this time but three....

3 divided 3 = 1 and 6 divided by 3 = 2, so the answer is $\frac{12}{24} = \frac{1}{2}$

That's a lot of steps, so it doesn't seem like simplifying is that simple. Ah, but it is! What if instead of looking for any old common factor like 2, we look for biggest factor both numbers have in common: the GREATEST COMMON FACTOR?

Let's try it again: $\frac{12}{24}$ What is the BIGGEST number that both 12 and 24 have in common?

Can't tell right away? Try factoring both and circle the biggest number they both have in common.

1, 2, 3, 4, 6, (12)

$$\frac{12}{24}$$

1, 2, 3, 4, 6, (12) 24

The biggest number they both share is 12, so let's divide 12 out of the top and bottom.

$$\frac{12 \div 12}{24 \div 12} = \frac{1}{2}$$

Voila!

Let's try that with another fraction:

1, 2, 4, (8) 16

1, 2, 3, 4, 6, (8) 12, 24

The GCF is 8

$$\frac{16}{24}\text{, so }\frac{16 \div 8}{24 \div 8} = \frac{2}{3}$$

and again

1, 3, (5) 15

1, (5) 25

The GCF is 5

$$\frac{15}{25}\text{, so }\frac{15 \div 5}{25 \div 5} = \frac{3}{5}$$

Now try it yourself:

Reducing

1. $\frac{2}{4} =$
2. $\frac{3}{9} =$
3. $\frac{4}{6} =$
4. $\frac{8}{12} =$
5. $\frac{7}{14} =$
6. $\frac{9}{36} =$
7. $\frac{10}{15} =$
8. $\frac{6}{10} =$
9. $\frac{27}{72} =$
10. $\frac{5}{75} =$
11. $\frac{14}{18} =$
12. $\frac{13}{39} =$
13. $\frac{9}{12} =$
14. $\frac{11}{44} =$
15. $\frac{17}{34} =$
16. $\frac{6}{12} =$
17. $\frac{8}{14} =$
18. $\frac{15}{60} =$
19. $\frac{48}{52} =$
20. $\frac{36}{48} =$

Improper Fractions to Mixed Numbers

So let's say you have a big honking fraction, and your teacher wants you to break it down to a mixed number. Ok, Ms. Crabapple! Coming right up.

Remember, since a fraction is really just a compact division problem, simply divide the numerator by the denominator to find out how many wholes you have. The REMAINDER is the number of pieces you have left.

E.g. $\frac{8}{3}$. In $\frac{8}{3}$ we have 8 thirds. If we divide 8 by 3 we see that 3 goes into 8 twice with 2 left over, or in this case two thirds left over.

$$\frac{8}{3} = 3\overline{)8} = 3\overline{)8}\ \text{(quotient } 2 \text{ r}2\text{; } 8 - 6 = 2\text{)} = 2\frac{2}{3}$$

Let's try that again:

$$\frac{23}{5} = 5\overline{)23} = 5\overline{)23}\ \text{(quotient } 4 \text{ r}3\text{; } 23 - 26 = 3\text{)} = 4\frac{3}{5}$$

And again:

$$\frac{78}{7} = 7\overline{)78} = 7\overline{)78}\ \text{(quotient } 11\text{; } 78 - 70 = 8,\ 8 - 7 = 1\text{)} = 11\frac{1}{7}$$

Now you try:

Improper Fractions to Mixed Numbers

Solve the following problems. Use scrap paper if necessary

1. $\frac{42}{4}$

4. $\frac{14}{5}$

2. $\frac{29}{3}$

5. $\frac{12}{11}$

3. $\frac{3}{2}$

6. $\frac{37}{6}$

Mixed Numbers to Fractions

What if you have a mixed number and you want to turn it back into an improper fraction?

Simply figure out how many pieces the whole number of your mixed number would break into by multiplying it by the denominator of the fraction part of your mixed number.

Like this: $1\frac{1}{5} = \frac{1 \times 5}{5} + \frac{1}{5} = \frac{5}{5} + \frac{1}{5} = \frac{6}{5}$

Or this: $6\frac{4}{5} = \frac{6 \times 5}{5} + \frac{4}{5} = \frac{30}{5} + \frac{4}{5} = \frac{34}{5}$

Or this: $2\frac{2}{9} = \frac{2 \times 9}{9} + \frac{2}{9} = \frac{18}{9} + \frac{2}{9} = \frac{20}{9}$

Now you try it!

Mixed Numbers to Improper Fractions

1. $4\frac{3}{4} =$

2. $1\frac{1}{3} =$

3. $5\frac{3}{5} =$

4. $2\frac{1}{2} =$

5. $3\frac{9}{10} =$

6. $15\frac{4}{5} =$

Adding Fractions

Adding and subtracting fractions with different denominators is another one of those points at which a lot of kids hop off the math highway—sometimes for good!

"Wait, I have to add just the tops of the fractions? Not the bottoms?? WHY??"

"Wait, I can only add the tops if the bottoms are the same? If the bottoms start our different from each other I have change them?? Me??? I'm outta' here!"

If you've ever thought like that, *Remain Clam!*, we're here to help. It's a little tricky, but we'll talk you through it.

When you are adding fractions, you are adding pieces. That's what the bottom, the denominator is all about. It tells you the size of the piece. Think of money. If you have a number of quarters on the table, you just count the number of quarters.

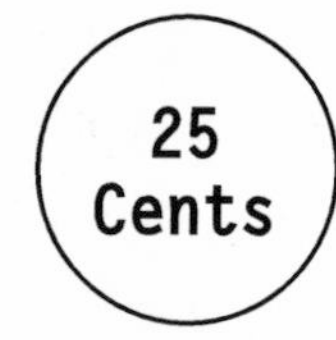

In the same way, if you have a number a quarter fractions, you merely add up the number that you have.

$$\frac{1}{4}+\frac{1}{4}+\frac{1}{4}=\frac{3}{4}$$

It even works if the you have two or more quarter grouped together and combine them with another group of quarters:

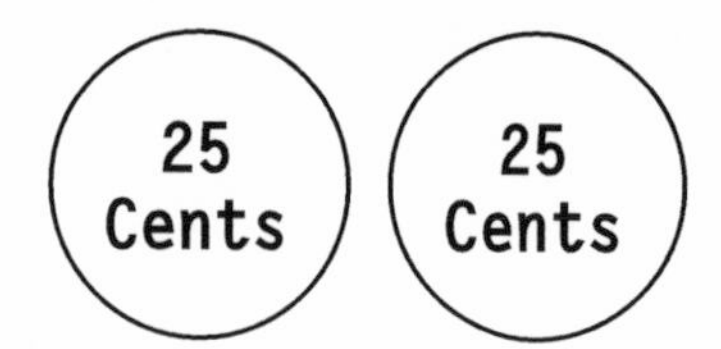

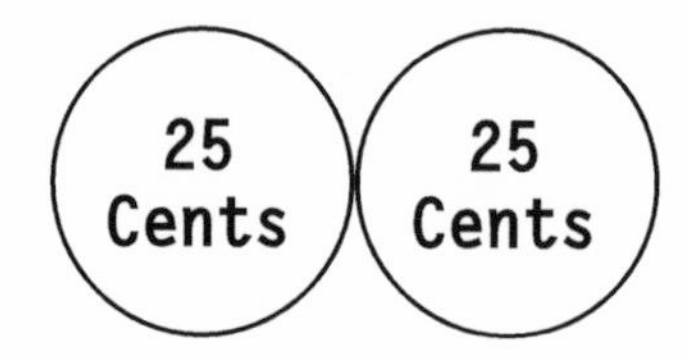

$$\frac{2}{4}+\frac{2}{4}=\frac{4}{4}$$

However, if you had a bunch of different coins on a table, say, 3 nickels, 2 dimes and one quarter, you could say you had 6 coins, but you couldn't say you have 6 nickels/dimes/quarters because there's no such thing. It's the same way when adding the fractions.

5 Cents 5 Cents 5 Cents + 10 Cents 10 Cents + 25 Cents = ?

$$\frac{3}{20}+\frac{2}{10}+\frac{1}{4}\neq \text{[DOES NOT EQUAL]}\ \frac{6}{20,10,4}$$

WHAT IS THAT ANYWAY? <u>NOTHING</u>!!

The way you add coins of different sizes is to make them equal the same size:

3 nickels = 15 cents

2 dimes = 20 cents

1 quarter = 25 cents

That we can add!

15 + 20 + 25 = 60 cents

It's the same with fractions, only instead of making the coins into the same value coin, we need to make the denominators into the same size pieces, in this case, just as with cents, 100 will work very well.

$$\frac{15}{100}+\frac{20}{100}+\frac{25}{100}=\frac{60}{100}$$

So, the goal in adding fractions is making sure that the denominators are all the same, and then adding JUST and ONLY JUST the numerators.

$$\frac{1}{2}+\frac{1}{3}$$

can't be added, but using the principal of anything over itself equals one, and one times anything equals itself, we can make each fraction look different but still really have the same value.

TOP TIMES TOP—BOTTOM TIMES BOTTOM

Multiplying fractions is a snap! Just multiply the top × the top and the bottom × the bottom. That's it!

$$\frac{1}{3}\times\frac{2}{9}=\frac{1\times 2}{3\times 9}=\frac{2}{27} \quad \frac{6}{7}\times\frac{3}{4}=\frac{6\times 3}{7\times 4}=\frac{18}{28}=\frac{9}{14}$$

If we want to find a common denominator for $\frac{1}{2}$ and $\frac{1}{3}$, just multiply the denominator or the first fraction with the denominator of the second fraction. Then, to keep things legit, we need to multiply the tops of each fraction by the same amount [so that we're really just multiplying by one].

$$\frac{1}{2}+\frac{1}{3}=\left(\frac{1}{2}\times\frac{3}{3}\right)+\left(\frac{1}{3}\times\frac{2}{2}\right)=\frac{3}{6}+\frac{2}{6}=\frac{5}{6}$$

or

$$\frac{1}{4}+\frac{1}{6}=\left(\frac{1}{4}\times\frac{6}{6}\right)+\left(\frac{1}{6}\times\frac{4}{4}\right)=\frac{6}{24}+\frac{4}{24}=\frac{10}{24}=\frac{5}{12}$$

or

$$\frac{2}{3}+\frac{1}{5}=\left(\frac{2}{3}\times\frac{5}{5}\right)+\left(\frac{1}{5}\times\frac{3}{3}\right)=\frac{10}{15}+\frac{3}{15}=\frac{13}{15}$$

Once you get good at this, there's an even better way of finding common denominators. Instead of automatically multiplying the denominators by each other to get a common denominator, try to find the LEAST COMMON MULTIPLES of the denominators. That is, look for the lowest number that both denominators go into.

For example,

$$\frac{1}{6} + \frac{1}{8} =$$

When you're starting out as a young fraction adder, you might just multiply the 6 and 8 and make your common denominator 48.

$$\frac{1}{6} + \frac{1}{8} = \left(\frac{1}{6} \times \frac{8}{8}\right) + \left(\frac{1}{8} \times \frac{6}{6}\right) = \frac{8}{48} + \frac{6}{48} = \frac{14}{48} = \frac{7}{24}$$

However, if you know your multiplication tables really well, you might realize that 6 and 8 both go into 24 and do this instead:

$$\frac{1}{6} + \frac{1}{8} = \left(\frac{1}{6} \times \frac{4}{4}\right) + \left(\frac{1}{8} \times \frac{3}{3}\right) = \frac{4}{24} + \frac{3}{24} = \frac{7}{24}$$

Doing things this way, you get better at knowing your numbers, you deal with smaller numbers AND you save yourself a step by not having to reduce at the end!

If you don't know your multiples so well, here's a simple way to find your LCM:

$$\frac{1}{8} + \frac{3}{10} =$$

You might want to just go with 8 × 10, but take a second to see if there's a better choice. Take the bigger number of the two denominators and list a few of its multiples:

$1 \times 10 = 10$

$2 \times 10 = 20$

$3 \times 10 = 30$

$4 \times 10 = 40$

$5 \times 10 = 50$

Then take a peek at them and ask yourself, "Is 10 a multiple of 8? Is 20? Is 30? Is 40?" *Ding, ding, ding!!* We have a winner!! The least common multiple of 8 and 10 is 40. 8 goes into 40 five times and 10 goes into 40 four times.

So,

$$\frac{1}{8} + \frac{3}{10} = \left(\frac{1}{8} \times \frac{5}{5}\right) + \left(\frac{3}{10} \times \frac{4}{4}\right) = \frac{5}{40} + \frac{12}{40} = \frac{17}{40}$$

Try it again:

Multiples of 15

$15 \times 1 = 15$

$$15 \times 2 = 30$$

$$15 \times 3 = 45$$

$$15 \times 4 = \textcircled{60}$$ (60 is also a multiple of 12!)

$$\frac{5}{12} + \frac{3}{15} = \left(\frac{5}{12} \times \frac{5}{5}\right) + \left(\frac{3}{15} \times \frac{4}{4}\right) = \frac{25}{60} + \frac{12}{60} = \frac{37}{60}$$

And again:

Multiples of 24

$$24 \times 1 = 24$$

$$24 \times 2 = \textcircled{48}$$ (48 is also a multiple of 16!)

$$\frac{5}{16} + \frac{3}{24} = \left(\frac{5}{16} \times \frac{3}{3}\right) + \left(\frac{3}{24} \times \frac{2}{2}\right) = \frac{15}{48} + \frac{6}{48} = \frac{21}{48}^{*}$$

LCM

Find the Least Common Multiple [LCM] of the following pairs of numbers.

1. 8 and 12
2. 12 and 18
3. 24 and 28
4. 12 and 30
5. 25 and 10
6. 21 and 9

SUBTRACTING FRACTIONS—SPOILER ALERT... IT'S THE SAME THING AS ADDING!

Make sure the denominators are the same and only subtract the numerators!

Dividing Fractions

$$\frac{1}{2} \div \frac{3}{4} = \frac{\frac{1}{2}}{\frac{3}{4}}$$

Division is really just multiplying by opposites. So to divide by a fraction, you just multiply by its opposite. The opposite of a fraction is called its reciprocal. To find the reciprocal of a fraction, just flip the top and bottom.

E.g., the reciprocal of $\frac{3}{4}$ is $\frac{4}{3}$

Once you've found the reciprocal of the fraction you want to divide, then just multiply your numbers together!

$$\frac{1}{2} \div \frac{3}{4} = \frac{\frac{1}{2}}{\frac{3}{4}} = \frac{1}{2} \times \frac{4}{3} = \frac{4}{6} = \frac{2}{3}$$

Dividing Fractions Practice

1. $\frac{1}{2}$ divided by $\frac{1}{4}$
2. $\frac{1}{2}$ divided by $\frac{1}{3}$
3. $\frac{1}{4}$ divided by $\frac{1}{2}$
4. $\frac{1}{4}$ divided by 2
5. $\frac{1}{6}$ divided by $\frac{1}{3}$
6. $\frac{1}{6}$ divided by $\frac{1}{6}$

Adding and Subtracting Fractions

Solve the following problems. Use scrap paper if necessary.

1. $\frac{3}{4}+\frac{1}{4}=$

2. $\frac{1}{7}+\frac{3}{7}=$

3. $\frac{6}{8}+\frac{3}{8}=$

4. $\frac{1}{2}+\frac{7}{2}=$

5. $\frac{2}{3}+\frac{4}{12}=$

6. $\frac{2}{16}+\frac{3}{8}=$

7. $\frac{4}{5}+\frac{4}{10}=$

8. $\frac{3}{7}+\frac{1}{2}=$

9. $\frac{2}{3}+\frac{1}{4}=$

10. $\frac{1}{8}+\frac{1}{9}=$

11. $\frac{2}{3}-\frac{1}{3}=$

12. $\frac{4}{8}-\frac{2}{8}=$

13. $\frac{11}{5}-\frac{1}{5}=$

14. $\frac{8}{9}-\frac{5}{9}=$

15. $\frac{3}{4}-\frac{4}{8}=$

16. $\frac{2}{4}-\frac{1}{2}=$

17. $\frac{2}{3}-\frac{5}{8}=$

18. $\frac{5}{7}-\frac{1}{4}=$

19. $\frac{1}{8}-\frac{1}{9}=$

20. $\frac{7}{8}-\frac{1}{4}=$

Practice

Multiplying and Dividing Fractions

1. $\frac{1}{3} \times \frac{1}{2} =$

2. $\frac{2}{3} \times \frac{3}{4} =$

3. $\frac{1}{7} \times \frac{1}{2} =$

4. $\frac{1}{6} \times \frac{3}{5} =$

5. $\frac{1}{4} \times \frac{3}{7} =$

6. $\frac{6}{7} \times \frac{1}{4} =$

7. $\frac{4}{11} \times \frac{1}{2} =$

8. $\frac{2}{3} \times \frac{9}{11} =$

9. $\frac{2}{5} \times \frac{15}{26} =$

10. $\frac{5}{6} \times \frac{18}{25} =$

11. $\frac{1}{2} \div \frac{1}{4} =$

12. $\frac{2}{5} \div \frac{2}{3} =$

13. $\frac{2}{7} \div \frac{5}{6} =$

14. $\frac{2}{9} \div \frac{7}{18} =$

15. $\frac{10}{11} \div \frac{3}{4} =$

16. $\frac{3}{4} \div \frac{9}{16} =$

17. $\frac{5}{8} \div \frac{5}{24} =$

18. $\frac{3}{7} \div \frac{6}{11} =$

19. $\frac{1}{3} \div \frac{4}{27} =$

20. $\frac{2}{5} \div \frac{8}{9} =$

Fractions Review—1

1. If eight people are coming to dinner and half of them are vegetarians, how many people are vegetarians?

2. If a recipe calls for one quarter of a pound of meat for four people and eight people are coming to dinner, how many pounds of meat must you buy?

3. If 18 lemons cost $3, how many lemons can you buy for $1?

4. One dollar is what fraction of three dollars?

5. $\frac{3}{4} =$

   A. $\frac{6}{9}$

   B. $\frac{3}{2}$

   C. $\frac{7}{14}$

   D. $\frac{12}{16}$

   E. $\frac{7}{8}$

6. Which is greatest?

   A. $\frac{3}{2}$

   B. $\frac{3}{3}$

   C. $\frac{3}{4}$

   D. $\frac{3}{5}$

   E. $\frac{3}{6}$

7. Which is least?

   A. $\frac{3}{17}$

   B. $\frac{3}{13}$

   C. $\frac{3}{8}$

   D. $\frac{3}{4}$

   E. $\frac{2}{17}$

8. A soup recipe yields 24 servings. It calls for 8 cups of water. If you want to make only 18 servings, how many cups of water will you need?

Answer __________________

9. What is one-third of 15?

Answer ________________

10. On Tuesday, Sandy's dad brought home a pizza for dinner. Sandy ate one third of the whole pie. If Sandy ate five slices, how many slices did the pizza pie have?

A. 16
B. 15
C. 14
D. 12

11. On the bus ride to school, Nikhil counted 60 cars, and 12 of them were taxis. What fraction represents the number of taxis Nikhil saw out of all the cars he counted?

A. $\frac{1}{6}$

B. $\frac{1}{5}$

C. $\frac{1}{4}$

D. $\frac{1}{3}$

12. Sonia has many shirts in her drawer. One quarter of her shirts are button-down, and the rest are t-shirts. If Sonia has six button-down blouses, how many t-shirts does Sonia have in her closet?

A. 32
B. 30
C. 24
D. 18

13. When Imani went to Times Square, she counted fifteen people eating pretzels. Of the fifteen people, she saw five of them eating their pretzels with mustard. What fraction is equivalent to the fraction of people eating pretzels with mustard?

A. $\frac{15}{35}$

B. $\frac{2}{6}$

C. $\frac{3}{10}$

D. $\frac{3}{12}$

14. Jacob has three best friends. After hanging out with all of them, he realized that two of them are shorter than he. What fraction of his best friends is shorter than he?

A. $\frac{12}{24}$

B. $\frac{9}{21}$

C. $\frac{18}{27}$

D. $\frac{6}{24}$

15. Anthony runs a mile every Monday through Friday. Last week, he reached his goal of running those miles in under ten minutes $\frac{3}{5}$ of the time. If he wants to achieve the same goal for the next four weeks, how many more sub 10-minute miles will he have run in those four weeks?

A. 9
B. 10
C. 11
D. 12

Fraction Review—2

1. $\frac{1}{8} \times 1 =$

2. $\frac{1}{8} \times 8 =$

3. $\frac{2}{8} \times 4 =$

4. $\frac{1}{3} \times \frac{1}{3} =$

5. $\frac{1}{3} \times \frac{2}{3} =$

6. $\frac{1}{3} + \frac{2}{3} =$

7. $\frac{2}{4} \times \frac{2}{3} =$

8. $\frac{4}{2} \times \frac{2}{2} =$

9. $\frac{2}{9} \times 9$

Fraction Review—3

1. Leyla is painting a wall. If she paints $\frac{1}{4}$ of it yellow, $\frac{1}{3}$ of it orange and the rest of it blue, what fraction of the wall will be blue?

2. If one-half of the students in one class like pizza best and one-third of them like cheeseburgers best, what fraction of the students like something else best?

3. Mary has a bucket of golf balls. One-third of them are white, and one-sixth of the white balls are striped. What fraction of the whole bucket of balls are white, striped golf balls?

Decimals

Believe it or not, decimals, like their close cousins fractions, were invented to make things ***easier***, yet many students are as confused by decimals as they are by fractions. Decimals are really just a specific kind of fraction—just as percents are.

Decimals are fractions with any power of ten [10, 100, 1000, 10,000, etc.] in the denominator.

For example,

.1 is really 1/10

.04 is really 4/100

.125 is really 125/1000

The decimal place a number starts [has its first digit on the right in] is that numbers denominator. For example, 24/1000 would be written as .024 because the third place to the right of the decimal is the thousandths place [see the boink above].

Here are some more examples:

2/100 = .02

16/10,000 = .0016

9/10 = .9

125/100 = 1.25

Now try some conversions of you own!

4/10 =

5/1000=

17/100 =

½ =

Decimals are Special Fractions

Just as, you can make a fractional connection from decimals to fractions very easily, you can also change fractions to decimals though the other way but not necessarily as easily.

Remember when we turned $\frac{1}{2}$ into .5?

$$.01 = \frac{1}{100}$$

$$.25 = \frac{25}{100} = \frac{1}{4}$$

If you can change the denominator of your fraction to a 10, 100, or 1,000 etc., then you can change your decimal into a fraction. For $\frac{1}{2}$ is there a way to change 2 to a 10? Yes, multiply by 5, and if you do it to the bottom, you have to do it to the top:

$$\frac{1}{2}\times\frac{5}{5}=\frac{5}{10}$$

so

$$\frac{1}{2}=\frac{5}{10}=.5$$

Let's try another one:

Let's try changing $\frac{3}{4}$ to a decimal.

For $\frac{3}{4}$ is there a way to change the denominator 4 to 10, 100, or 1,000 etc.? 4 doesn't go into 10, but it does go into 100 if we multiply it by 25, and if you do it to the bottom, you have to do it to the top:

$$\frac{3}{4}\times\frac{25}{25}=\frac{75}{100}=.75$$

How about $\frac{2}{5}$?

5 can be made into 10 by multiplying it by 2, so:

$$\frac{2}{5}\times\frac{2}{2}=\frac{4}{10}=.4$$

What happens when we have fractions whose denominators can't be turned into 10s, 100s, 1,000 etc.?

That's when we remember that fractions are really little division problems, and instead of using a bridge fraction, we divide the numerator by the denominator and get our answer as a decimal, we convert the fraction to a decimal in one step.

When the numerator is smaller than the denominator, it's hard to think of the fraction as a division problem because you may not know how to divide numbers by numbers bigger than they are yet. Don't worry, we'll teach you. It's no big deal as long as you're neat and careful and you know the secret. Hint: It's what decimals are for!

$$\frac{1}{8}=8\overline{)1}=?$$

But wait, you can't do that....But yes, you can...

DIVIDING LITTLE BY BIG

This is yet another one of those points on the math highway at which many kids take the off ramp.

"Wait, you want me to divide a little number by a bigger number? Me??? I'm outta' here!"

One of the reasons it's hard to divide little numbers by bigger numbers is that it's hard to imagine numbers not being whole. In fact, many numbers aren't.

We can express those numbers as mixed numbers, 3 ¾ , or as whole numbers with decimals, 3.75.

Think about when you buy something that's in dollars and cents. Sometimes you pay $3.00 for a slice of pizza. Sometimes you pay $3.75 [if you get anchovies, yum!].

The decimal portion of the number represents a proper fraction of some sort...in this case $\frac{75}{100}$ or $\frac{3}{4}$.

Now back to $\frac{1}{8}$. How do we divide it?

To convert a fraction into a decimal by division:

- Place the numerator inside the division house

$$8\overline{)1}$$

- Add a decimal point to the right of the number you're dividing into

$$8\overline{)1.}$$

- Add some zeroes to the right of the decimal place while you're at it

$$8\overline{)1.00}$$

- Pretend the decimal point isn't there and act like you're dividing 8 into 10, but keep running the decimal point down as you subtract and on top as you put your answers there.

$$\begin{array}{r} .1 \\ 8\overline{)1.00} \\ \underline{-.80} \\ .20 \end{array}$$

[Now you see why you need to be neat!]

- After you subtract your first partial quotient from your numerator, bring down the remainder, add a zero to that if need be and keep dividing. For all fractions, keep dividing until you get a remainder of zero or until your answer starts to repeat itself forever. To show that you know it's repeating, put a bar over the parts of the answer that repeat.

$$\frac{1}{8} = 8\overline{)1.000} = .125$$

```
       .125
1/8 = 8)1.000
       -.80
        .20
       -.16
        .040
        .040
           0
```

Repeating Decimals

When it comes to dividing into decimal places, many students fear that they might end up dividing forever. That is really, really not true. In fact, all deimal portions of answers will either end or repeat very quickly. In fact, the most you will ever have to divide out will be one place less than the number you're dividing by.

$$\frac{1}{3} = 3\overline{)1.000} = .\overline{333}$$

```
       .333
1/3 = 3)1.000
        -.9
         .10
        -.09
         .010
        -.009
         .001
```

The bar over the numbers in a decimal value means those numbers repeat forever.

e.g. $\frac{1}{3} = .\overline{333} = .333333$

$\frac{1}{6} = .1\overline{66} = .166666$

$.\overline{142857} = .142857142857142857$

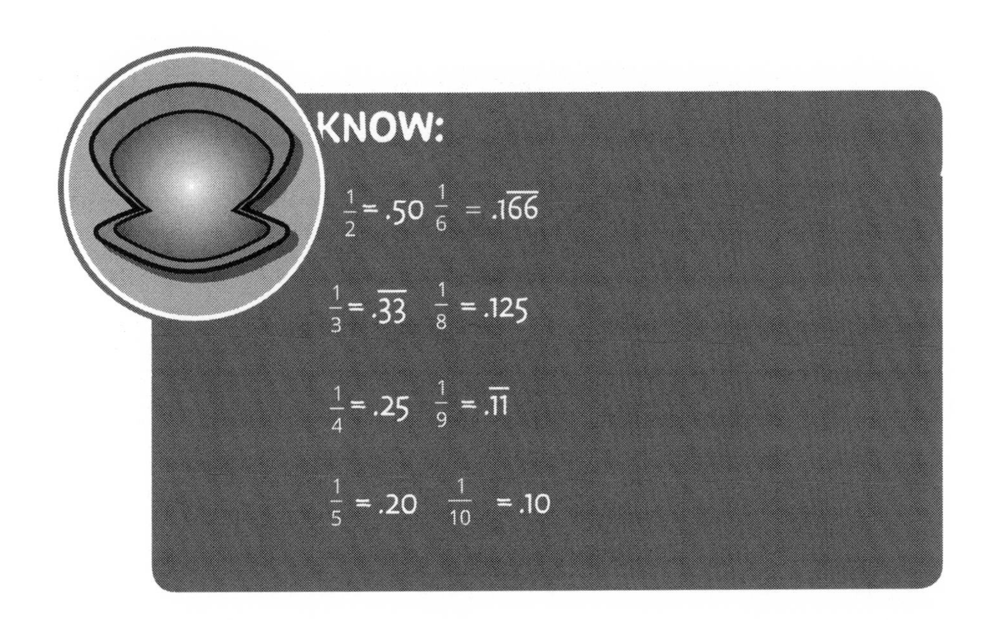

Fractions to Decimals, Decimals to Fractions

1. $\frac{1}{2}$ =

7. 0.8 =

2. $\frac{1}{3}$ =

8. $0.\overline{6}$ =

3. $\frac{3}{4}$ =

9. 0.25 =

4. $\frac{1}{5}$ =

10. $0.\overline{8}$ =

5. $\frac{4}{6}$ =

11. 0.5 =

6. $\frac{5}{8}$ =

12. 0.75 =

Fractions to Decimals Word Problems

1. Chloe bought a dozen eggs at the grocery store. Unfortunately, she did not check them for cracks until she got home. She discovered that 0.25 of the eggs had cracks. How many of her eggs were cracked?

   A. $\frac{1}{4}$
   B. $\frac{1}{3}$
   C. 3
   D. 4

2. Marcy has 12 apples. Of them, eight are green. How would you represent the fraction of green apples as a decimal?

   A. 0.9
   B. 0.8
   C. 0.75
   D. $0.\overline{6}$

3. Luis has 16 pairs of shoes. 14 of these pairs are old. How would you express the fraction of pairs of shoes that are new as a decimal?

   A. 0.875
   B. 0.2
   C. $0.1\overline{6}$
   D. 0.125

4. Last week, Jackson's family ordered takeout for more than $\frac{2}{3}$ of the nights in the week. How many nights could they have ordered takeout?

   A. 2
   B. 3
   C. 4
   D. 5

5. Priya collected as many fallen leaves as she could carry on the walk home from school. When she got home, she counted 56 leaves. Of these leaves, 37 were yellow and 19 were orange. If the fraction of yellow leaves can be written as a decimal as 0.66071429, which fraction comes closest to expressing the number of yellow leaves?

   A. $\frac{5}{6}$
   B. $\frac{3}{4}$
   C. $\frac{2}{3}$
   D. $\frac{3}{5}$

6. Noah plays outfield on his baseball team. At Saturday's game, he caught 0.2 of the other team's fly balls. If the opposition hit a total of 15 fly balls, how many of them did Noah catch?

   A. $\frac{1}{5}$
   B. $\frac{1}{3}$
   C. 2
   D. 3

Make Friends with Tens

Multiplying and dividing by factors of ten is super easy. Just ignore the zeros! Most students get scared when they see 12,000 × 4,000. Of course, most of those same students wouldn't have any trouble with 12 × 4. In reality, it's the same problem!

$$12{,}000 \times 4{,}000 = 12 \times 4 \times 1{,}000 \times 1{,}000 = 48 \times 1{,}000{,}000 = 48{,}000{,}000$$

How did I know that 1,000 × 1,000 =1,000,000? That's easy! Anytime you multiply a multiple of ten times a multiple of ten, just count the zeros to find out what your new place value will be! In this case, 1,000 × 1,000 *yields six zeros, so it equals* 1,000,000.

The easiest and neatest way to multiply multiples of 10 is to separate out any integers besides zero and multiply them, and then add the number of zeros involved to the end of that problem.

E.g. 25,000 × 30 = 25 × 3 *and four zeros* = 750,000

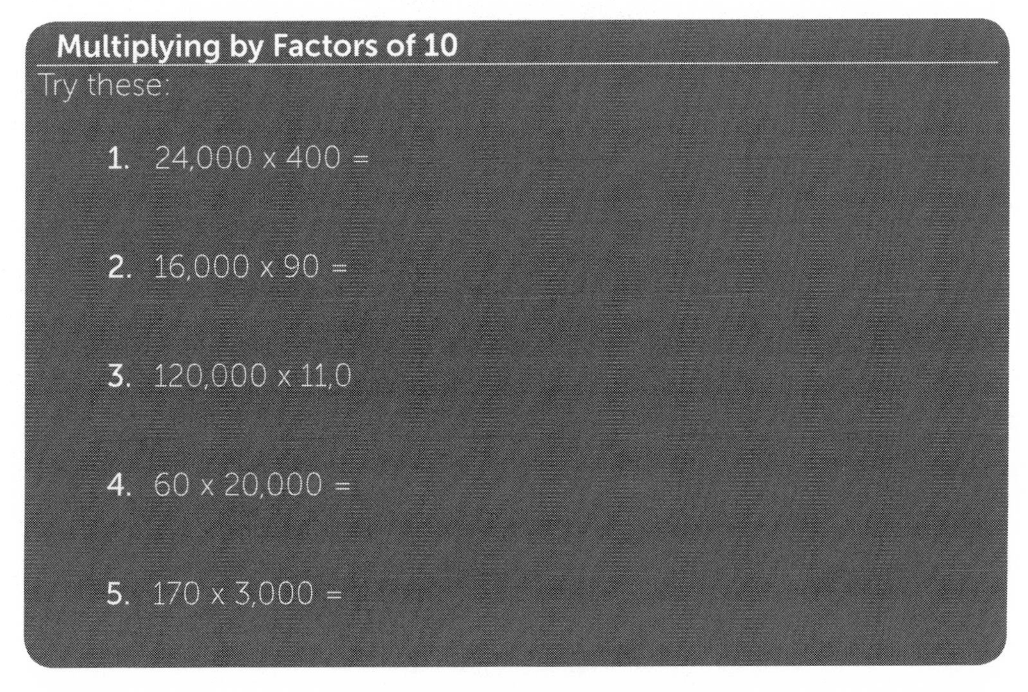

Tens Places

100,000	10,000	1,000	100	10	1
one hundred thousand	ten thousand	thousand	hundred	ten	one

Each tens places is ten times greater than the one to its immediate right.

Decimal Places

1	.1	.01	.001	.0001	.00001
one	tenth	hundredth	thousandth	ten-thousandth	hundred-thousandth

Each decimal place is ten times greater than the one to its immediate right.

Rounding

Rounding is a super easy way to simplify numbers. Here's what you need to know.

- There is no such thing as "Rounding Up" or "Rounding Down" – IT'S ALL JUST ROUNDING.
- Rounding to a digits place—say the ones place—means if the preceding digit [in this case the tenth's place digit] is 5 or more, then the digit you are rounding goes up. If it is less than five, the digit stays the same. Simple as that.
- So,

4.5 to the nearest ones place equals 5

AND

4.4 to the nearest ones place equals 4

- Here are the other various "places" you might be asked to round to, the place in bold.
    - Tens: **1**0
    - Hundreds: **1**00
    - Thousands: **1**,000
    - Ten Thousands: **1**0,000
    - Hundred Thousands: **1**00,000
    - Millions: **1**,000,000

Rounding

1. Round 0.944 to the nearest tenth. __________
2. Round 1,230 to the nearest thousand. __________
3. Round 0.98 to the nearest tenth. __________
4. Round 67,403 to the nearest hundred. __________
5. Round 0.7654 to the nearest hundredth. __________
6. Round 0.8564 to the nearest thousandth. __________
7. Round 2,378,960 to the nearest million. __________
8. Round 56,789 to the nearest ten thousand. __________
9. Round 2.356 to the nearest tenth.. __________

Place Value and Rounding

Write the place value of the digit in bold.

1. 130,**4**56 ______________________
2. **7**,365,980 ______________________
3. 8,6**5**4 ______________________
4. 0.**9**76 ______________________
5. 0.47**3** ______________________
6. 2,**8**90,475 ______________________
7. **7**8,361,304 ______________________
8. **5**6,492 ______________________
9. 3,9**8**6 ______________________

Understanding Digits Problems

1. How many times larger is the 7 in 47,652 than the 7 in 4,071?

2. The value of the 6 in the hundreds place of 106,698 is what fraction of the six in the thousands place?

3. Write a number with six in the hundred thousands place.

4. In the numbers 43,082 and 7,126, which one has the greater value in the hundreds place? How much greater is it?

5. Identify which digit is in the ones, tens, hundreds, etc. place in the number 5,086,342.

6. What would the following number be if the value of the tens place were zero: 54,382. How much would its value change?

Finding Patterns Intellectually[35]

Some problems in math require that you know a formula or a set of relationships in order to be able to solve them—like many geometry problems. Other problems require that you figure out the formula or pattern involved. A good way to discover a pattern is the way scientists do it.

- Create a hypothesis
  - Make a guess as to how you think the pattern might be formed (are the numbers increasing or decreasing by addition? Subtraction? Multiplication? Division?)
- Test the hypothesis through trial and error
  - Try your pattern or the pattern given on ***every*** answer choice
- Be thorough
  - Don't poop out after trying two or three answers and guess "D" out of laziness. Get to "E"!

Often in these problems, the hypothesis is given to you. Then it is merely a question of testing the various possible solutions offered.

All of these patterns involve basic math operations. Most of us like to test addition and multiplication first; however, don't be afraid of trying subtraction and division. More important, try to be able to see and test for patterns that might COMBINE operations [add one then multiply by two, etc.]. Other patterns might even change how much the numbers are increasing or decreasing each time.

Here is a simple example:

Find the pattern and fill in the blank

16, 20, 24, ___, 32

This is pretty straight forward: 20 is 4 more than 16

24 is 4 more than 20, so the blank must be 28

Check it to make sure it fits: 16, 20, 24, 28, $28 + 4 = 32$!

Here's a trickier one:

2, 5, 11, 23, 47, ___

5 is three more than 2, but 11 is not three more than 5.

5 is 2.5 times 2, but 14 is not 2.5 times 5.

However, if we combine operations, we might notice that 5 is just one away from 2×2, and 11 is just one away from 2×5, and so on.

Now you can figure the blank out yourself.

[35] Having an idea and testing it!

Pattern Problems

1. Which of the following sequences of numbers follows the pattern "add 7" if the first number is 16?

   A. 16, 22, 29, 36, 43, 50
   B. 16, 23, 31, 38, 45, 52
   C. 16, 24, 30, 37, 44, 51
   D. 16, 23, 30, 37, 44, 51
   E. 16, 23, 31, 38, 45, 52

2. Write a number sequence of at least six numbers whose pattern is "subtract 6" when the first number is 99.

3. Which of the following sequences does NOT follow a consistent pattern?

   A. 82, 70, 58, 46, 34, 22
   B. 128, 64, 32, 16, 6, 3
   C. 13, 19, 26, 32, 39, 45
   D. 4, 8, 12, 16, 20, 24, 28
   E. 100, 87, 74, 61, 48, 35

4. Which number goes in the blank: 16, 32, 48, ___, 80, 96?

5. Write a sequence of at least six numbers whose pattern is "add 9" when the first number is 23.

MUST KNOW

GEOMETRY

Geometry

There is a basic core of geometry you need for most problems from here to high school. However, if you learn very well the few things that you are required to know, then you will be in great shape for whatever geometry questions come your way for a long time to come!

The Basics

There are THREE DIMENSIONS that we can see:

Length || Width || Height

Shapes and objects with **two dimensions** are essentially flat [if they rise or have any thickness at all, they're not really 2D]: paper, screens [even though things projected on them might look 3D], maps, floors, streets, rectangles, triangles, circles, etc.

Shapes and objects with **three dimensions** rise, at least slightly, from their 2D bases. E.g., cans, cones, pyramids, people, trees, cars, etc.

Point

A point marks a place in space [on your page, in the air, on a white board, etc.]. It has no size, only location.

Lines, Rays & Segments

The first thing to know about geometry is the answer to this question:

What is the shortest distance between two points?

The ancient answer to this question is **a line.**

In spirit, that answer is correct. Technically, however, the shortest way to connect two points is using a straight line **SEGMENT**.[1]

Line

A line continues infinitely—that means forever—in both directions.

Line Segment

A line that ends on both sides at two separate points.

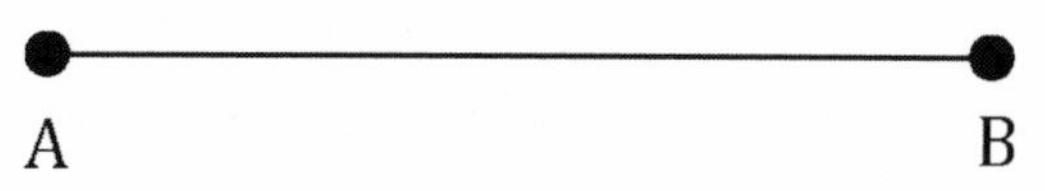

Ray

A line that ends at a point in one direction and continues infinitely in the other.

Parallel & Intersecting Lines, Segments & Rays

When two or more lines, segments or rays are drawn so that they never cross, then those lines, segments or rays are ***parallel***.

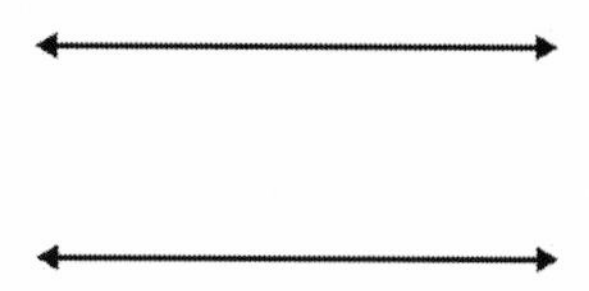

When two or more lines, segments or rays are drawn so that they cross at one point, then those lines, segments or rays are ***intersecting***. Simply enough, the point at which two or more lines, segments or rays intersect is call the ***point of intersection***.

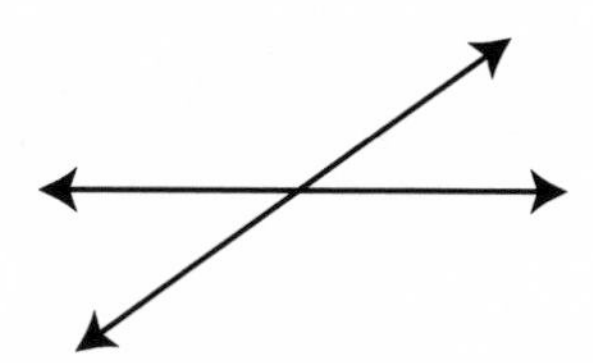

When two lines, segments or rays intersect, they form angles at the point of intersection.

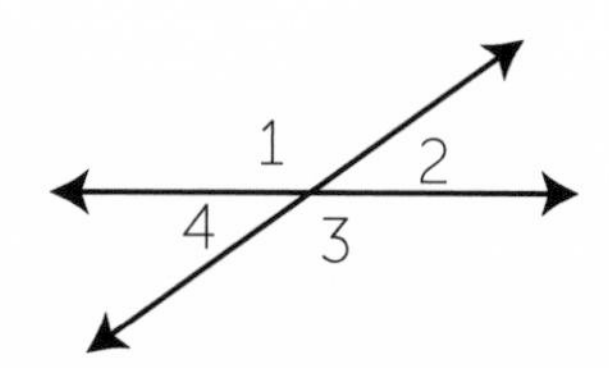

Angles

An angle is formed when two rays intersect at one point. The point of intersection is called the **vertex**. You can make an angle using almost anything: your thumb and forefinger work great for this. The crook between your thumb and forefinger makes a natural vertex.

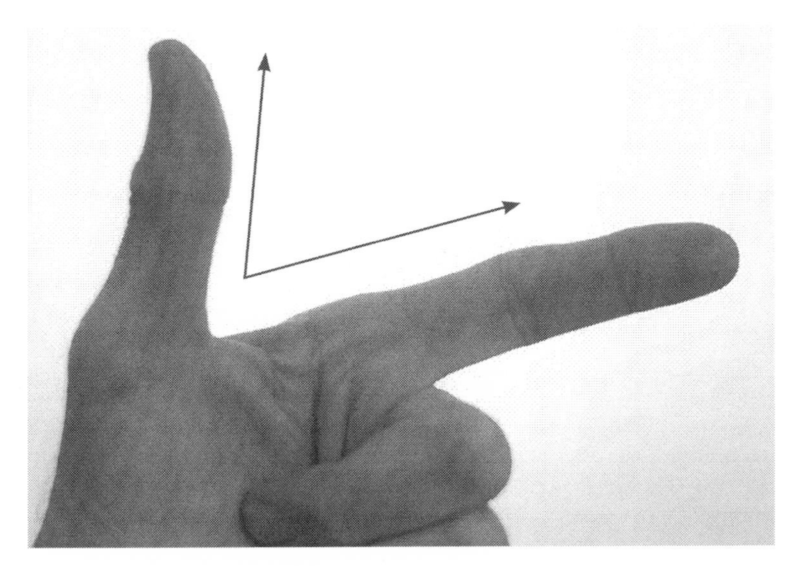

If the rays of your thumb and forefinger are very close together, the measure of the angle they form is very small. The **wider** apart the fingers—rays—are, the bigger the angle. If your thumb could rotate all the way around and meet your index finger on the other side, that would make a circle.

We measure angles by pieces of a circle called degrees. There are 360° in a circle—the little ° above the 360 means degrees.

WHY 360 DEGREES?

No one really knows why, but it probably has something to do with the fact that ancient calendars used 360 days for a year. Astronomers arrived at 360 days by watching the stars revolve around the North Star—one degree each day.

Also, 360 has a lot of factors [figure them out!] and that makes doing a lot of basic geometry much easier.

Right Angles

When the two rays of an angle form an "L," then the angle is said to be a RIGHT angle. Right angles measure 90° and the rays are said to be "perpendicular" to each other.

A little box in the corner of an angle that looks like a right angle means it is a right angle!

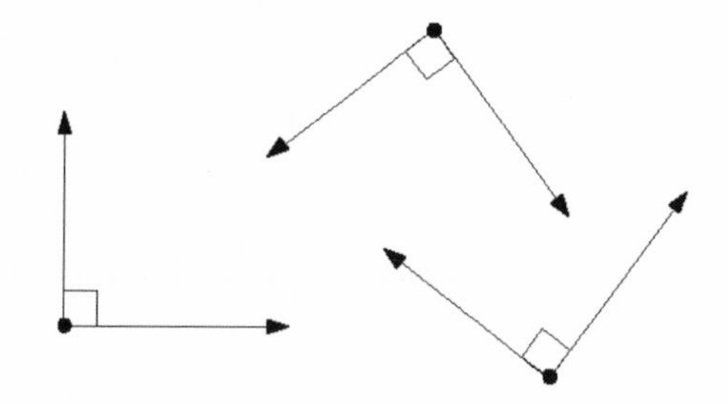

Acute Angles

Acute angles are angles that measure between 0° and 90°. It's as simple as that!

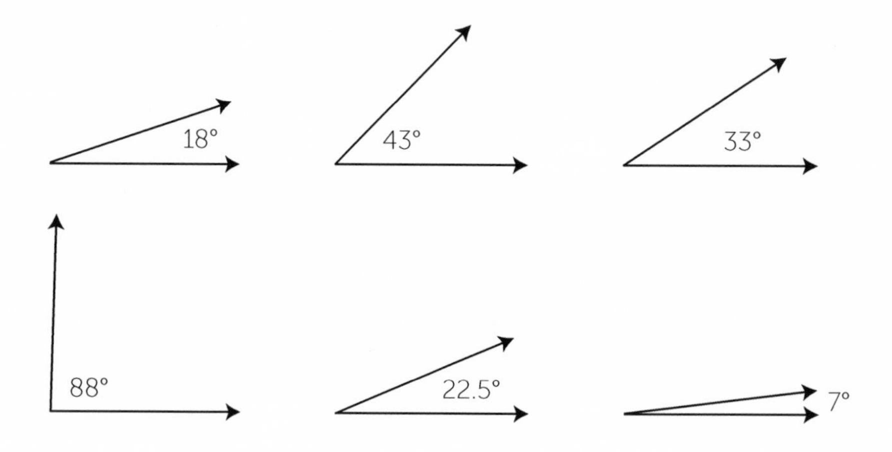

Obtuse Angles

Obtuse angles are angles that measure between 90° and 180°.

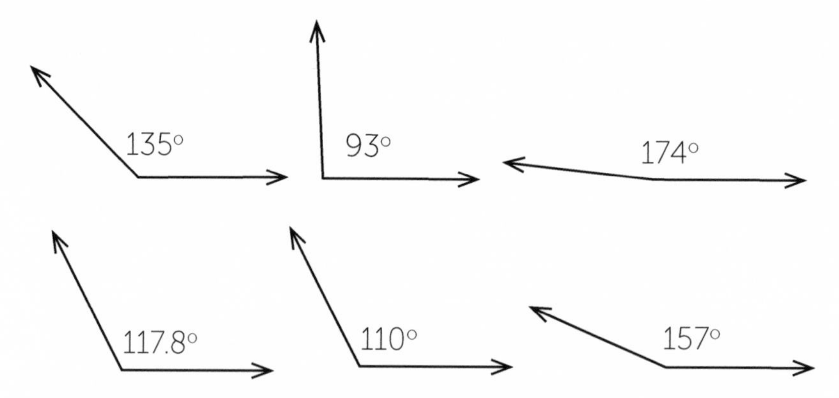

Straight Angles

Like snakes hiding in the grass, straight angles like to hide in line segments, rays or lines. Even though they don't look like angles [because you don't always see the vertex], lines, segments or rays make excellent angles, and they all measure 180°!

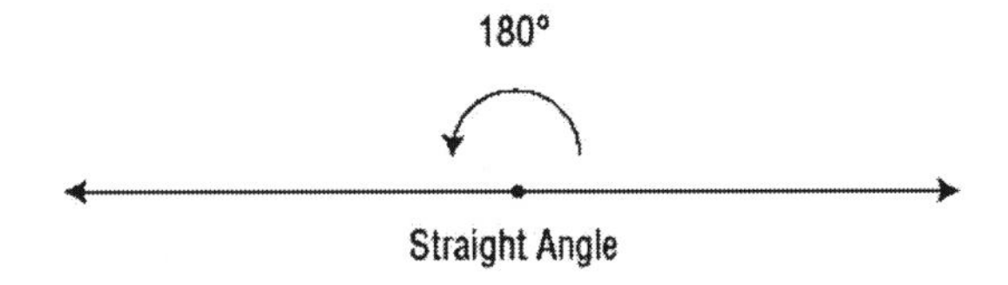

Interior Angles

Interior angles are angles that are on the *inside* of shapes!

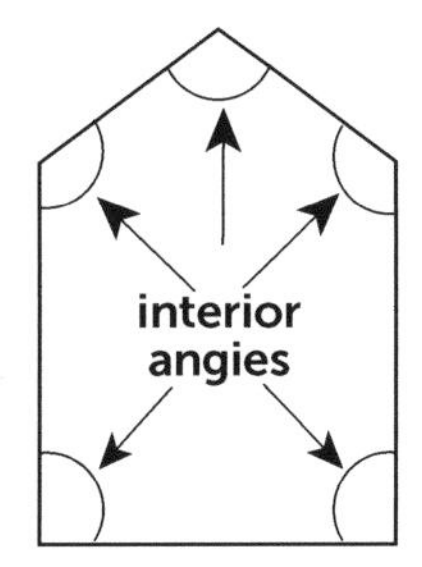

Lines of Symmetry

A line of symmetry is a line that you draw from side to side through the middle of the shape that leaves each side of the line exactly the same. So, if you were to look at a mirror put on a line of symmetry, it would look like the other side was there. For example, if you were to fold a sandwich along a line of symmetry, each half would be the same and nothing would fall out of it.

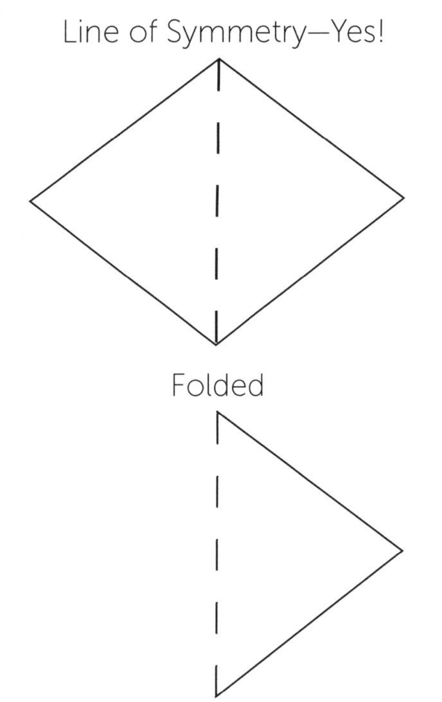

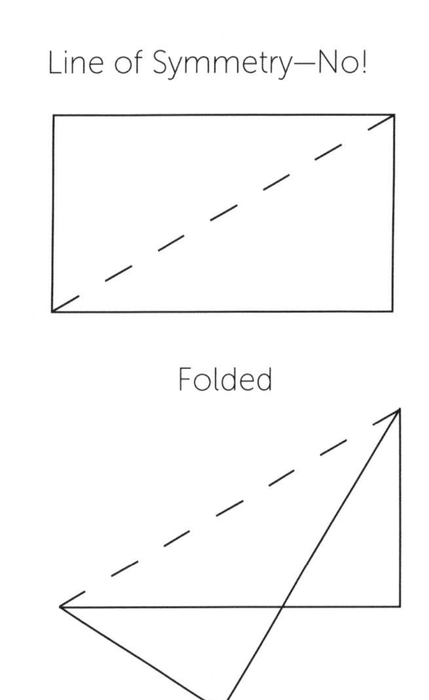

Symmetry

Please draw all lines of symmetry on the following shapes—if possible:

Polygons

Polygons are 2-D [flat] shapes made of intersecting line segments. They are generally named for the number of sides they have.

Triangles—Triangles are polygons with three sides ["tri" means three!] and three interior angles. The sum of the three angles in a triangle **always** equals 180°.

Equilateral Triangle—In an equilateral triangle all sides are equal and all angles are equal. Since all angles are equal and the three interior angles of a triangle add up to 180° then each angle in an equilateral triangle equals 60°.

Quadrilaterals—Quadrilaterals have four sides and four interior angles. The sum of the four angles in a quadrilateral equals 360°. There are many kinds of quadrilaterals. Some of them you probably know.

Trapezoid—A trapezoid has two sides that are parallel.

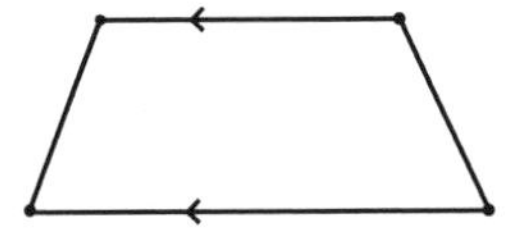

Parallelogram—A parallelogram has two pairs of parallel sides and each pair of opposite angles is equal.

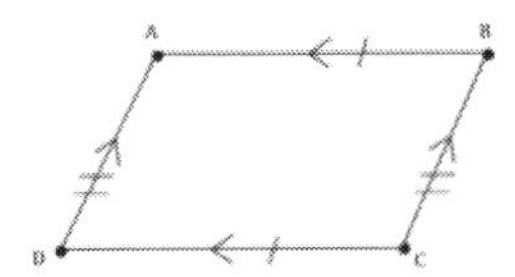

Rhombus—A rhombus is a special kind of parallelogram. All its sides are equal, but all its angles do not have to be. If a rhombus has all equal angles, then those angles are 90°, and the rhombus is a square!

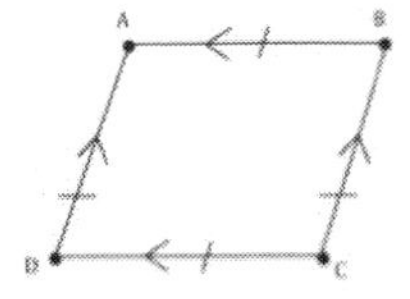

Rectangle—A rectangle is a special kind of parallelogram. It has two pairs of equal sides, each pair of opposite corner angles is equal, AND all those corner angles are 90°.

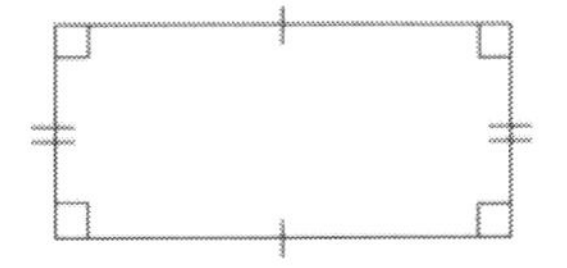

Square—A square is a special kind of rectangle [which is a special kind of parallelogram]. A square is a rectangle whose sides are all equal to each other.

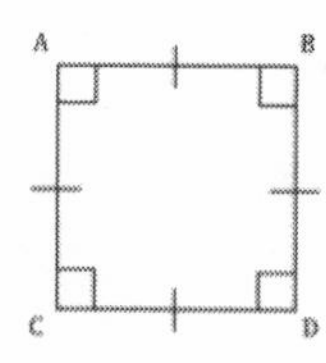

Pentagon/Hexagon/Heptagon/Octagon...

A pentagon is a five-sided polygon.

A hexagon is a six-sided polygon.

A heptagon is a seven-sided polygon.

An octagon is an eight-sided polygon.

If a polygon has all equal sides and all equal interior angles, then it is called a ***regular*** polygon.

More Triangles

1. In a **right**[2] triangle, the side opposite the 90° angle [and therefore the longest] is the hypotenuse—"c."

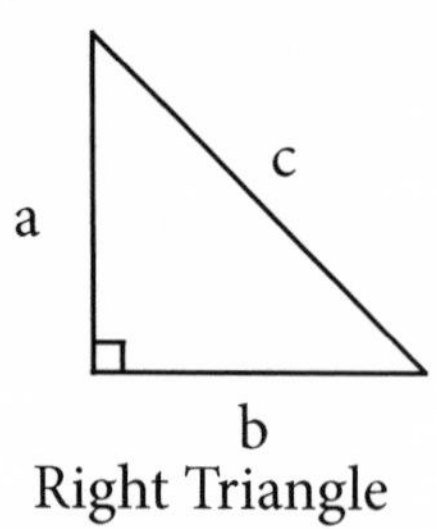

Right Triangle

2. In similar triangles all angles are congruent[3] to their counterparts in the other triangle and all sides are in equal ratios to one another.**Some Triangles**

3. An **isosceles** triangle has two equal sides and two equal angles opposite them.

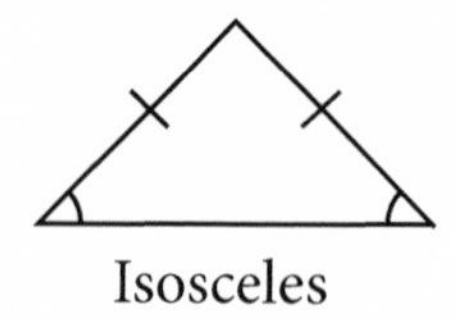
Isosceles

Shape Questions

1. Please explain what a polygon is. Draw two examples.

2. Please explain what a quadrilateral is. Draw two examples.

3. Please explain what a parallelogram is. Draw two examples.

4. Please explain what a trapezoid is. Draw an example.

5. Please match the shapes on the left with the group or groups they belong to on the right

a. Square	i. Polygon
b. Triangle	ii. Quadrilateral
c. Parallelogram	iii. Parallelogram
d. Quadrilateral	iv. Rectangle
e. Circle	v. None of the above
f. Rhombus	
g. Trapezoid	
h. Octagon	
i. Rectangle	
j. Hexagon	

Area

Area is the space inside a shape.

The two main areas you need to know are the area of a rectangle and the area of a triangle. The area of a square is the same as the area of a rectangle because a square is a rectangle. It is a special rectangle: one with all sides equal!

Area of a Rectangle = Length x Width or Base x Height

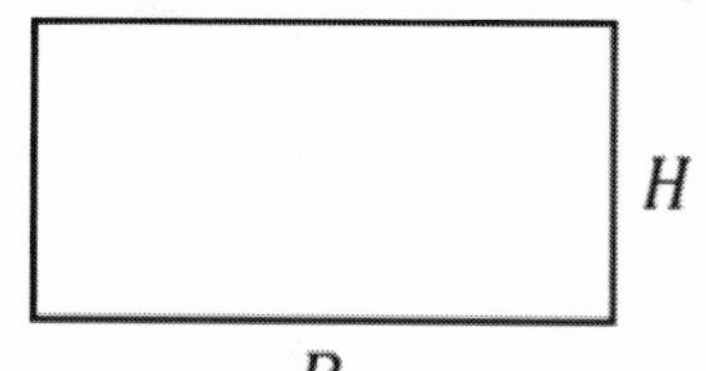

are given a picture and given information about that picture, be sure to fill that information in on the figure so you get a clear idea of what's going on in that picture. It REALLY helps!

Make Like a Gunfighter and DRAW!

If you are NOT given a picture, make your life easier and simply draw one!

You would be surprised how many students skip this step, but it makes solving the problem SO MUCH EASIER if you can see what's going on.

Fill in Formulas!

Geometry problems are MUCH easier to solve if you write down the formulas for the specific shapes as those things are mentioned. Once you write out that formula, then it's just a matter of filling it in as you go. It's sort of like following a recipe. If you have the right recipe and follow the steps, you can't screw up!

Fortunately, on a lot of geometry problems they give you the correct formulas, so you just need to remember to fill in the information for them as you go.

NOW... Let's put it all together! Use diagrams, formulas and math to solve the following problem.

E.g., Rona has a mandrake garden that is 3 feet wide and 9 feet long. She wants to enclose her garden with a row of roses. If rose edging costs $40/yard, how much will it cost her to do this?

Perimeter = 2 Length + 2 Width

1 Yard = 3 Feet

Draw a diagram below with information from the question:

Now, do the math to find the answer.

Practice

Area and Perimeter—Drill Set

1. Find the area of a rectangular room that measures 5 yards by 7 yards.

2. A rectangular lawn is 45 feet long and 90 feet wide. What is the perimeter in feet?

3. Find the area and perimeter of a rectangle with a length of 14 yards and a width of 12 yards.

4. The area of a rectangle is 25 sq. cm. What is the total area of 5 such rectangles?

5. Find the perimeter and area of a square with a side 11 meters.

6. The length of a square is 8 cm. How many such squares are needed to form a rectangle of length 24 cm and width 16 cm?

Measurements, Units and Conversions

There are three types of things we usually measure: distance, weight and volume.

- Distance measures how long something is.
- Weight measures how heavy something is.
- Volume measure how much space something occupies.

Just as the rest of the world plays one kind of football and we play another, most of the rest of the world uses one system of measurement and we use another. Most of the world uses the **METRIC** system, but we use the **CUSTOMARY** system.

The **METRIC** system is based on multiples of the number 10, so it can be increased and decreased easily by powers of 10.

Metric Measures include:

Distance:	Meters
Weight:	Grams
Liquid Volume:	Liters

Metric Units include:

Kilo [1000]—Hecto [100]—Deca [10]—UNIT NAME [1]—Deci [.1]—Centi [.01]—Milli [.001]

E.g., grams:

- **Milligram = .001 Gram**
- **Centigram = .01 Gram**
- **Decigram = .1 Gram**
- **GRAM**
- **Decagram = 10 Grams**
- **Hectogram = 100 Grams**
- **Kilogram = 1000 Grams**

The **CUSTOMARY** system, like the **DEGREE** system, is very old and is based on numbers with many factors, like 12 and 32, that can be easily split into many whole number pieces.

CUSTOMARY MEASURES include:

Distance:	**12 inches = 1 foot**
	36 inches = 3 feet = 1 yard
Weight:	**16 ounces = 1 pound**
Liquid Volume:	**8 ounces = 1 cup**
	16 ounces = 2 cups = 1 pint
	32 ounces = 4 cups = 2 pints = 1 quart
	128 ounces = 16 cups = 8 pints = 4 quarts = 1 gallon

Measurement and Conversion—Drill Set

What does each unit measure (weight, length, liquid volume, etc.)?

1. inches ____________________

2. ounces ____________________

3. feet ____________________

4. pounds ____________________

5. kilograms ____________________

6. kilometers ____________________

7. miles ____________________

8. meters ____________________

9. liters ____________________

10. grams ____________________

11. gallons ____________________

12. cups ____________________

13. centimeters ____________________

14. yards ____________________

Conversions

1. 36 inches is equal to how many feet?

2. 5 feet 6 inches is equal to how many inches?

3. 2 meters is equal to how many centimeters?

4. 32 ounces is equal to how many pounds?

5. 3 pints is equal to how many cups?

6. 1 kilometer is equal to how many meters?

7. 400 centimeters is equal to how many meters?

8. 6 pounds is equal to how many ounces?

Protractors and Rulers

Protractors and Rulers are great tools! With them you can do A LOT of things. You can draw plans for bridges and rocket ships, you can build go-carts and castles, or you can find out how tall you are or how far you've jumped—to name just a few things!

Protractors and Rulers are pretty straightforward to use—which is why they've been around for hundreds of years without changing much. No need!

Protractors and Rulers are so old and have been around for so long that sometimes we forget to teach students how to use them. We just assume they were born knowing. That, of course, is silly. However, once we show you how to use them, it will seem like you've known how to use them forever!

RULERS

A ruler is a usually a long, thin rectangle made of wood, plastic, metal or sometimes, as on this test, paper. A ruler is cut to a specific length—one foot, one yard, one meter, 100 cm, etc.—and then that length is divided by lines into smaller distinct units.

If the ruler is a foot long, that length is divided into inches, and each inch is divided by smaller lines into fractional parts: half inch, quarter inch, eighth inch. Each part is one half of the other, so everything stays nice and even.

If a ruler is divided into centimeters, then the centimeter will usually only be divided into ten pieces—millimeters.

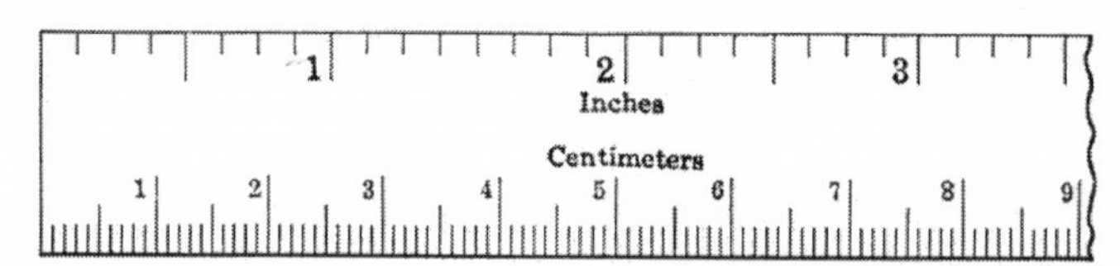

To measure a line, a side of an object, or the length of a wall, person, or distance, put one end of the ruler at the beginning of the thing you are measuring and note the point on the ruler at which that length ends. Then figure out how far you've gotten!

If the end of your ruler is slightly worn [as often happens], you can sometimes get more accurate results by starting your measurement on a whole inch number, seeing where you get to, and then subtracting by the number you started with.

Measuring Lines

Use your ruler to measure each line to the nearest eighth of an inch:

1. ⊢——⊣

2. ⊢————————⊣

3. ⊢——————————⊣

Use your ruler to measure each line to the nearest centimeter.

4. ⊢——⊣

5. ⊢——————⊣

6. ⊢—————————⊣

Protractors

Most protractors are semi-circles that allow you to measure angles or draw your own angles. Since a circle is 360°, half-circle protractors can measure up to 180°. The protractor usually has a little hole along the flat side and can generally measure angles in either direction. That is, they can go from 0°-180° left to right or right to left; it does not matter which way the angle is drawn!

If you are given an angle to measure, place the hole at the bottom of the protractor over the vertex of the angle. Align one ray of the angle on the bottom edge of the protractor, in line with 0° on the right or left. Remember, it doesn't matter which way the ray is facing!

Once you have lined up one ray with 0°, see where the other ray is pointing. That will tell you the measure of your angle! If your angle is too small to reach a number on the protractor, place your ruler over the ray to extend it, and see where the ruler hits on the protractor.

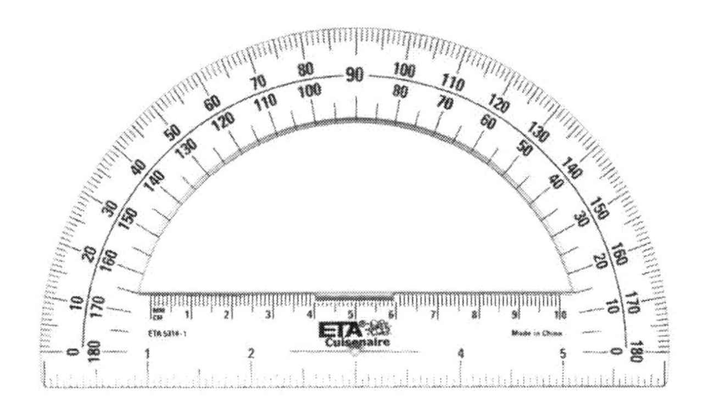

Measuring Angles

Measure each angle below with a protractor and identify as acute, right, obtuse or linear.

1.

2.

3.

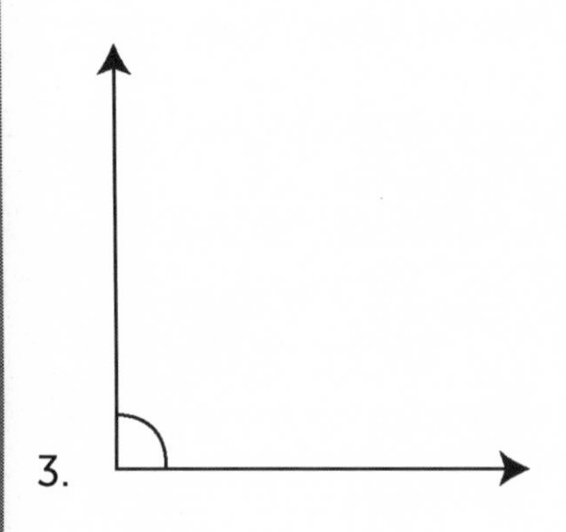

4.

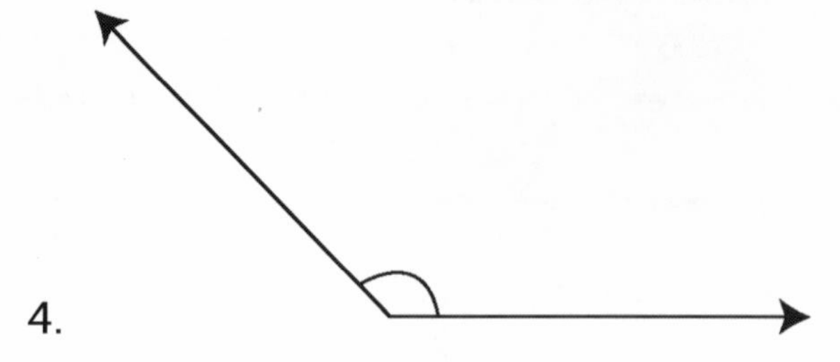

5.

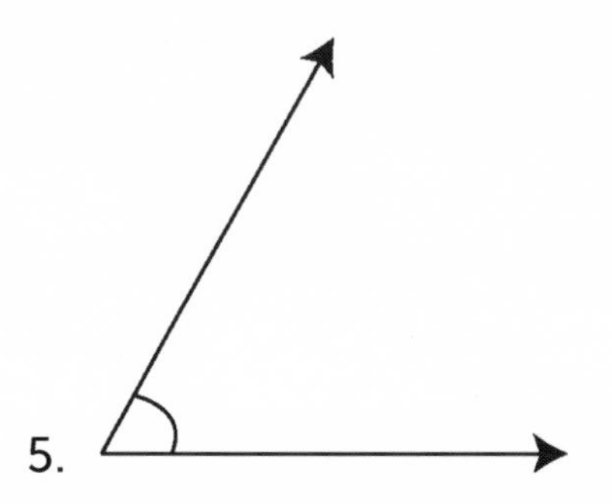

6.

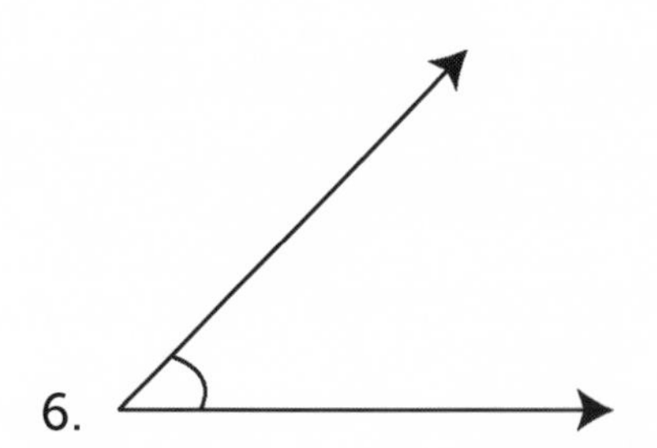

Data Analysis

From the Common Core through the SATs and ACTs, learning to read and interpret graphs and charts has become a big thing. Just as with reading comprehension, it is important to learn to read ALL the information in the tables/graphs/charts provided word-for-word AND number for number in order to understand what the tables/graphs/charts are trying to tell you. Just like a story or an essay, every set of data has a point to make, and it is your job to figure out what that point is.

Student	Number of Video Games Owned
Julio	8
Maxine	4
Lars	5
Justine	1
Vincent	10
Mary	7

If you look at the table above, it's pretty easy to understand the information it's presenting: It tells us how many video games each of six different student owns. Maxine, for example, has four, and Lars has five.

However, when we have a lot of data, it can sometimes be difficult to understand what it all means. In that case, it can be useful to find a way to present the same information graphically (that means with a picture, which is why we call such pictures of information "graphs").

There are three kinds of graphs we're going to cover. Let's start with the bar graph.

A bar graph is used to compare different amounts of something. You could, for example, use a bar graph to show how many video games each student in a class has. You could use it to show how many students said particular movies were their favorite. As long as you are comparing different amounts of the same thing, you can use a bar graph.

How To Read & Draw Graphs

For some reason, most younger students read graphs differently from adults and older students. When you are looking at graphs, it is important to understand that values are measured by the intersection of the lines, NOT the spaces on a graph:

YES **NO**

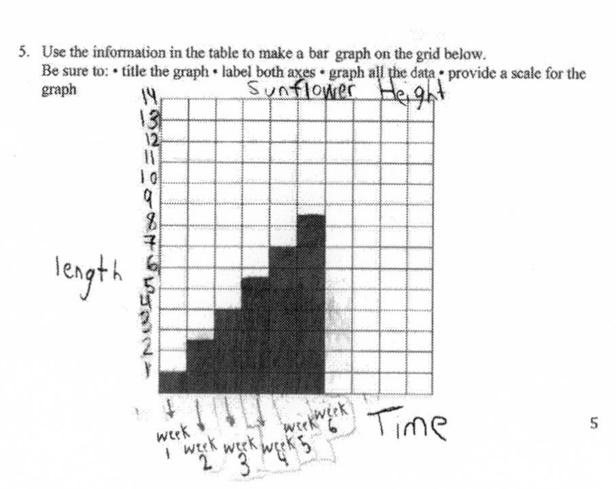

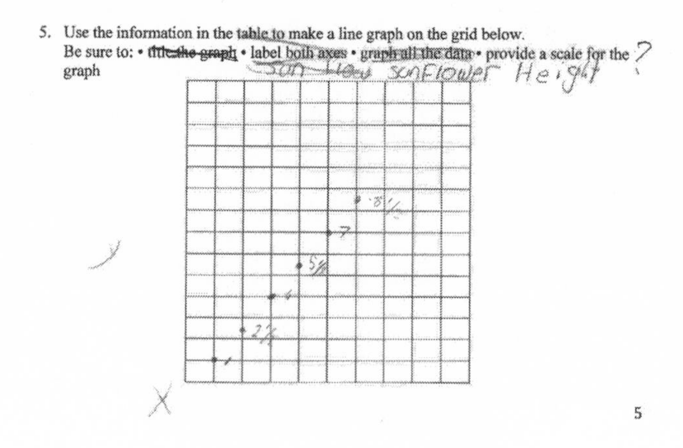

Bar Graphs

Below are two bar graphs that represent the video games owned by the students.

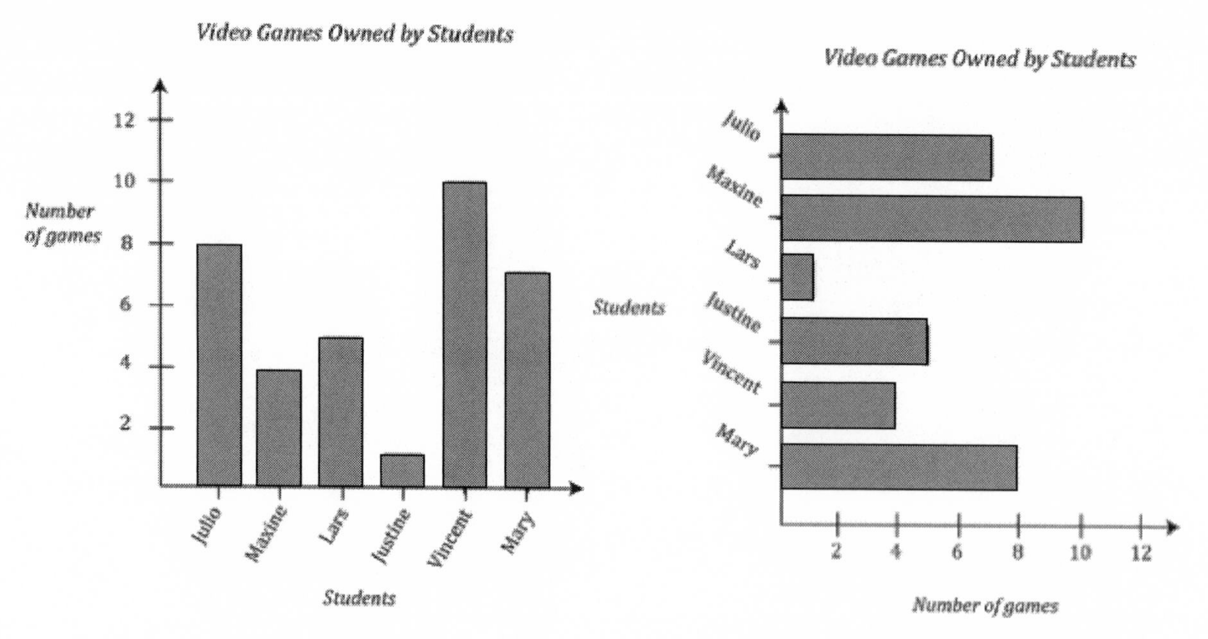

As you can see, a bar graph can go from bottom to top or from left to right. Both graphs show the same information that we found in the original table. Vincent's bar is the longest—it reaches 10—because he is the student with the most video games; Justine's bar, however, reaches only 1 because she has only one video game.

Line Graphs

But sometimes the data we're given isn't suited for a bar graph. If we want to see how something changes over time, it's best to use a line graph.

Check out the data below.

Days	Number of Flowers on a Magnolia Tree
1	4
2	7
3	9
4	10
5	11
6	11

It is not immediately obvious how the passage of time and the number of flowers on the tree are related, so we make a line graph out of it.

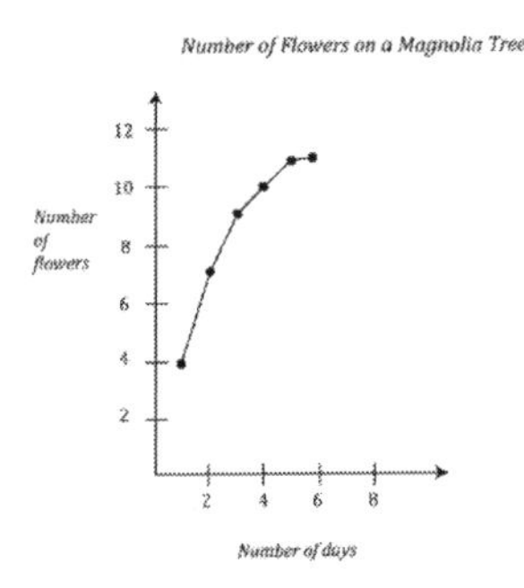

It is now clear that the number of flowers on the tree increases at first and then gradually reaches a peak [top point] of eleven, where it stays. If you want to see how something changes over time, it's best to use a line graph.

Line Plot

The final kind of graph we're going to discuss is called a line plot (not to be confused with a line graph). This kind of graph is especially good at showing how often something happens—the frequency of an event. The following line plot shows sea depths in kilometers as found by a research crew.

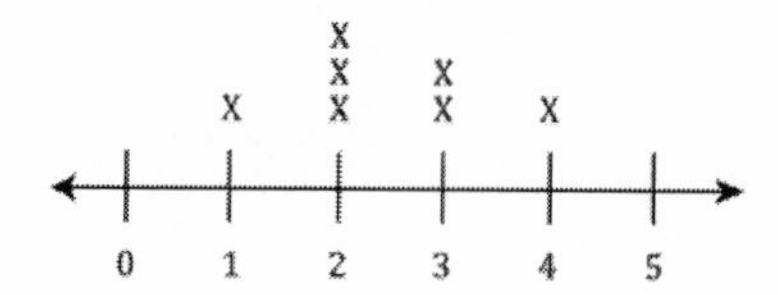

Each x above a number represents how many times the crew found that depth. Therefore, since there is no x above 5, there was no point with a depth of 5 kilometers. Since there are three x's above 2, there were three locations with a depth of 2 km.

So remember: if you're comparing amounts of the same thing, use a bar graph. If you're showing change over time, you a line graph. And if you want to show frequency, use a line plot.

Data Analysis Questions

Use the bar graph below to answer the following three questions.

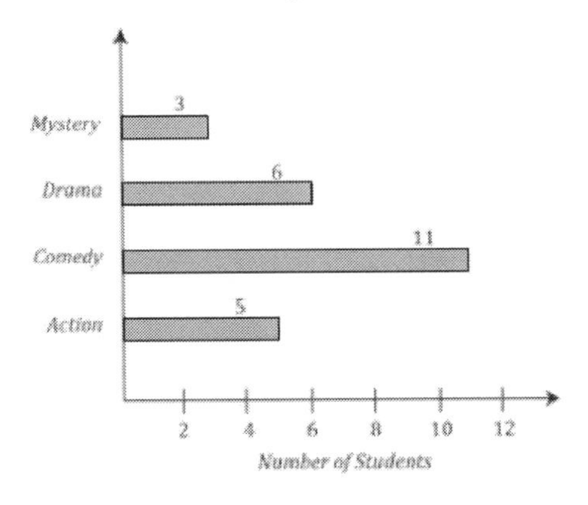

1. Which kind of movie do the students like best?

Answer_____________

2. How many students prefer drama than prefer mystery?

Answer_____________

3. Which two genres combined are as popular as comedy?

Answer_____________

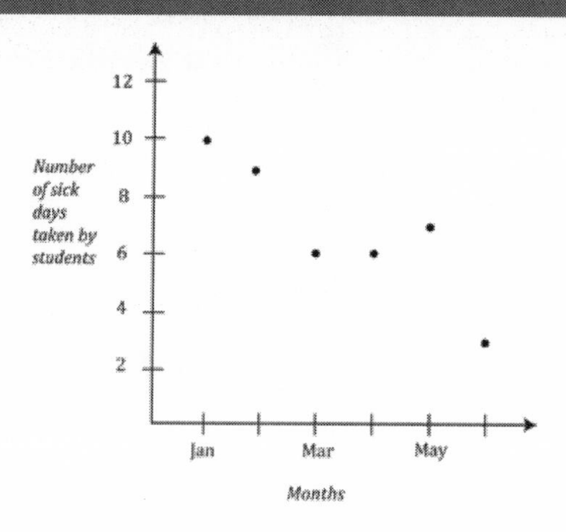

Use the line graph above to answer the following three questions.

4. Which two months had the same number of sick days taken by students?

Answer_____________

5. How many more sick days were taken in February than in June?

Answer_____________

6. After which month was there the greatest change in the number of sick days taken?

Answer_____________

The line plot below shows the amount of rainfall, in inches, received on different days. Use it to answer the following three questions.

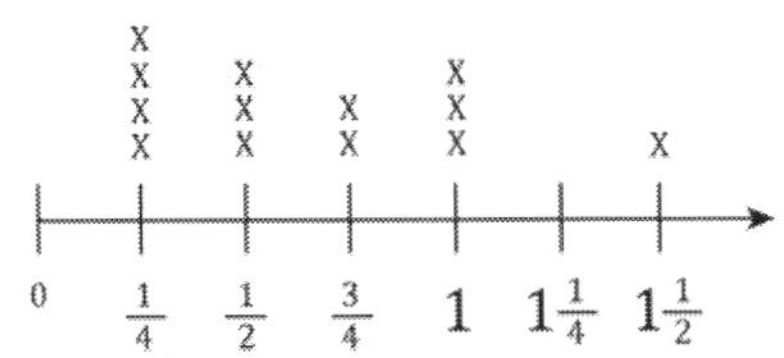

7. Which amount of rainfall was the most common?

Answer______________

8. Which amount of rainfall occurred exactly twice?

Answer______________

9. Which two amounts of rainfall occurred the same number of times?

Answer______________

Geometry Review—1

1. Jill's bedroom measures exactly 15 feet by 18 feet. If Jill wants to put a carpet on the floor, how much carpeting is needed?

   A. 33 square feet
   B. 270 square feet
   C. 715 square feet
   D. 829 square feet

2. Which letter has a line of symmetry?

   A. G
   B. S
   C. J
   D. M

3. The diameter of a circle painted by Bill is 2 feet. What is the area of the circle?

   A. 0.5 π square feet
   B. π square feet
   C. 2 π square feet
   D. 4 π square feet

4. How many sides does a quadrilateral have?

   A. 3
   B. 4
   C. 5
   D. Any number of sides greater than 3

5. What is the area of the figure to the right?

   A. 4 square units
   B. 8 square units
   C. 16 square units
   D. 64 square units

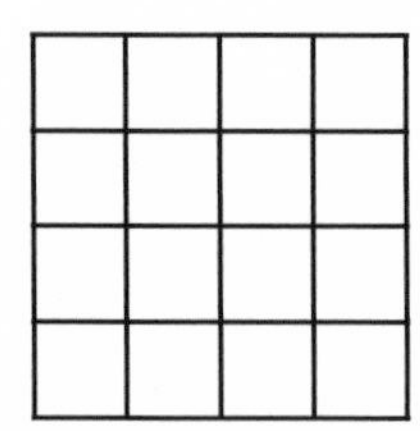

6. What is the sum of the least number of degrees in an obtuse angle added to the greatest number of degrees in an obtuse angle?

   A. 179 degrees
   B. 180 degrees
   C. 270 degrees
   D. 268 degrees

7. Amy's room measures 768 square feet. Which of the following could be a correct measurement of Amy's room?

   A. 34 ft by 41 ft
   B. 22 ft by 32 ft
   C. 24 ft by 32 ft
   D. 24 ft by 44 ft

8. Paul drew a square with an area of 121 square inches. What is the perimeter of this square?

   A. 132 inches
   B. 120 inches
   C. 44 inches
   D. 22 inches

Geometry Review—2

1. The diameter of a circle painted by Bill is 2 feet. What is the length of the radius?

   A. 6 feet
   B. 13.5 feet
   C. 4 feet
   D. 1 foot

2. Bill's house has a garden that is in the shape of a square. If each side of the garden is 17 feet, then what is the perimeter of the garden?

   A. 68 feet
   B. 98 feet
   C. 105 feet
   D. 289 feet

3. If the height of a rectangle is 9 kilometers and its length is 24 kilometers, what is the area of the rectangle?

   A. 66 square kilometers
   B. 216 square kilometers
   C. 324 square kilometers
   D. 432 square kilometers

4. Classify the relationship of the lines to the right.

   A. Parallel
   B. Perpendicular
   C. Intersecting
   D. Congruent

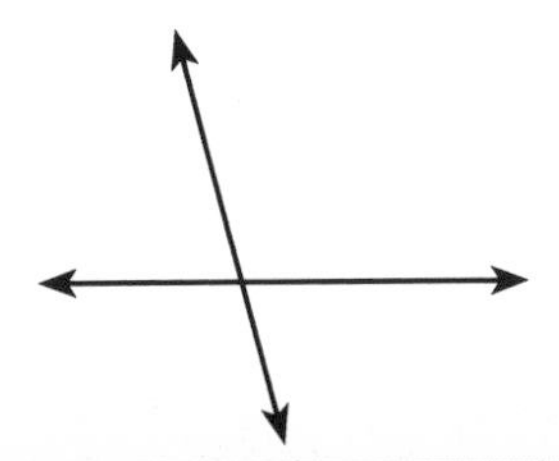

Practice

5. Name the polygon to the right.

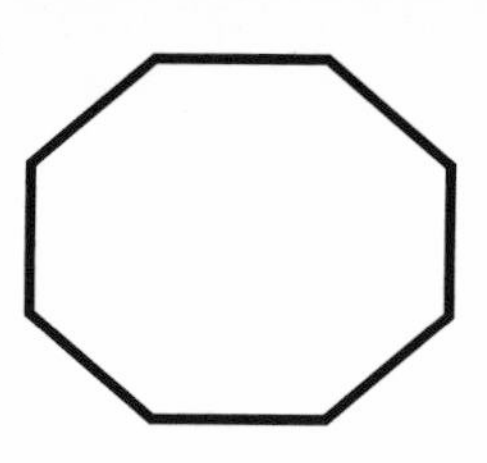

A. Decagon
B. Octagon
C. Heptagon
D. Hexagon

6. How many of the pairs of lines to the right will intersect?

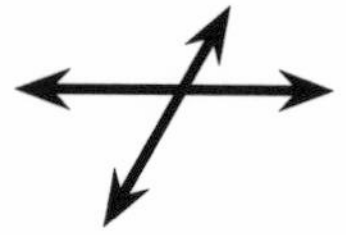
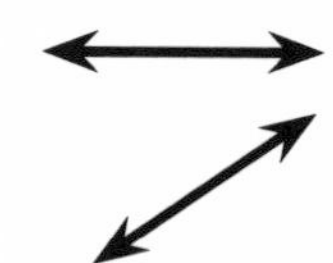
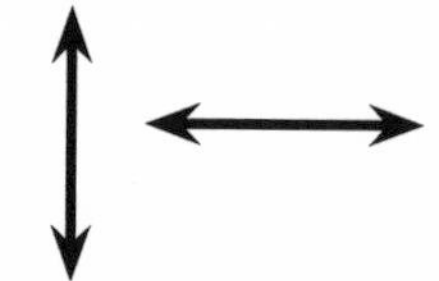

A. Zero
B. Two
C. Three
D. One

7. Find the perimeter of a pentagon if all of the sides equal 8 yards.

A. 24 yards
B. 32 yards
C. 40 yards
D. 64 yards

8. When it is 8 o'clock, what type of angle is the smaller angle formed by the minute hand and the hour hand on the face of the clock?

A. Acute angle
B. Obtuse angle
C. Right angle
D. Straight line

9. What is the perimeter of the triangle to the right?

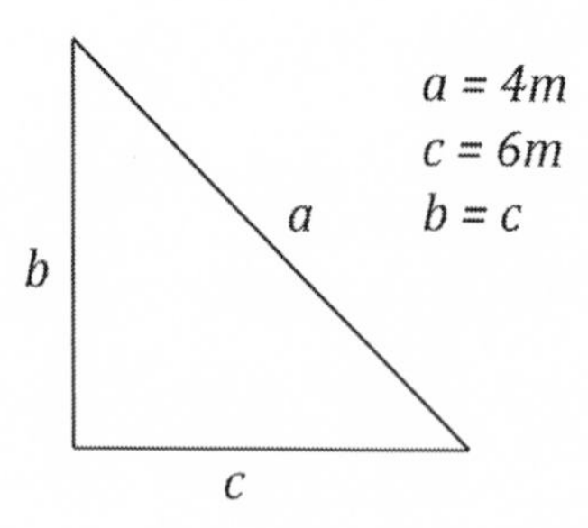

$a = 4m$
$c = 6m$
$b = c$

A. 10 m
B. 16 m
C. 24 m
D. 32 m

10. A diagram included 10 hexagons, 6 circles, 12 decagons, 12 squares, and 11 rays. How many polygons are in the diagram?

A. 10
B. 34
C. 35
D. 51

11. A polygon has 13 sides. How many vertices[4] does the polygon have?

A. 6
B. 13
C. 26
D. None of the above.

12. An angle of 16° is ______

A. A line segment
B. Parallel
C. Right
D. Acute

13. Which of these is a right angle?

A. 72 degrees
B. 90 degrees
C. 141 degrees
D. None of the above.

14. Please find the area of a triangle with a height of 5 and a base of 3.

Answer ___________

15. What is the shortest distance between two points?

Answer ___________

[4] plural of vertex

16. What does each angle measure in an equilateral triangle? Why?

Answer ___________

17. A shape has two pairs of parallel sides and two pairs of opposite, equal angles. What is this shape called?

Answer ___________

18. One side of an equilateral triangle measures 7 inches. What do the two other sides measure? Why?

Answer ___________

SHORT AND EXTENDED MATH

Your MATH test will have short-response and extended-response questions. These questions require that you respond to them by writing out all the steps you take to arrive at an answer.

This means you MUST write out all the figuring and calculations that you make even if they seem incredibly obvious to you. You must also write all this information out clearly and efficiently.

How to Write Math

A funny thing about how we learn math is that we are not always taught some important things like: how to write out math in a productive way!

One important thing to remember on the short and extended questions of this test is that you are not graded simply on whether or not you get the correct answer. You are graded on your process—how you do things. You can even receive partial credit for your process! So it is important to write out every step of your work in detail.

You may not think so, but even if you're not getting partial credit it helps you to write out every step of your process. Sometimes students think they are smarter if they can do math steps in their heads, but students often end up making mistakes when they do this. Who is smarter: the student who carefully writes out all the steps, checks her work and gets the answer right, or the student who does everything in his head only to get the answer wrong?

EASY ON THE ERASER

Almost every student I have ever known is concerned about time on their tests. To this end they often hurry when they don't need to and make careless mistakes. However, in spite of how much they worry about time, almost as many students spend too much time erasing every darn little misstep they make with their pencils.

And most students don't just erase. They sit there and painstakingly erase every last mark. And then blow the eraser bits away. Then erase a little more...Or sometimes, students start a problem, realize a part of it is wrong, and then instead of just erasing the part that's wrong, they erase the whole problem and start from scratch...Or sometimes a student writes a 1 and needs a 4 and, instead of simply changing the 1 into a 4, they erase the 1 [painstakingly] and then write 4. [I've also seen students erase "minus" signs in order to write in "plus" signs!]

It's enough to make an old man [me] cranky.

Try to think of time and erasers as precious...so don't waste either. Don't be afraid to:

1. Cross out [neatly].
2. Erase only the parts that really need erasing.
3. Get creative and reuse, rewrite and repurpose numbers and signs instead of erasing.

What to Write

People who grade your tests do not know you; they are not your mom, dad, grandparents or teachers. They do not know what is inside your head. They will not guess what is in your head, and it will cost you points. You may think something is obvious, so you don't need to write it—but it is **not** obvious, and you **do** need to write it.

Writing out means you need to **label** everything [for example, don't write 3; write $3], and you MUST [forever and always] complete your equations and not leave them hanging in space.

Before you start to answer your question, take a moment to plan how you're going to go about answering it—just like you plan your essay!

When you start to write stuff out, please make sure that you write neatly and in even rows and columns. Do not write over printed material or curve and trail off into the margins. It is almost certain that the straighter and clearer the work is written out, the straighter and clearer the answers you get [and the straighter and clearer the mind writing them!]

One last thing to know. Even if you're stumped by a question, just setting up a few equations or listing the parts of the problem might get you some points. So by all means, WRITE SOMETHING!

HOW TO WRITE OUT MATH—IN TEN STEPS!

1. Begin writing from the top left of your blank space.
2. Write across from left to right.
3. Be sure to write clearly, neatly and not too small or big.
4. Don't waste too much time erasing.
5. Don't write over print or trail off into margins.
6. Label all your terms.
7. Complete all your equations.
8. Show all your equations.
9. Check all your work and show that too.
10. No matter what: WRITE SOMETHING!

WRITE IT OUT JUST LIKE THIS:

Sample Student

...with her new job in May and only has time to walk her dog 20 minutes ...many minutes will she spend in the month of May walking her dog? There ... in May. Express your answer in **minutes**.

620min

31
× 20min
00 min
+ 620min
620min

13. Jeremiah gives $\frac{1}{4}$ of his rainbow bands to his little brother. He has 88 rainbow bands. How many does he give to his brother?

Answer 22rainbowbands

88 ÷ 2 = 44
88 ÷ 4 = 22
44 ÷ 2 = 22

14. What percent of his rainbow bands does Jeremiah have left after he has given $\frac{1}{4}$ to his brother?

Answer 75percent

88rainbow bands = 100percent
gives away $\frac{1}{4}$ of them $\frac{1}{4}$ = 25 percent
100percent − 25percent = 75percent

Questions 15 & 16

A school cafeteria receives 1700 packaged lunches, and the cafeteria needs to feed 225 students a day.

15. How many days will the cafeteria be able to feed all the students for?

Answer 7days

225 × 2 = 450
225 × 4 = 900
225 × 5 = 1,125
225 × 6 = 1,350
225 × 7 = 1,575

DO NOT WRITE IT OUT LIKE THIS:

Sample Student

...ny donates 935 pencils to a school. The pencils ... venly among 9 classrooms. The rest of the pencils ...o the library.

Which statement below correctly describes how the pencils are divided?

A. 103 pencils to each classroom and 8 pencils to the library

B. 108 pencils to each classroom and 8 pencils to the library

C. 130 pencils to each classroom and 8 pencils to the library

D. 133 pencils to each classroom and 8 pencils to the library

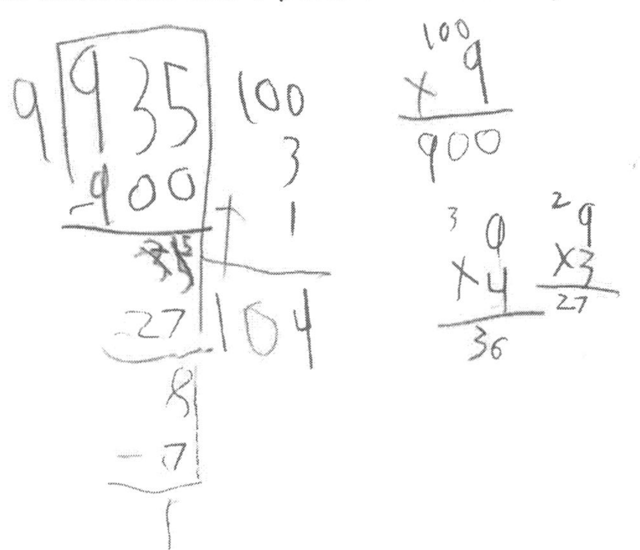

Word Problems—Short Answer—1

1. Michelle has 16 friends and she wants to give them each 16 cookies. How many cookies will she need to bake? **Show your work.**

   Answer _______ cookies

   Michelle learns after she bakes the cookies that one in four of her friends is on a diet and won't eat cookies. How many cookies will she therefore have left over?

   Answer _______ cookies

2. Josiah has 180 Legos and he wants to divide them equally between his 12 friends. How many Legos does each friend get? **Show your work.**

   Answer _______ Legos

3. Christine has 9 jars and 180 beads. She wants to put the same number of beads in each jar. How many beads will she put in each jar? Show your work.

Answer _______ beads

4. Joseph has 8 cats and 208 treats. He wants to give each cat the same number of treats (but not all at the same time!) How many treats will each cat get? Show your work.

Answer _______ treats

Joseph finds there are four more cats than he expected. If he wants to give them all the same number of treats, how many treats will be left over at the end?

Answer _______ treats

5. Miranda wants to put a carpet in her living room, which measures 14 feet by 17 feet. What is the area of the carpet will she need to get? Show your work.

Answer _______ square feet

6. Geronimo has 4 siblings. The family has a dog who needs to be walked once a day. If Geronimo and his 4 siblings take turns walking the dog, how many days will each of them walk the dog in one year? Show your work.

Answer _______ days

7. Ms. Linda has 360 books for her classroom. She can fit 90 books on each bookshelf. How many bookshelves will she need? Show your work.

Answer _______ books

8. Shania has 4 boxes of crayons. Each box contains 64 crayons. How many crayons does she have in all? Show your work.

Answer ________ crayons

9. Mary bought 4 bags of Skittles. Each bag contains 156 Skittles. How many Skittles does she have in all? Show your work.

Answer ________ Skittles

10. Mary wants to divide the Skittles between herself and her sister. How many Skittles will each of them get?

Answer ________ Skittles

Word Problems—Short Answer—2

1. Kelly's room is 9 feet 6 inches wide. How many inches wide is her room? Show your work.

Answer ________ ***inches***

2. Marcia and her friends ordered pizza, and they have some leftovers. There is $\frac{1}{2}$ of a pepperoni pizza, $\frac{2}{3}$ of a pineapple pizza and $\frac{1}{4}$ of a cheese pizza left. How much pizza is left? Show your work.

Answer ________ ***pizza***

3. Please list the factors of 60.

4. A square has a side that is 6 inches long. Please find the perimeter of this square. Use the formula Perimeter = 2(Length + Width) [this means 2 times the sum of length and width]. **Show your work.**

Answer ________ inches

5. A rectangle is 6 inches wide. It has a perimeter of 42 inches. What is the length of the rectangle? Show your work.

Answer ________ inches

6. Marie wants to decorate her room with posters only in shapes that have at least one pair of parallel lines. Which shapes could she use?

7. Marie's brother, Joshua, also wants to decorate his room, but he wants to use only shapes with no parallel sides. Which shapes could he use?

8. Please list five units that measure length.

9. How many degrees must the angles in a triangle add up to?

10. How many degrees must the angles in a rectangle add up to?

11. What is the difference between the sum of the degrees in the four angles of a rectangle and the sum of the degrees in the three angles of a triangle?

12. Taylor's mom has 316 jelly beans that she wants to divide equally among Taylor and her two brothers. How many jelly beans can each child get? Is there a remainder? Show your work.

Answer _______ jelly beans

Remainder (if any) __________

Questions About Math Multiple Choice & Short Answer Questions

Please answer the following questions in complete sentences.

1. What is your general approach for approaching the Math multiple-choice section?

2. When solving a multiple choice question, what should you do?

3. When solving a short or extended response question, what is the most important thing to do besides finding the correct answer?

4. What is your general approach for tackling a short or extended answer question?

5. What should you do if you don't know how to solve a multiple choice question? A short or extended response question?

6. Is it worth it to guess even if you can't eliminate any answers?

7. What are some ways you can check your answers?

8. What are some good ways to manage your time on the math sections?

9. What should you do if you aren't sure how to solve a short or long response question?

10. Is it possible to get partial credit on the short and extended response sections? How can you do this?

Scoring on the State MATH Tests

There are two points available for most non-multiple choice math questions, and here's how you'll be graded.

2 Points.

- You get the right answer!
- You show your work.
- Only tiny errors in your work that leave no doubt that you understand the concepts being tested.

1 Point.

- You don't answer all aspects of the question completely.
- You get the right answer but you don't show all your work.
- You get the wrong answer, but your work shows that you understood the concepts in question.

0 Points.

- You're totally wrong.
- You show no work.
- You get the right answer but your work shows that you have no understanding of the material.

There are also some longer math questions, and these are worth three points. They're evaluated for the same things as the 2 point questions, there are just more ways of getting partial credit.

3 Points.

- You get the right answer.
- You show your work over the different steps of the problem.
- Irrelevant errors in your work.

2 Points.

- Correctly answer most parts of the question.
- May not have the right answer, but used the correct procedures.
- May have some small misunderstanding of the principles in question.

1 Point.

- May do some parts of the question correctly, but get the question wrong and show little understanding of the material.
- May get the right answer but show little to no work required.

0 Points.

- Nothing right!

PART III

The Toddler & the Threshold

1 TAKING THE TEST: BEFORE & AFTER

Keep in mind: no matter how well you do on your tests [unless you score perfectly], it will always seem like everyone else has done better. Things will seem this way for two very good reasons:

- Kids who do well on their tests are much more likely to talk about their scores than kids who don't.
- Also, kids who don't score well on their tests are much more likely to lie about their scores.

2 Everyone Lies About Her Scores

The only motive other students have in speaking to you right before a test is to give you some of their anxiety. How much your friends love and support you doesn't matter; everyone is in survival mode, and everyone is just trying to unload anxiety as quickly and easily as possible. Short of throwing up, making other people nervous seems to help best. So kids will tell other kids things like "Did you hear there might be Roman Numerals on this test?" or "Did you hear that there might be poetry in the Reading Comprehension this year?" all in the hopes of seeing that burst of fear in their best friends' eyes. It doesn't even matter that you tell yourself they're full of baloney—it's too late—you just got a dose of their anxiety right into your veins. In order to avoid this happening, smile and wave to your friends and acquaintances before a test, but DO NOT engage them in conversation. Talk to them AFTER the test.

EXAMICIDE

3 If You Run into People You Know Before You Take Your Test, Do Not Talk to Them!

When my sons were just starting to walk, their balance was incredibly precarious. They toddled down our hallways, perilously[42] swaying from foot to foot until they reached the threshold to the living room. Invariably, stepping on and over that tiny threshold was, for them, akin to climbing Mount Kilimanjaro. That little bump would upset their tentative[43] balances, and they'd come crashing down on their diapered rears.

While you're taking the test, if you hit a bump, you must be more resilient than a toddler, if only because you have no diapered butt to fall on. If you see a new kind of math problem or there's a reading passage the meaning of which completely eludes you, DON'T FREAK. Just take your best shot at it:

- ELIMINATE bad answers,
- GUESS, and then
- MOVE ON and FORGET ABOUT THAT PROB-LEM!

Don't let one tough question ruin the rest of the test—put it out of your mind.

[42]- dangerously
[43]- uncertain, faltering

CHAPTER SIX

GAME DAY

Ok—You've Learned The Material And The Test, Now Let's Play!

At Last—Studatuta's Guide to Guessing

How to Guess

As I've gotten older and crankier, I have become less interested in teaching kids how to guess because, for the most part, it's really much more productive for me to spend my time teaching them how not to have to guess.

However, in spite of everyone's best efforts, sometimes there are those questions that we just can't figure out. In those situations, we need to grab our guts and guess! Below is a summary of some of the ideas I have touched upon throughout this book and a few new ideas on how to guess and how not to guess.

Six Steps to Better Guesses

These guidelines are not always right, nor are they meant to overrule any answers you may have figured out on your own. These are just some ideas of what to do if you have no idea what to do!

1. In math: Close is Wrong! Unless you are asked to round to begin with, if you get an answer, and your answer isn't among the answer choices, DON'T guess the number that's closest to your answer. Pick any other number.
2. In math: on a hard problem that you don't know how to solve, do not just guess the answer that turns out to be the sum or product of the numbers in the question. Don't "just" do anything.
3. In general: if you are a lousy guesser, figure out what your guess normally would be and then pick something else.
4. In general: don't plan to "come back later." Guess right away, but put a little "g" next to the questions you guess on [in your test book, not your answer sheet]. That way, you can go back, but only if you really need to and have the time.
5. In general: do not waste time guessing. Instead of "thinking" about your guess, flip a coin in your head, pick that answer, and MOVE ON!
6. In general: guessing should be fun [about as fun as anything ever is on these tests]. Don't overthink it; just relax and pick one!

Don't Change Your Game!

So you've remembered to get a good night's sleep, eat a good breakfast and relax, and now at last you're ready to take your test. Now remember: play exactly the same way you've practiced. DO NOT change your game just because "now it's real!"

Veal Parmigiana

When the proctor calls "Five minutes," it is almost impossible not to react as if she just said, "Five seconds until the ceiling collapses!" It might help, however, if you pretend she's saying "Veal Parmigiana" instead and react accordingly. Mmmmm,

Veal Parmigiana.

REMEMBER: There is NOTHING to be gained by going faster at the end of your test. For most tests the questions at the end are harder, so going faster will only improve your chances of getting them wrong. Better to take your time and get two correct than to rush and get five wrong.

Besides:Five Minutes Is a Very Long Time

Sit and watch the clock for five minutes. It will feel like an eternity. Try doing it for just a minute. You will be amazed.

The Letter: Here's What I Send to All My Students Before Their Tests. Now I'm Sending It to You.

To all my geniuses:

Congratulations on all your hard work and good thinking in the run-up to your test. You have prepped well, and now you're ready for the real thing. I just wanted to write you with a few things to be aware of come test day and the night before:

The night before, please relax. It is not the time to try to learn or review anything. Before dinner you might want to review your old tests or look over your last essays, but then: have some pizza, watch a movie and go to bed at a decent hour [but not so early that you end up tossing and turning in bed].

On Game Day, please arrive on time (or even early), and make sure you have with you:

a. Pencils
b. Snack/Water
c. Brain

Walk into your classroom like you own the joint. Float above everyone's anxiety. Whatever silly, annoying questions kids are fretting about, DO NOT ENGAGE. Everything will be sorted out, and you will be in your seat shortly.

When you see your friends before your test, try not to speak with them too much. As much as your friends love you, they will mostly be looking to offload anxiety onto you. No one needs more anxiety.

Remember: play exactly the same way you've practiced. DO NOT change your game just because "now it's real!"

Again: Don't change what you've been doing! We've prepped you for a test of reading comp, math and writing. If your test seems different from those you have been practicing on, it's probably nerves. These things never vary that much! If something is actually different, it's different for everyone. Just keep going until you start to feel comfortable. If an early question seems hard, it does not mean that all the others ones will be harder; sometimes it's just difficult to get going. Try reading through the example problem or run through math formulas in your mind to get your head in the game.

Take each question as it comes and answer it to the best of your ability – don't worry about how things are different from what you expected. Remain Clam!

And also remember: It doesn't matter if you hit a bumpy patch—it matters how you respond to it!

1. Guess and Don't Obsess.
2. Forget about it, and
3. Move on, because—
4. All the questions afterwards are far more important!

Finally: You have practiced, you know the test...Now go out there, stick to your game plan and ace the test!

REMAIN CLAM!!

Best,

Studatuta

Test Taking and Time—More Thoughts
Subway Stories

WHEN I WAS WISE

I got to the turnstiles. My train was already in the station, doors open. I took out my wallet to get my Metrocard, but it wasn't in its usual place. For some reason, I did not rifle through my wallet like a madman as I would have done the other 99% of the time. Instead I said to myself, "The train is already gone. Put it out of your mind. What is the most efficient way to find the card?" With a weird poise, I stopped, took the business and credit cards out of my wallet and systematically flipped through them. In seconds, I found the Metrocard, slid it through the turnstile and got on the train!

WHEN I WAS NOT SO WISE

I took the wrong subway line to meet a friend in Lower Manhattan. The stop I ended up getting off at was not far from my destination, but Lower Manhattan is full of tiny, winding streets. I was already running late, so I rushed out of the subway. At the exit was a large "YOU ARE HERE" map of the neighborhood. I paused for a nanosecond and thought about studying the map. My un-clam mind shouted, "You don't have time to read the map!!" So I didn't.

Of course, I got lost. Instead of taking one minute to read the map and ending up maybe five minutes late, I rushed and ended up 20 minutes late!

OUTRO

When I started tutoring, I was just a few years older than my students. I was a fine, if rough, writer and painter, and a wildly undisciplined and fairly indifferent math student. Now, I am more often than not a few years older than my students' parents, a somewhat more polished writer and artist, and a really excellent basic-math kind of guy. In spite of how everyone likes to yammer about "kids nowadays," I can honestly say that kids are the same. Mostly, as far as I can tell, only the nature of distractions has changed. Otherwise, the song remains the same: some students are engaged, some are checked out, some are only interested in hanging out. For many, education is something you get through or at best a means to an end. For others, it's a job: a responsibility you tend to during the day and evenings, and nothing more. In my experience, the rarest creature of all is the engaged student.

The engaged student is interested in the material either because she finds it interesting or because it *might* be interesting. The engaged student doesn't decide this is boring or that is boring or that isn't me. The engaged student samples *everything*, gives it a fair shake and moves on or not. The engaged student doesn't just learn stuff for a test and then do a memory dump the next day. The engaged student actually learns stuff.

As much as this book has been an appeal to students to REMAIN CLAM! on their tests, it has also [not so secretly] been an appeal to students to engage: to face the work in front of them head-on and not spend all their time trying to find a way around it. I hope this book has inspired students to read in depth and write out and complete equations, to admit when they don't know something and figure it out, look it up or ask someone!

The payoff for all this engagement is more than just a guarantee of marvelous scores on your tests; it is also a great way to learn how to use your mind—now and beyond these tests. So, by all means:

Engage!! [and *REMAIN CLAM!*]

ANSWERS

READING

"Zeami Motokiyo and Noh Theater" on page 29

1. C
2. B
3. A
4. B
5. D

"Which Literary Device?" on page 40

1. Metaphor
2. Personification
3. Simile
4. Personification/(onomatopoeia)
5. Personification
6. Hyperbole
7. Imagery
8. Alliteration
9. Simile

"First Day of School" on page 41

1. C
2. A
3. C
4. C
5. A

Peter Pan"Dramatic Text: PETER PAN Scene" on page 45

1. D
2. A
3. D
4. B
5. C
6. C
7. A

WRITING

"Classify Parts of Speech Practice" on page 60

1. noun
2. proper noun
3. noun
4. adjective
5. noun/verb
6. verb
7. adverb
8. adverb
9. adjective
10. adjective
11. proper noun
12. noun
13. proper noun
14. adjective

15. noun/verb
16. proper noun
17. proper noun
18. proper noun
19. adverb
20. proper noun

Part B

For
And
Nor
But
Or
Yet
So

"Contraction Practice 1" on page 65

1. Sam isn't coming to the library with us.
2. Don't you want something to eat?
3. We've been working on this project all month.
4. It's starting to feel like spring.

"Contraction Practice 2" on page 66

1. She'd
2. Couldn't
3. Won't
4. He's
5. We'd
6. I've
7. You're
8. We'll
9. Shouldn't
10. She's
11. It's
12. I'd
13. That'll
14. Who's
15. Didn't
16. They're
17. He'd
18. We're
19. Wouldn't
20. They'd
21. I'm
22. You'll
23. That'd
24. She'll
25. You'd
26. That's
27. What're
28. He'll
29. It'd
30. I'll

"Possessive Pronoun / Adjective Practice" on page 69

1. Its
2. Theirs
3. Mine
4. Her
5. Yours
6. His, mine

7. Their
8. Its
9. Your; ours
10. My
11. Its
12. Hers
13. Their
14. Our
15. Their
16. Hers
17. Its
18. Mine
19. Our
20. Your
21. His
22. Hers
23. His
24. Its

"Possession" on page 69

1. All the boys' bicycles are gone.
2. The dancer's dress was made of silk.
3. Did the cat eat the Smith family's food off of the table?
4. Marta plays on the girls' basketball team.
5. Matthew and Marsha's toys are all over the floor.
6. The hero's arrows aimed for the villain's heart.
7. The family of dragons breathed fire on the heroes' shields.
8. The heroes' horses' heads were covered in flameproof armor.
9. The boys went to the girl's party and danced with her friends.
10. Some of the girl's friends danced while her other friends played Frisbee.
11. Unfortunately, it was the girl's dog's Frisbee.
12. The girl's dog chased its Frisbee, much to all her friends' fear.

"Apostrophe and Possession Practice" on page 71

1. Who's the party's candidate for vice president this year?
2. The fox had its right foreleg caught securely in the trap's jaws.
3. Our neighbor's car is an old Chrysler, and it's just about to fall apart.
4. In three week's time we'll have to begin school again.
5. Didn't you hear that they're leaving tomorrow?
6. Whenever I think of the stories I read as a child, I remember Cinderella's glass slipper and Snow White's wicked stepmother.
7. We claimed the picnic table was ours, but the Smiths' children looked so disappointed that we found another spot.
8. It's important that the kitten learns to find its way home.
9. She did not hear her children's cries.

10. My address has three 7's, and Tim's phone number has four 2's.

11. Didn't he say when he would arrive at Arnie's house?

12. It's such a beautiful day that I've decided to take a sun bath.

13. She said the watch Jack found was hers, but she couldn't identify the manufacturer's name on it.

14. Girls' clothing is on the first floor, and the men's department is on the second.

15. The dog's bark was far worse than its bite.

16. The moon's rays shone feebly on the path, and I heard the insects' chirpings and whistlings.

17. They're not afraid to go ahead with the plans, though the choice is not theirs.

18. The man whose face was tan said that he had spent his two weeks vacation in the mountains.

19. I found myself constantly putting two c's in the word process.

20. John's 69 Ford is his proudest possession.

"Capitalization Practice" on page 74

1. I like to go to McDonald's on Tuesdays after soccer practice.
2. Meredith says it is silly for me to go to McDonald's after soccer because fast food is not healthy.
3. My mom said after I finished my homework I could watch SpongeBob.
4. At soccer practice, I hurt my ankle, so I am going to see the doctor on Wednesday morning.
5. I go to Sunshine Elementary School, and my teacher's name is Mr. Oliver.
6. My favorite book is The Star-Bellied Sneeches by Dr. Seuss.
7. One day I want to go to Africa and see a real tiger.
8. For dinner last night I ate pizza from Domino's.
9. This weekend I need to study for my spelling test before I play video games.
10. I made my favorite stuffed animal at Build a Bear, and I named her Daisy.

"Homophone Practice—1" on page 78

1. Which...Witch
2. There....their...They're
3. Too...to...two
4. write...right
5. It's....its
6. Whether...weather

"Homophone Practice—2" on page 78

1. two, one
2. sole
3. whether
4. it's
5. you're
6. here

7. our
8. than
9. pedal
10. some
11. dye
12. pears

"Compound Word Questions" on page 80

1. A lot
2. every day
3. cannot
4. All together
5. some time
6. Everyday...sometime

"Reading 1" on page 94

Proofread this story. Correct any errors.

The little old lady lived by the river. She had many friends among the animals in the woods. T**hey** came to her house every mornin**g,** and every morning **she** fed them. One day the animals came to the little old **lady's** house, but she **wasn't** there. The bird tapped on the window pane, but no one answered. **The** deer knocked on her door with their **hooves**, but still she did not answer. What had happened to the old lady**?** All the animals were **deeply c**oncerned.

"Reading 2" on page 94

Proofread this story. Correct any errors.

Goober is my worst student. She wears too **many** sock**s**. **Goober's** brain is filled with too many thing**s**. Some of the things in Goober'**s** brain **are**: dust bunnies, pillows, candles and smelly socks. I also think that **Goober** is too big to **fit** in my office.

"Reading 3" on page 94

Poppa wasn't like other grandpas. He didn't live in Florida or play golf or visit us at regular times like Thanksgiving or the 4th of July. Like our dad, he traveled all around the world, had amazing adventures and told us all about them. He didn't give us presents at regular times either, like on our birthdays or at Christmas. He had Poppa's holidays.

Sometimes he would just show up in the middle of the week and announce "Happy February 17th day!" No one else knew that February 17th was a holiday—so we had it all to ourselves. My brother Simon and I loved it. Our mom was not so thrilled. Most of the time Mom loved Pops like crazy, but sometimes she wished her dad would be a teeny bit more like the other grandpas who read the paper, sat on benches and celebrated regular holidays like Labor Day.

"Reading 4" on page 95

There are so many fun **subjects** in school. *It is so hard to pick a favorite subject* ***(Cut: this is a zero sentence)***. However, overall my absolute favorite subject is reading.

Why is reading my favorite subject? Well, that is because**,** one, it is fun to do. Two, what do I do when I am sad**? R**ead! Someone should write a song about that **(Cut: this sentence is off-topic)**. And last, three, I love to get **wrapped** up in a good story.

It is fun **to be read to by Mom and Dad** once in a while. Also, at school we have **literature** groups (book clubs). However, there is homework **(cut: off-topic)**. Our teacher reads to us too, but after that we discuss it.

Reading in the **ELA,** in my opinion**,** doesn't count as real reading, **nor** do **the** practice tests. That is because they have questions about **the readings**. Also, there aren't chapters or **plot** twists, and worst of all, no cliffhangers! Information **books** sort of count as real books. Also, in my opinion, picture books don't really count as real books. **Biographies** such as the ***Who Was...*** books do count as real books. They may **have pictures,** but it's OK.

In conclusion, reading is my favorite subject. It is fun for the whole family **and the class.**

"Blood" on page 99

1. C
2. D
3. B
4. B
5. A

"CHAPTER I. Murder at the Manor" on page 104

1. C
2. B
3. D
4. A

"Rock Climbing" on page 108

1. D
2. C
3. B
4. A
5. C
6. B

"Ski Trip" on page 114

1. D
2. C
3. D
4. D
5. A

"Barber Surgeons" on page 120

1. D
2. B
3. C
4. A
5. C

"Serena Williams" on page 125

1. C
2. B
3. C
4. A
5. D

"Video Games as Art" on page 132

1. D
2. C
3. B
4. A

"The Little Ghost" on page 145

1. C
2. B
3. B
4. D
5. A

"Shadwell Stair" on page 146

1. B
2. A
3. B
4. D
5. B

Math

"Addition" on page 165

1. 66
2. 86
3. 21
4. 30
5. 63
6. 95
7. 98
8. 171
9. 33

"Subtraction" on page 166

1. 108
2. 216
3. 435
4. 809

"Stack and Add" on page 167

1. 781
2. 288
3. 2,347
4. 288
5. 56,581
6. 17,295

"Stack and Subtract" on page 169

1. 83
2. 191
3. 2,612
4. 5,666
5. 23

"Stacking Practice" on page 173

1. 150
2. 294
3. 1,372
4. 2,133
5. 7,872
6. 2,244

"Division Practice" on page 175

1. 123
2. 113
3. 102
4. 1,155
5. 99 r 6
6. 202 r 1

"Inequality Practice Set" on page 177

1. <
2. >
3. <
4. <
5. <
6. >
7. >
8. >
9. >
10. <
11. >

12. <

"Factoring Practice" on page 180

1. 1, 2, 3, 4, 6, 8, 12, 24
2. 1, 2, 3, 4, 6, 9, 12, 18, 36
3. 1, 2, 4, 5, 10, 20
4. 1, 3, 5, 15
5. 1, 2, 3, 4, 5, 6, 10, 12, 15, 20, 30, 60
6. 1, 2, 3, 4, 6, 8, 9, 12, 18, 24, 36, 72

"Recognizing Equivalents" on page 184

1. 4
2. 8
3. 15
4. 10
5. 7
6. 7
7. 16
8. 27
9. 16
10. 20
11. 8
12. 12

"Reducing" on page 192

1. $\frac{1}{2}$
2. $\frac{1}{3}$
3. $\frac{2}{3}$
4. $\frac{2}{3}$
5. $\frac{1}{2}$
6. $\frac{1}{4}$
7. $\frac{2}{3}$
8. $\frac{3}{5}$
9. $\frac{3}{8}$
10. $\frac{1}{15}$
11. $\frac{7}{9}$
12. $\frac{1}{3}$
13. $\frac{3}{4}$
14. $\frac{1}{4}$
15. $\frac{1}{2}$
16. $\frac{1}{2}$
17. $\frac{4}{7}$
18. $\frac{1}{4}$
19. $\frac{12}{13}$
20. $\frac{3}{4}$

"Fraction Modeling" on page 185

1. A
2. B
3. D
4. D
5. B
6. D
7. A
8. D
9. C
10. D
11. A
12. B

"Improper Fractions to Mixed Numbers" on page 194

1. $10\frac{1}{2}$
2. $9\frac{2}{3}$
3. $1\frac{1}{2}$
4. $2\frac{4}{5}$
5. $1\frac{1}{11}$
6. $6\frac{1}{6}$

"Mixed Numbers to Improper Fractions" on page 195

1. $\frac{19}{4}$
2. $\frac{4}{3}$
3. $\frac{28}{5}$
4. $\frac{5}{2}$
5. $\frac{39}{10}$
6. $\frac{79}{5}$

"LCM" on page 199

1. 24

2. 36
3. 168
4. 60
5. 50
6. 63

"Adding and Subtracting Fractions" on page 201

1. 1
2. $\frac{4}{7}$
3. $\frac{9}{8}$
4. 4
5. 1
6. $\frac{1}{2}$
7. $\frac{6}{5}$
8. $\frac{13}{14}$
9. $\frac{11}{12}$
10. $\frac{17}{72}$
11. $\frac{1}{3}$
12. $\frac{1}{4}$
13. 2
14. $\frac{1}{3}$
15. $\frac{1}{4}$
16. 0
17. $\frac{1}{24}$
18. $\frac{13}{28}$
19. $\frac{1}{72}$
20. $\frac{5}{8}$

"Multiplying and Dividing Fractions" on page 202

1. $\frac{1}{6}$
2. $\frac{1}{2}$
3. $\frac{1}{14}$
4. $\frac{1}{10}$
5. $\frac{3}{28}$
6. $\frac{3}{14}$
7. $\frac{2}{11}$
8. $\frac{6}{11}$
9. $\frac{3}{13}$
10. $\frac{3}{5}$
11. 2
12. $\frac{3}{5}$
13. $\frac{12}{35}$
14. $\frac{4}{7}$
15. $\frac{40}{33}$
16. $\frac{4}{3}$
17. 3
18. $\frac{11}{14}$
19. $\frac{9}{4}$
20. $\frac{9}{20}$

"Fractions Review—1" on page 203

1. 4
2. 0.5 pounds
3. 6
4. $\frac{1}{3}$
5. D
6. A
7. E
8. 6 cups
9. 5

"Fraction Review—2" on page 206

1. $\frac{1}{8}$
2. 1
3. 1
4. $\frac{1}{9}$
5. $\frac{2}{9}$
6. 1
7. $\frac{1}{3}$
8. 2
9. 2

"Fraction Review—3" on page 207

1. $\frac{5}{12}$
2. $\frac{1}{6}$
3. $\frac{1}{18}$

"Fractions to Decimals, Decimals to Fractions" on page 212

1. .5
2. $.\overline{3}$
3. .75
4. .2
5. $.\overline{6}$
6. .625
7. $\frac{4}{5}$
8. $\frac{2}{3}$
9. $\frac{1}{4}$
10. $\frac{8}{9}$
11. $\frac{1}{2}$
12. $\frac{3}{4}$

"Fractions to Decimals Word Problems" on page 213

1. C
2. D
3. D
4. D
5. C
6. D

"Multiplying by Factors of 10" on page 215

1. 9,600,000
2. 1,440,000
3. 1,320,000,000
4. 1,200,000
5. 510,000

"Rounding" on page 216

1. 0.9
2. 1,000
3. 1.0
4. 67,400
5. 0.77
6. 0.856
7. 2,000,000
8. 60,000
9. 2.4

"Place Value and Rounding" on page 217

1. hundreds
2. millions
3. tens
4. tenths
5. thousandths
6. hundred thousands
7. ten millions
8. ten thousands
9. tens

"Understanding Digits Problems" on page 217

1. 100
2. $\frac{1}{10}$
3. Answers may vary, but: 6xx,xxx
4. 7,126; 100
5. 5 = millions, 0 = hundred thousands, 8 = ten thousands, 6 = thousands, 3 = hundreds, 4 = tens, 2 = ones
6. 54,302. It would be 80 smaller

"Pattern Problems" on page 219

1. D
2. 99, 93, 87, 81, 75, 69, 63, etc.
3. B
4. 64
5. 23, 32, 41, 50, 59, 68, 77, 86

"Symmetry" on page 228

1. Square: 4 lines of symmetry
2. Rectangle: 2 lines of symmetry
3. Pentagon: 5 lines of symmetry
4. Hexagon: 6 lines of symmetry
5. Triangle: 3 lines of symmetry
6. Circle: trick question – infinite lines of symmetry
7. Smiley Face: 1 line of symmetry
8. Lightning Bolt: 0 lines of symmetry

"Shape Questions" on page 231

1. A CLOSED shape with at least 3 sides and 3 vertices and straight lines.
2. A polygon with 4 sides.
3. A quadrilateral with 2 pairs of parallel sides.
4. A quadrilateral with 1 pair of parallel sides.
5. a. i, ii, ii, iv

   b. ii
   c. i, ii, iii
   d. i, ii
   e. v
   f. i, ii, iii
   g. i, ii
   h. i
   i. i, ii, iii, iv
   j. i

"Area and Perimeter—Drill Set" on page 234

1. 35 square yards
2. 270 feet
3. A = 168 square yards; P = 52 yards
4. 125 square centimeters
5. P = 44 meters ; A = 121 square meters
6. 6 squares

"Measurement and Conversion—Drill Set" on page 236

1. length
2. weight/volume
3. length
4. weight
5. weight/mass
6. length
7. length
8. length
9. liquid
10. weight/mass
11. liquid
12. liquid
13. length
14. length

"Conversions" on page 237

1. 3600 seconds

2. 20 quarts
3. 420 inches
4. 3 meters
5. 160 ounces
6. 8,000 liters
7. 4 pints
8. 600 hectograms
9. 2,500 centimeters
10. 540 inches
11. 1,440 minutes
12. 56 pints
13. 2 gallons
14. 8 yards
15. 300 seconds
16. 2 minutes
17. 4 feet
18. 4 pounds
19. 2 (US) tons
20. 4,400 yards
21. 100 centimeters
22. 5 yards
23. 86,400 seconds
24. 63,360 inches

"Measuring Lines" on page 239

1. 1 ½ inches
2. $3\frac{7}{8}$ inches
3. 5 inches
4. 4 cm
5. 8 cm
6. 12 cm

"Measuring Angles" on page 240

1. 160 degrees, obtuse
2. 30 degrees, acute
3. 90 degrees, right
4. 135 degrees, obtuse
5. 60 degrees, acute
6. 45 degrees, acute

"Geometry Review—1" on page 248

1. B
2. D
3. B
4. B
5. C
6. C
7. C
8. C

"Geometry Review—2" on page 249

1. D
2. A
3. B
4. C
5. B
6. C
7. C
8. B
9. B
10. B
11. B
12. D
13. B
14. 7.5
15. a straight line
16. 60 degrees; each angle in an equilateral triangle is the same, and the total must be 180 degrees
17. parallelogram
18. 7 inches; all sides in an equilateral triangle are identical

"Data Analysis Questions" on page 245

1. C
2. B
3. D
4. C
5. A

1. B
2. B
3. C
4. D
5. A

"Word Problems—Short Answer—1" on page 260

1. 256 cookies; 64 cookies

2. 15 Legos
3. 20 beads
4. 26 treats; 4 treats
5. 238 square feet
6. 73 days
7. 4 bookshelves
8. 256 crayons
9. 624 skittles; 312 skittles

"Word Problems—Short Answer—2" on page 264

1. 114 inches
2. $\frac{17}{12}$ of a pizza
3. 1, 2, 3, 4, 5, 6, 10, 12, 15, 20, 30, 60
4. 24 inches
5. 36 square inches
6. 15 inches
7. squares, rhombuses, trapezoids, parallelograms, rectangles
8. triangles, circles, pentagons,
9. inches, yards, feet, meters, kilometers
10. 180 degrees
11. 360 degrees
12. 180 degrees
13. 105 jelly beans; remainder = 1

APPENDIX A

READING COMPREHENSION– NUTS & BOLTS

Nuts & Bolts of Reading Comprehension

1. Read the passage.

2. Keep reading until you've got your Two T's. Usually you'll know your Theme and Thesis by the first few sentences of the second paragraph, but sometimes the author doesn't spit them out until much later. Hang in!

    a. Make sure you are clear on what the topic [THEME] truly is: just because they're talking about *bananas*, it doesn't mean that the topic is really *bananas*.

    b. Make sure you are clear on what the author's viewpoint [THESIS] is: i.e., look for the "but." Just because the author writes "most people think bananas," it doesn't mean the author thinks "bananas." In fact he probably thinks "not bananas."

3. Once you've established what the "but" and/or author's point is, you will see that **every** body paragraph is designed to support that point.

4. Occasionally, authors will devote a body paragraph to a contrary example—something that seems to contradict their point of view. Authors do this in order to:

    a. Seem fair—they want to create the appearance of examining all sides of an argument and demonstrating their awareness of them, or

    b. Strengthen their point—by raising and then ultimately dismissing or diminishing contrary points of view, authors hope to reinforce the strength of their own point of view.

5. Every passage makes one and only one point, and most of the questions hinge on your being aware of what that point is.

6. Answering the questions:

    a. Read the question,

    b. Paraphrase the question so as to be sure you know what it's asking,

    c. Determine ***your*** answer to the question. If you don't have one, look back to the passage. Don't flip back to the question until you've figured something out. Then:

    d. Once you have an answer in mind:

        i. Read the answers given.

        ii. Eliminate any answers that seem wrong outright.

        iii. If you find the answer during your first read-through of the answers—pick it.

        iv. If you don't find the answer you want but have one or two choices left, look closely at the remaining answers and try to find one or two words in an answer that would make it **wrong.**

        v. If you are still left with more than one answer choice, pick the answer that seems qualified the most [some, often, occasionally, etc.] **and** the most like previous answers to other questions in the section, and then,

        vi. **Move on!** Don't spend too much time on a question you're totally clueless about. The longer you spend on a reading comprehension question, the more likely you are to waste time, energy and points. If you don't know the answer, guess and GTHOOT![45]

APPENDIX B

ESSAY PROCESS & STRUCTURE

How to Structure Extended Essay

1. **Intro Paragraph**
   a. WHAT YOU BELIEVE—

   The passage suggests that although machines can be very helpful, they do not solve all our problems

   b. WHY YOU BELIEVE IT—

   Machinery does not solve all our problems because it often causes new problems even as it eliminates others.

   c. HOW YOU WILL SET ABOUT PROVING YOUR WHY.

   Numerous examples in the passage demonstrate the limits and negative impacts of machines among all the good they do.

   d. BRIEFLY MENTION YOUR EXAMPLES

   Among these, the discussions of robots and cell phones show how machines often do more harm than good.

—Everything after your intro is meant to prove your WHY—

2. **Body Paragraphs**
   a. Paragraph 2 — Example 1—Robots
      i. Topic sentence—

      Robots are the perfect example of machines not solving problems.

      ii. Cite SPECIFIC details from the passage and quote them appropriately
         a. As the author says in line 8, "Many robots...
         b. The author also adds in line 16, "Not only do robots harm humans, but..."

      iii. Conclude—Though robots can be threatening there are other more dangerous machines out there.

   b. Paragraph 3 — Example 2—Cell Phones
      i. Topic sentence—

      Cell phones contribute to users' distraction problems.

      ii. Cite SPECIFIC details from the passage and quote them appropriately
         a. As the author says in line 32, "Many cell phones..
         b. The author also adds in line 48, "Not only do cell phones do everything for us, but..."

      iii. Conclude—Though cell phones make our lives easier, they make it harder for us to solve problems ourselves.

   c. Paragraph 3a — Example 3 [if you have a good 3rd example and time, use it. If not, just mention it as additional proof in conclusion along with any other possible examples you might have.]

3. **Conclusion**—Recap your WHAT and WHY and then add in any extra observations you may have on thetopic.

   As shown above through the author's mention of robots and cellphones, machines do not always make life better or easier.

   It is obviously false because of the "because" stated above [Paragraph 1, Sentence 2] and proved with the examples above.

   Although some may say it is true because of "some contrary reason," this reason only serves to make topic even more false because "some reason of your own to contradict the contrary."

4. **Over-read**—Re-read what you've written.
   a. Make sure there are no blatant grammatical errors.
   b. Make sure that the essay is reasonably legible.
   c. Make sure that paragraphs are clearly delineated.

APPENDIX C

MULTIPLICATION & DIVISION TIPS

2

Most everyone can multiply an even number by 2 fairly comfortably, but we often get stuck when multiplying an odd number by 2. One good approach is to simply double an even number just above or below your number and then add or subtract two.

E.g., 2 x 19
Think of (2 x 20) and subtract 2, so
2 x 19 = (2 x 20)–2 = 40 – 2 = 38

E.g., 2 x 37
Think of (2 x 36) and add 2, so
2 x 37 = (2 x 36) + 2 = 72 + 2 = 74

Of course you may also double the ten's digit and then double the one's digit:
2 x 37 = (2 x 30) + (2 x 7) = 60 + 14 = 74

Dividing by 2

Just as with multiplication, most of us can divide an even number by two fairly easily but have trouble dividing an odd number by two. One thing to keep in mind is that there are only ever two remainders possible when dividing by two: zero and one. An even number divided by two always has a remainder of zero, and an odd number divided by two always has a remainder of one (which becomes 0.5 if we continue dividing), so the best way to divide an odd number by two is to go to the even number below your number, divide that number by two, and add to your answer!

E.g., 45 ÷ 2

Think of (44 ÷ 2) and add .5, so

45 ÷ 2= (44 ÷ 2) + .5 = 22 + .5 = 22.5

3

To determine if a number is divisible by 3, simply add all the digits in the number. If their sum is a multiple of 3, then the number is a multiple of 3.

E.g., 2,132
The digits of 2,132 are 2, 1, 3 and 2, and their sum is 2 + 1 + 3+ 2 = 8, SO 2,132 IS NOT divisible by 3.

E.g., 366
The digits of 366 are 3, 6 and 6, and their sum is 3 + 6 + 6 = 15; 15 is a multiple of 3, so 366 IS divisible by 3.

4

A number is divisible by 4 if the number formed by its last two digits is divisible by 4. E.g., 9,872 is divisible by 4 because 72 is. [Answer = 2,468] 834 is not because 34 is not divisible by 4.

5

All multiples of 5 have a units digit of 0 or 5.

To multiply a number by 5, simply multiply the number by ten and divide it by 2.
In 24 x 5, 24 becomes 240, which is then divided by 2 to give the product 120!

To divide a number by 5, simply divide the number by 10 and multiply that by 2!
In 245 ÷ 5, 245 becomes 24.5, which is then multiplied by 2 to give the quotient 49!

6

A number is a multiple of 6 if its digits add up to a multiple of 6 and the number is even.

E.g., 846
The digits of 846 are 8, 4 and 6, so 846 is divisible by 6 because 8 + 4 + 6 = 18, and 846 is an even number.

E.g., 1,942
The digits of 1,942 are 1, 9, 4 and 2 so 1,942 is NOT divisible by 6 because 1 + 9 + 4 + 2 =16, and 16 is not a multiple of 6.

9

A number is a multiple of 9 if its digits add up to a multiple of 9.

The digits of 17,658 are 1, 7, 6, 5 and 8, so 17,658 IS divisible by 9 because 1 + 7 + 6 + 5 + 8 = 27, and 27 is a multiple of 9.

To multiply a single-digit number by 9, simply make the ten's digit of the product one less than the number you're multiplying 9 by, and then make the one's digit whatever adds to the ten's digit to make 9. That sounds much harder than it is.

In other words, in 9 x 7, the ten's digit would be 6 [one less than 7] and the one's digit would be 3
[because 6 + 3 = 9], so 9 x 7 = 63!

NERD FACT: The digits of the first 20 multiples of 9 [except 99] all add up to 9!

11

The first nine multiples of 11 are simply that number repeated: 11 × 2 = 22, 11 × 3 = 33, 11 × 4 = 44, etc.

To multiply a two-digit number by 11, simply split that number and put the sum of its digits in between the original digits.

E.g.	15
	×11
split the 15 to make it	1__5
then take 1 + 5 [6] to make	165

Other examples—

	27
	×11
	2__7
2 + 7 = 9, so	297
	35
	×11
	3__5
3 + 5 = 8, so	385

When the sum of the digits of the number is greater than 10, simply carry the 1 as you would in regular addition.

```
   94
  ×11
9+__4
```

9 + 4 = 13, so 3 becomes the middle digit and 1 gets added to 9 to make 10: 1,034

```
    94
   ×11
9+1 3 4
```

```
  94
 ×11
1034
```

Acknowledgments

Translating more than two decades of teaching into a coherent form that includes equations and illustrations has proven a vast undertaking. Many people have helped make this book and the others in the series possible. Among them, in no particular order, are Ian Fiedorek, Brandon Huang, Emma Chin, Rachel Dennis, Bill Lauck and Angie Cohn and the great and powerful Beth Servetar. Most of all I'd like to thank Paul Ketchum whose intellectual oversight and inventive editing makes it all possible. Over and above the brilliant contributions of all these wonderful people, I am grateful to all my students past and present who have allowed me into their amazing minds long enough to learn how to teach them better.

Also available:

Remain Clam! Test Taking & the Student Mind: Middle School Entry Test Edition

Remain Clam! Test Taking & the Student Mind: Hunter Edition

Remain Clam! Test Taking & the Teenage Mind: 7th Grade State Test Edition

Remain Clam! Test Taking & the Student Mind: SHSAT Edition

Remain Clam! Test Taking & the Teenage Mind: SAT Edition

Remain Clam! Test Taking & the Teenage Mind: ACT Edition

About the Author

Stuart Servetar is from Brooklyn, NY. He grew up in Rockland County, NY, and attended Wesleyan University in Middletown, CT, where he studied English Literature. After briefly studying fine art at Pratt Institute, Stuart settled in New York City to write, paint and eventually tutor. When the Berlin Wall came down, Stuart headed to Eastern Europe and lived in Prague for a number of years. There he painted, taught English and was the food critic for *The Prague Post*. Upon returning to New York City, Stuart continued to paint and became the art critic for *The NYPress*. From there he wrote art criticism for a number of local, national and international publications. He also resumed tutoring. In 2006, Stuart formed ibidPREP in order to bring his approach to tutoring and test prep to a wider cross-section of students. Today, ibidPREP offers classes and individual tutoring throughout the New York metropolitan area and across the U.S. via Skype.

01292020

Made in the USA
Columbia, SC
01 July 2020